helenbacks
;;; '70

FROM THE
KITCHEN
OF

Helen Wike

The Cooking of India

Foods of the World

The Cooking of India

by

Santha Rama Rau

and the Editors of

TIME-LIFE BOOKS

photographed by Eliot Elisofon

TIME-LIFE BOOKS, NEW YORK

THE AUTHOR: Santha Rama Rau *(far left)* was born in Madras, India, and is the daughter of a distinguished Indian diplomat, Benegal Rama Rau. As a child she went to school in England, and later lived in South Africa, the United States and Japan. A graduate of Wellesley, she is an internationally known author whose books include *Home to India, East of Home, View to the Southeast, Remember the House* and *Gifts of Passage*. In 1956 she adapted E. M. Forster's *A Passage to India* for successful runs on the stage in London and New York.

THE CONSULTANT: Devika Teja, who prepared the recipes for this book and the accompanying Recipe Booklet, learned to cook in her mother's kitchen in Goa. Later, she came to the United States to study voice at the Conservatory of Music of the University of Southern California at Los Angeles. While there, she met and married Jaskaran S. Teja, a native of the Punjab in North India. He studied at Harvard and later joined India's foreign service. Since then, they have been stationed in London, Prague, Oslo, New Delhi, Moscow and New York, where he currently is First Secretary in the Indian mission to the United Nations.

THE PHOTOGRAPHER: Eliot Elisofon *(far left)* is a gourmet, painter and well-known LIFE photographer. In preparing this book, he traveled through India and Pakistan, photographing and sampling the food of both countries.

THE PAKISTANI AUTHOR: Mohammed Aftab, who wrote the Pakistan chapter of this book, is correspondent for TIME and LIFE in Rawalpindi.

THE CONSULTING EDITOR: Michael Field, who supervised the writing of recipes for this book, is one of America's foremost culinary experts. His books include *Michael Field's Cooking School* and *Michael Field's Culinary Classics and Improvisations*.

THE COVER: Fresh chutneys, made with highly seasoned vegetables and fruits, lend a zest to Indian meals. (See the Recipe Index for a varied selection of chutneys.)

TIME-LIFE BOOKS

EDITOR: Maitland A. Edey
Executive Editor: Jerry Korn
Text Director: Martin Mann
Art Director: Sheldon Cotler
Chief of Research: Beatrice T. Dobie
Picture Editor: Robert G. Mason
Assistant Text Directors: Harold C. Field, Ogden Tanner
Assistant Art Director: Arnold C. Holeywell
Assistant Chief of Research: Martha T. Goolrick

PUBLISHER: Rhett Austell
Associate Publisher: Walter C. Rohrer
Assistant Publisher: Carter Smith
General Manager: Joseph C. Hazen Jr.
Business Manager: John D. McSweeney
Production Manager: Louis Bronzo

Sales Director: Joan D. Manley
Promotion Director: Beatrice K. Tolleris
Managing Director, International: John A. Millington

FOODS OF THE WORLD

SERIES EDITOR: Richard L. Williams
Series Chief Researcher: Helen Fennell
EDITORIAL STAFF FOR THE COOKING OF INDIA
Associate Editor: William K. Goolrick
Picture Editor: Grace Brynolson
Designer: Albert Sherman
Assistant to Designer: Elise Hilpert
Staff Writers: Gerry Schremp, Ethel Strainchamps
Chief Researcher: Sarah B. Brash
Researchers: Julia Johnson, Barbara Leach, Myra Mangan
Test Kitchen Chef: John W. Clancy
Test Kitchen Staff: Fifi Bergman, Sally Darr, Leola Spencer

EDITORIAL PRODUCTION
Color Director: Robert L. Young
Assistant: James J. Cox
Copy Staff: Rosalind Stubenberg, Eleanore W. Karsten, Florence Keith
Picture Department: Dolores A. Littles, Joan Lynch
Traffic: Arthur A. Goldberger

The text for this book was written by Santha Rama Rau, recipe instructions by Michael Field, picture essays and appendix material by members of the staff. Valuable assistance was provided by the following individuals and departments of Time Inc.: Editorial Production, Robert W. Boyd Jr.; Editorial Reference, Peter Draz; Picture Collection, Doris O'Neil; Photographic Laboratory, George Karas; TIME-LIFE News Service, Murray J. Gart; Correspondents Dan Coggin and James Shepherd (New Delhi).

Contents

The Recipe Booklet that accompanies this volume has been designed for use in the kitchen. It contains all of the 58 recipes printed here plus 50 more. It also has a wipe-clean cover and a spiral binding so that it can either stand up or lie flat when open.

A Passage to India's Cooking

Ibegan my writing career when I was 19, at Wellesley College, with a book called *Home to India*. I was feeling far from "Home," and knew I would be returning after I graduated, but somehow it seemed necessary to me at that time to put down on paper something of what I felt about my own country. The book began with my return from boarding school in England and with my grandmother wondering despairingly wherever in India she would find a man tall enough to marry me (I'm just under five feet eight; she was just under five feet). Since I was scarcely 16 at the time, the matter didn't seem of primary importance to me, and I made the mistake of saying so. She replied severely that she had been half my age when *she* married.

The episode is still fresh in my mind, and I remember my grandmother's answer rather shook me, even though I had known it for years. I kept a decorous silence during the rest of the family greetings and comments, and immediately after those formalities, we were all ushered into the dining room for an elaborate meal that included all the favorite dishes of my childhood. In a way, these minor incidents summed up the two major preoccupations of my grandmother—and millions of other Indian women of all classes as well. Marriage and food.

It was really from that moment that I began to realize how forgetful I had become about my country, how much there was to learn and relearn, and how ill-equipped I was to grasp even a small part of it. In the two years that followed, I started on what I now think of as my "real education" about India, and it left me with a lifelong, indelible engagement with that impossible, diverse, wonderful, muddled, extraordinary, exciting and maddening country so that even after years of foreign travel—even after being married to an American (who was six feet tall)—it will forever remain "Home" in my mind.

I know that I have had certain advantages in trying to write about India. To begin with, my father was in the Indian civil service and at one time happened to be stationed in Madras, far south on the east coast of the Indian peninsula. Equally fortuitous, my mother (always a decisive and progressive woman, if not an outright rebel) was at college in Madras—the first girl of the Kashmiri Brahmin community to insist on higher education. It was there that the two families met, and the elders, my grandparents, arranged the marriage between, on one side, a very beautiful, if unpredictable, daughter for whom they had practically given up hope of finding a suitable match —after all, she was over 21—and, on the other, a brilliant and stubborn son who insisted that he wanted an *educated* bride, not simply a conventional housewife. It was considered a most unorthodox contract, the first of its sort in India, between a family from the far North and another from the far South, totally different in every way, even language. (To this day my parents speak to each other in English, their only common tongue.) Only one fact made it acceptable or possible at all: both families belonged to the same caste, Brahmin, and both to the same subcaste of Brahmins, Saraswat.

My father's work compelled him to travel a great deal. And in India, where conditions sometimes were too isolated or too rugged for him to take my mother, my sister and me along, we went to stay in the more stable households of grandmothers (North or South), or with married aunts, or other close relatives scattered here and there about the country. If what Freud or the Jesuits say is to be believed, then it was the experiences and indoctrination of those six years of early childhood that formed me, that gave me whatever little fundamental response or instinctive understanding I may have, not of India so much as of life in India. I know they also left me with an abiding, if exasperated, love of the place.

Later, my father's diplomatic assignments took us to England and various European capitals and then to South Africa with trips back and forth to India in between. After that I came to Wellesley, and by the time I graduated and went back home again, the country was in a state of turmoil, on the brink of moving painfully from being a colony—"the brightest jewel in the British crown"—to becoming entirely independent.

The following year my father was appointed Independent India's first Ambassador to Japan, and from there was later sent as Ambassador to Washington. Four years passed before I returned to India, this time to find a country struggling with problems—in some ways more massive than those of the fight for freedom—of establishing a viable, independent nation that could honorably deal with all its many special minorities, its religions, characters, provincial loyalties, and still battle with its overwhelming problems of economics, education, housing, health and, most of all, food.

From that time on, wherever I happened to live or travel, I felt I had to return to India at more or less regular intervals, for a year, a few months, whatever I could. Some atavistic urge made me feel, for example, that my son *had* to be born in India, at my parents' house, in the accepted Indian tradition. And for the last couple of years India has remained, and I hope will continue to remain, my "Home" in all the ways that matter.

One point that is, probably, more relevant to this book than my own feelings about my country, requires at least a little explanation. My life in India, at whatever stage, would have to be considered a "privileged" one—not unaware or unaffected by the way that the enormous majority of India's 520 millions live, and certainly far from affluent by American standards, but truly representative only of that social and economic layer of the moderately well-off that lies, as thin as the skin on boiled milk, over the daunting poverty of the mass of Indians.

This book, then, is mostly an account of the best food that I know from the sort of homes I have lived in or visited, and with a few exceptions, not the daily fare of India's villagers, about 80 per cent of the country's inhabitants. There are no "great" restaurants or famous chefs in India as there are in, say, France, to guide one in formulating a nationally accepted "great cuisine." Relatives, friends, friends of friends, acquaintances and some professional cooks have, in their generosity, provided much of my material. Yet, one must remember that while India provides a poor living for the majority of its people, in its diversity, grandeur and humanity it does offer them a rich life.

—*Santha Rama Rau*

7

I

Two Grandmothers and Their Kitchens

An Indian morning begins very early. I can remember from my childhood in my grandmother's house in North India, somewhere between dreams and waking, the sounds of that large household coming slowly to life at 5 or 5:30 in the eerie gray before daybreak. During the Hot Weather, as we called it, meaning specifically the months of spring and early summer, before the monsoon rains broke, the whole family—great-grandmother, grandparents, uncles, aunts, cousins, children, visiting relatives—all slept out in the large walled courtyard behind the house on light wooden-framed beds webbed with tape. From there, inside my filmy tent of mosquito netting, I could hear the rhythmic creaking of the old wooden wheel of the well outside the courtyard walls where blindfolded oxen were plodding round and round, drawing up the water for the day's needs of cooking, drinking, washing, bathing. A gentle clatter of pots and pans and the sweet fragrance of wood smoke issuing from the kitchen, a separate building opening off the courtyard, made a busy counterpoint to my grandmother's soft chanting of her morning hymns from the prayer room in the main house.

At about 6 o'clock her clear voice, accustomed to complete command within the small realm of her family, summoned us all to the sweet, milky tea accompanied by fruit that began our day. In the cold North Indian winter, the tea sometimes would be made in a samovar, spiced with cloves and cinnamon and ginger, rich with honey, to give us strength and warm us through the chill hours. For my grandmother's household was Kashmiri Brahmin, which meant that its members belonged to the highest Hindu caste and had come from the country's northernmost—now disputed—province. Even

8

In an austere middle-class kitchen a South Indian woman fries tortilla-like breads called *chapatis (Recipe Index)* over the charcoal stove on which she does all of her cooking. Beside her are vegetables—eggplant, okra and beans—that will be served with the *chapatis*. The stacked brass and copper pots at right hold water for cooking and drinking. Cooking and serving vessels are on the lower shelves behind her, while the top shelf holds containers of regularly used staples—rice, wheat, lentils, flour, spices, pickles and tamarind.

though the family had fled the oppression of Muslim invaders about three centuries earlier (to settle, inappropriately enough, in another Muslim stronghold, Allahabad) and even though many of its members had never even seen Kashmir, still their food and eating habits remained implacably Kashmiri. They retained the Kashmiri samovar and method of brewing green tea (which Kashmiris shared with the Russians on their northern frontier, across the massive stretch of the Himalayas). My family continued to eat the elaborate Kashmiri meat dishes, cooked in *ghee* (clarified butter) rather than the vegetable oils used in much of the rest of India. Instead of rice, the staple of South India, they preferred to prepare the many kinds of "bread" made from wheat but radically different from Western bread.

In all of this, their fierce sense of their origins, their strong feeling for the "Kashmiri Brahmin community" remained undiminished even though they were exiled in uncomprehending, if not actually hostile territory. So intense was this feeling that it never allowed them to realize that their food, like their manners, language, even in some cases, their dress, had been strongly influenced by centuries of Muslim rule both in Kashmir and later in Allahabad. Unlike most Brahmins in India they ate meat (though not beef); on the rare occasions when they served rice it was in the form of one of the wonderfully aromatic *pulaus* (imaginative variations of the Persian *polo*, or pilaf). They delighted in serving an iced sherbetlike mixture of fruit juices, a drink they had adopted from the Moghul courts of North India. Still, they were Hindus and Brahmins, and no matter how long they lived in Allahabad, they would never be anything other than Kashmiri.

My grandmother's kitchen was a very special place. First of all, like the kitchen of any orthodox Hindu home, it had to be spotlessly, almost neurotically clean. Nobody was allowed to enter it with his shoes on; my grandmother herself had to bathe and put on clean clothes before she could go in, and we younger children, considered as yet unpredictable and possibly lax in the thoroughness of our washing habits, could go no farther than the doorway. Inside, you could quite literally and safely have eaten off the floor—in fact the kitchen floor was the object of very special consideration, though this part is rather difficult to explain to foreigners who are apt to be repelled by the methods and the materials used to ensure its purity. In almost any Hindu kitchen (except, of course, recently, and in the big cities) the floor has a base of dried mud, over which a thin layer of fresh cow dung is spread by hand. Let me quickly add that cow dung sets within half an hour into a smooth, compact surface almost as hard as cement. It is entirely odorless as soon as it dries, and, according to firmly entrenched Indian tradition, it has antiseptic qualities. So far I have never heard this contradicted by even the most germ-conscious people, who may dislike the idea, but are helpless against the continued, and apparently innocuous, use of cow dung. In any case, my grandmother, who wouldn't have listened to ignorant Western objections, was so convinced of its efficacy that the kitchen floor had to be resurfaced with cow dung after every meal because, of course, there were bound to be minor spills and drips in the course of the cooking that couldn't be allowed to remain for a second longer than necessary. Luckily there were enough bullocks and cows on the property to provide a fresh daily supply.

Across a large part of the back wall of the kitchen was the *chula,* or stove, which involved another sort of tradition. The foundation of the *chula* was a sort of hollow brick cube, with holes in the top to serve as burners, and another hole near the floor in front through which the *chula* could be fed firewood, charcoal or dried cow-dung cakes (yes, it is used for fuel as well), depending on the type and strength of heat required. All this could be built by a bricklayer or one of the menservants, but the tricky part was the plastering and surfacing of the *chula* inside and out. First, mud had to be applied, molded, thickened in places, almost sculpted to provide the right draft for the fire, the right draw for each burner and the right distribution of heat. Then the drying process had to be carefully supervised to forestall cracks, and finally the *chula* had to be surfaced inside and out with cow dung. All this was supposed to be done by the woman of the house, for it was considered both an art and a valuable skill. One of my aunts, I remember, had quite a local reputation for expert and elegant *chula* building.

On one side of the *chula* was a low earthen platform covered with a bed of cow-dung ash, which retains its heat for a long time and is used to keep pots of food warm, to dry cooked rice, and for baking. Without an oven, our method of baking used to be simply to place the food in a pan in the hot ash and spread a layer of glowing charcoal or more ash on the cover. On the other side of the *chula* there was a wooden stool, about four inches high, on which my grandmother sat, the big round board and rolling pin on the

11

ground in front of her, as she prepared the thin wheat cakes, rather like tortillas, that have to be served absolutely fresh and can be made only after people have already sat down for their meal and everything else is ready.

In a corner of the kitchen were the two massive stone disks of the *chakki,* a kind of mill. One was set flat in the floor, while the other, on top of it, had a wooden handle on the rim and two holes near the center; into these holes one of the women in the family would slowly trickle handfuls of wheat while a servant pushed the handle. The top stone would turn round and round on the bottom one, grinding the grain in between and producing the flour for the day's needs. Next to the *chakki* was the smaller, flat, grinding stone and pestle, treated with particular respect as it was used for the spices that had to be freshly ground every day in the right combination for whatever dishes were to be cooked. These intricate mixtures of ground or whole spices, mild or strong, so bland as to be almost imperceptible or sharp enough to scald your palate, are called *masalas.* They are the unquestioned heart, the genius of Indian cooking. Through the choice of spices, through their proportions and blending, a good Indian cook expresses imagination, ingenuity, individuality, subtlety, adventurousness. So important are the *masalas*—and so vital is cooking among the talents of a Hindu girl—that in some parts of India a bride stands on a grinding stone for some of the preliminary wedding ceremonies while prayers and blessings are intoned and formal offerings of flowers and spices on silver trays are made to her. The stone under her bare feet is the symbol that from now on she will be the mistress of her own household. In other places a stone mortar and pestle are a traditional part of a bride's possessions when she goes to live in her husband's home. It is understood that it would be an unnecessary hardship for her to have to learn the character and quirks of new equipment for such an essential aspect of her duties.

Another corner of the kitchen was set apart as the area where food and dishes were washed, and all across one wall was a long shelf on which, in a gleaming array, were kept the pots and pans and cooking utensils. Dozens of *degchis,* saucepans of different sizes and depths, were stored here, all without handles, all made of highly polished brass, silvered on the inside to keep any brassy taste from reaching the food, and resilvered every month just to be sure. The *karhais,* shallow bowls with rounded bottoms and two handles, again made of silvered brass, were used exclusively for frying. The *tavas,* very heavy iron pans only slightly curved at the rim, were used for different kinds of wheat cakes. There were, as well, large earthenware pots needed for a few special dishes that had to be cooked for a long time, sometimes overnight, and required a very low and even heat. And then there were the cooking implements, which along with the usual spoons and different sizes of kitchen knives included the essential *karchi,* a long-handled iron ladle used for liquid foods, and the *tambakhash,* a flat iron disk that was sometimes perforated. Attached to a long handle, it was used for stirring dry things and foods that need air, for frying and for extracting any item from hot oil. Also, of course, there were tongs and pincers of different shapes and sizes, some for shifting glowing charcoal, for lifting lids on *degchis,* and huge curved ones to grip the entire *degchi* and remove it from the burner.

Opening off the kitchen was the storeroom, and its contents gave sur-

India and Pakistan

U.S.S.R.

AFGHANISTAN

CHINA

Khyber Pass

Kabul River

Landi Kotal
Peshawar
Kohat
Khewra
Lahore

JAMMU
AND
KASHMIR

Srinagar
Islamabad
Rawalpindi

PAKISTAN (WEST)

HIMACHAL PRADESH
Simla
PUNJAB
Chandigarh
HARYANA

HIMALAYAS

Brahmaputra River

SIKKIM
NEPAL
BHUTAN
ASSAM
Shillong

NAGALAND
Kohima

Indus River

DELHI — Delhi
New Delhi

Mathura
Fatehpur Sikri
Jaipur
Jodhpur

UTTAR PRADESH
Agra
Lucknow

Jumna River

RAJASTHAN

Hyderabad
Karachi
Tatta

Allahabad
Banaras
Ganges River

Patna

PAKISTAN (EAST)

Imphal
MANIPUR
Agartala
TRIPURA

Ahmedabad
GUJARAT

Bhopal

BIHAR

WEST BENGAL
Calcutta

Dacca

BURMA

MADHYA PRADESH

INDIA

GOA, DAMAN AND DIU
DADRA AND NAGAR HAVELI
Silvassa

MAHARASHTRA

ORISSA
Bhubaneswar

ARABIAN SEA

Bombay

BAY OF BENGAL

Hyderabad

ANDHRA PRADESH

Panaji
GOA, DAMAN AND DIU

MYSORE
Bangalore
Mangalore
Calicut

Madras

PONDICHERRY

Malabar Coast

KERALA
Cochin
Trivandrum

TAMIL NADU

Cape Comorin

CEYLON

INDIAN OCEAN

⊛ National capitals
✪ Other capitals
• Other cities and towns

0   100   200   400 miles

Continental India is divided into 17
states and seven federally administered
union territories, whose boundaries and
capitals are shown on the map above.
Although India is only one third the size
of the United States, its population of
500 million is two and a half times as
great. It is a land of startling contrasts
and contradictions: of jungle and desert,
feast and famine, and people who range
in color from the jet-black Dravidians of
the South to the pale Aryans of the
North. Most Indians (83 per cent) are
Hindus; they eat no beef, and members
of the higher castes are rigid vegetarians.
Pakistan, which was formed in 1947
when India achieved independence, is
divided into two provinces—West
Pakistan and East Pakistan—which are
separated by 1,000 miles of Indian
territory. Most of Pakistan's 100 million
people are Muslims. In contrast with the
Hindu vegetarians to the south, these
Muslims depend upon beef and lamb as
mainstays in their everyday diet.

prising clues to the kind of life we led in that household. Enormous brass urns, with covers (against insects), held the month's grain supply—usually about 75 pounds of wheat, rice, millet and maize. Smaller jars contained a dozen different varieties of lentils. Another huge vessel was filled with *ghee*, made at home by boiling down mountains of crude butter from buffalo milk for hours, until all the water had been evaporated and all the impurities burned out, and the final waxy, fragrant grease could be stored almost indefinitely without refrigeration—for of course we didn't have refrigeration; we didn't even have electricity. There was also cooking oil for vegetables —only meat was cooked in *ghee*—and containers of white sugar, unrefined brown sugar and molasses. Then there was the year's supply of fruit pickles kept in special stone jars that were supposed to be completely moistureproof, an important consideration because no water was ever allowed to touch the pickles as it might rot them. At the appropriate season, all the women in the house would help in making the pickles, preserving tiny green mangoes, limes, chilies, *anvlas* (sharp-tasting fruit about the size and shape of gooseberries), in oil with different mixtures of spices to flavor each one properly. Certain vegetables—cauliflower, carrots, turnips or anything without a mushy texture—were better pickled in brine, with ground mustard, turmeric and chili powder used as flavoring.

Another household activity was the dehydrating of vegetables during the winter months when they were plentiful and cheap. In addition to vegetables from our own garden, my grandmother would buy large quantities of cauliflower, cabbage, *muli* (a kind of large, mild horseradish), turnips, two kinds of chick-peas, and the two Kashmiri favorites, lotus seeds and *methi*, a leafy green herb, fenugreek, a little like highly flavored spinach. Regretfully, the Allahabad climate was too dry for the large Kashmiri mushrooms. With that exception, however, we followed the usual pattern of washing and slicing the vegetables, and then spreading them out on reed mats to dry in the sun of the courtyard before they were stored for use in the Hot Weather when all vegetables except potatoes vanished from the markets. Similarly, dried apricots, raisins, dates and figs were kept to be eaten during the season when fresh fruit would become unobtainable.

Finally, in the storeroom were kept the crucial reserves of dry spices that would be needed for *masalas* for months to come—dried chilies, coriander and cumin seed, black pepper, ginger and turmeric root, saffron, cloves, cardamom, cinnamon—all the wonderfully romantic names, evocative reminders of the great spice trade with "the Indies," which flourished in the 16th and 17th Centuries when Portuguese, Dutch and British traders, adventurers and pirates came in search of India's fabulous wealth. The fresh spices—leaf coriander, green chilies or ginger, for example—had, of course, to be bought each day as they were required. The spice vendor, butcher and fishmonger used to come to the house, and the morning would be punctuated by their visits and the brisk, canny bargaining of my grandmother.

In all matters concerning food my grandmother was the undisputed authority. Her uncompromising dictum, which still echoes in my childhood memories, was: "No Hindu woman worth her salt gives an order to a servant that she cannot carry out herself." It was directed with special emphasis toward the preparing, cooking and serving of food. I cannot remember a

Opposite: Before the stately Rambagh Palace Hotel, which once was a residence of the Maharaja of Jaipur, a North Indian nonvegetarian meal is served in the accustomed style. The food is contained in small silver bowls called *katoris*, on a silver tray known as a *thali*. Starting with the tall *katori* at the back of the *thali* and moving clockwise, the foods shown here are: a rice dish called *pulau;* mutton curry; curried peas and potatoes; raw onion and tomato; curried peas and cheese; mutton *kofta* (meatballs made of mutton) garnished with edible silver leaf; curried cauliflower; and carrot *halva* garnished with silver leaf. In the center are unleavened wheat-flour breads that are known as *parathas*.

Continued on page 18

The basic ingredients for *paan (above)*
are the betel nut, betel leaves and
spices. Some *paan* makers include
lime paste or tobacco; others add
powdered precious stones (which are
supposed to make one more virile).

1 Silver *paan* box
2 Pink (dyed) coconut
3 Betel-nut slivers
4 Aniseed
5 Silvered betel nuts
6 Tobacco
7 Cardamom
8 Unsilvered *paan*
9 Silvered *paan*
10 Betel-nut cutter
11 Cardamom
12 Lime paste
13 Cloves
14 Silvered aniseed
15 Betel nuts and pumpkin seeds
16 Betel leaves

A Pair of "Paan" Handlers and a Do-It-Yourself Digestive

On almost every street in India you will find shops that sell *paan*, a digestive and
breath freshener that is chewed more avidly by Indians than Americans chew
gum. The word *paan* means leaf, and in this case it refers to a betel leaf wrapped
around a betel nut, a specialty of tropical Asian countries that is seasoned with a
variety of spices. The ingredients for *paan* vary widely—the shop on the opposite
page sells seven varieties. In India you can buy it ready-made or purchase the
ingredients and make it yourself. To prepare it you slice the betel nuts, add lime
paste (powdered lime and water), cardamom, pink (dyed) coconut, and other
ingredients, then wrap them in a silvered betel leaf, and fasten the leaf with a
clove. Chewed between or after meals, *paan* turns the mouth a telltale red (a
temporary, harmless effect of the betel nuts), but leaves a clean, refreshing taste.

With a hand-cranked grater held in place by her foot, an Indian woman reams out a coconut to provide flavoring for a vegetable curry.

day when she did not both supervise the organization of every meal and cook the main dishes herself. Nobody ever thought of going to a restaurant or entertaining anywhere except at home. Indeed, it wasn't until many years later that I knew that there *were* restaurants and public eating places. Somehow the whole life of that remote Allahabad household, its privileges and duties, its wildly divergent personalities and its strong family feeling, its pleasures and responsibilities, its festivals and celebrations, were given stability and a sense of tradition by the regular procession of the meals we shared, the daily ritual that taught me something about the proper conduct of a Hindu home.

At almost the other end of the country, as far as it could possibly be in atmosphere, history, climate and surroundings from Allahabad and its setting in the vast northern plains, my other grandmother made her home near Mangalore, a small and charming port town on the lushly tropical southwest coast of the Indian peninsula. She too was a Brahmin, and she too observed the rules and duties that Hindu tradition assigned her. The feeding and care —especially the feeding—of her family were her primary concerns. And though she matched her Allahabad counterpart in her passion for cleanliness (an aspect, to her, of religious purity), and spent as much time and energy in the correct functioning of her kitchen, any resemblance ended there.

The land, climate and custom impose their own terms, and the food that issued from the two kitchens, Northern and Southern, was as different as the landscape, as the manners and habits of the people. Although in principle and in layout the two kitchens were much alike, the differences in equipment were significant. First of all, my Southern grandmother was a strict vegetarian—even eggs were not permitted in her house because they counted as "meat" and might contain embryonic life, which one was forbidden to destroy. So there were none of the heavy knives for meat cutting, and the long, thin silver spoon for extracting marrow from lamb bones was missing. Yet a coconut scraper, unheard of in the North, was an absolute essential. It was a low rectangular wooden stool with a strong metal prong at one end. You sat on the wooden part, and scraped the meat from the coconuts on the sharp, jagged points of the metal projection.

My South Indian grandmother preferred to use cooking utensils made from copper (silvered on the inside), and foremost among these was her steam cooker, a tall *degchi* into which a metal disk fitted halfway down, perforated to let the steam from the boiling water in the lower section reach the food in the top part. Many important items of the South Indian cuisine are cooked over steam—a technique virtually unknown in the North. She had, besides, a number of implements that would have been baffling to a North Indian: an iron press to make a kind of vermicelli from rice flour; a wooden gadget that squeezed out the dough for *murukkus*, which when fried provides a crisp, seasoned, salty snack about the shape of a very large pretzel; a large perforated ladle through which a batter made of chick-pea flour was forced into hot oil to produce the slender little curls of *saive;* a coffee grinder, of course, and a brass coffee maker, for tea was never served here, but coffee had to be roasted and ground fresh each day. Even her mortar and pestle were differently shaped—a deep stone bowl with an oval pestle so fat that it almost filled the cavity of the bowl. Much more practical, she claimed, because it re-

Coconut sweets, in varied forms, are a favorite Indian delicacy. The diamond-shaped and square confections in the foreground include coconut *barfis*, shredded coconut cooked with milk and sugar, and milkless coconut sweets. The half-moon sweets at the right are *karanjias*, pastries filled with grated coconut and sugar. At the center are bowls of grated coconut and coconut milk, along with three different kinds of coconut graters, including the turtle-shaped grater at the right.

quired less exertion in the grinding of spices than the Northern variety.

The contents of her storeroom were equally instructive about the differences of living, of taste, of necessity between North and South. There was, for instance, no wheat, although there were several kinds of rice, and certainly a container of pounded rice. There were a far greater amount and variety of lentils. There were large supplies of sesame and coconut oil, and a relatively small stock of *ghee* for use in cooking a few dishes, and also for pouring a spoonful at a time over boiled rice, much as one uses a pat of butter in the West. Pickles were kept in huge porcelain jars, which were believed to be a legacy to the southwest coast from the days in the 15th Century when there was an active trade with China. In flavor and texture the pickles were totally different from those of the North, and they included a couple of Mangalore specialties—green peppercorn and bitter lemon pickles.

It was both unnecessary and impractical, because of the humidity, to dry vegetables in Mangalore. They are available in abundance and in a dizzying variety all year round, except for the brief period of the heavy monsoon. Traditionally, however, certain varieties of gourds and squash are blanched and packed in salt to be used as the occasion arises, and green chilies are often soaked in curds, dried in the sun and stored to be used, fried crisp, as a garnish to a regular meal. Mango and jackfruit pulp (from the fruit of a tree that grows in this part of the world and is closely related to breadfruit) are dried and stored, and so are dates and raisins, but only a few of the spices, for South Indians use much more fresh spicing than Northerners.

Continued on page 22

Bombay is a heavily congested city with a population of 4.1 million where some residents live in modern high-rise apartments and others are crammed six or more into a single room. In the evenings people like to go down to Chowpatty Beach, in the heart of the city, and stroll along the water's edge, go wading at low tide in the Arabian Sea, or watch the yogis bury themselves in the sand. When the notion strikes them, the strollers may stop at one of the *bhelpuri* stands on the beach and enjoy one of India's favorite snacks. Made of puffed rice, lentils, chopped onions, herbs and chutney, *bhelpuri* is served in varying combinations with wheat-flour chips. A variation can be found in the Recipe Index.

At Allahabad there were mango and guava orchards, but the garden of the Mangalore house contained only one mango tree. Yet the garden produced much better jackfruit, cashews, tamarind, bananas (both the huge red kind for cooking and the tiny, honey-sweet "butter bananas" of the South), papayas, bitter lemons and the inescapable coconut palms, called the "tree of wealth" because every part can be profitably used.

In the serving of meals in both households a certain order of precedence was maintained—guests and men first, then children, then women, and last of all, after everyone else had finished, my grandmothers would eat, usually alone, usually in the kitchen. If this order seems to Westerners lacking in courtesy to women, Indians view it in quite another way. Confident of her secure position within her family domain, it is a sign of graciousness for an Indian woman to serve her menfolk first, a matter of dignified deference rather than a sign of subservience.

The table would be set with *thalis,* round, shallow trays, silver for special occasions, brass for everyday, and on the *thalis* there would be a number of small matching bowls containing different preparations of meat, fish, chicken, vegetables, lentils, curds, chopped raw vegetables, and in the middle either a little hill of rice, or some form of bread. For really large celebrations —a marriage or an important festival—when a couple of hundred people might be invited to dinner, we sat on the floor and ate from banana leaves instead of *thalis,* and used little earthenware bowls that could be thrown away after the meal. In any case, everything was served at the same time and you decided for yourself in what order or combination you wanted to eat the various dishes. Servants and the women of the house refilled the little bowls as they were emptied, replenished the rice or brought in fresh relays of the breads still too hot to touch.

Of course we used no cutlery because in the usual Indian way we always ate with our fingers. It may sound like a messy habit, but once you are used to it, you are apt to feel much as connoisseurs of Japanese and Chinese food feel about using chopsticks. The food, for no definable reason, just tastes better. (There is a story that the Shah of Iran, on a visit to India, was so taken by the custom that he remarked that to eat with the spoon and fork was like making love through an interpreter.)

Eating with your fingers is in no way a difficult technique, but a few rules and a certain etiquette go with it. North Indians are apt to feel that Southerners are hopelessly lacking in refinement and delicacy in their manner of eating because they will plunge their whole hand into their food if they feel like it. South Indians, if they bother to give the subject any thought, often feel that no decadence or absurdity is too extreme to be unexpected from those finicky people from North India who never allow their food to creep past the first knuckle.

Yet nowhere in traditional India would you use your left hand in eating, even if you are left-handed, for the left hand is considered unclean. You should always allow yourself to be served, never attempt to help yourself —your right hand, with which you are eating, will leave the serving spoon sticky, and you mustn't touch it with your left. Never offer anyone food from your *thali,* even if it is in one of the little bowls and you haven't touched it. All the food that is placed on your *thali* becomes *jutha* the moment you receive it. There is no precise English equivalent of *jutha*. I suppose "polluted" comes closest though it doesn't carry the overtones of hygienic observance or caste consciousness. To offer your *jutha* food to someone else would be either a gesture of extreme intimacy—a mother to her child, a husband to his wife—or an unpardonable social insult. As a rule, only untouchables can eat *jutha* food, and in the South the feeling about it is so intense that such food would not even be exchanged among family members.

At the end of an Indian meal, water and a bowl are brought around for you to wash your hands, and finally comes the ceremony of *paan* making. One of the women in the house will bring out the *paan-daan*, sometimes a plain metal box, sometimes a beautifully chased or filigreed silver casket, which holds in its many small compartments the *paan*, or betel leaves, and all the dozens of ingredients from which to choose the filling. A *paan* may be very elaborate, with betel nut, strips of perfumed coconut, saffron, tobacco, cardamom, cloves, aniseed and many other spices wrapped in the betel leaves and covered with silver leaf, or it may be quite simple, containing only lime paste (powdered lime and water) and betel nut. In either case it is considered a digestive and an astringent to remove the taste of food from the mouth. It is also one of the minor elegances of Indian life, for the filling and wrapping of the betel leaf are traditionally supposed to be the most graceful activity in which a woman's hands can be engaged. In the highly formal society of Hyderabad in the old days, when family elders were arranging a marriage for a young man, one of the qualifications and accomplishments they carefully considered in their quest for a suitable bride was her skill in making *paan*.

Nowadays, of course, such refinements become rarer and rarer as Indian life and the whole social structure changes. The households of both Allahabad and Mangalore are disbanded, all my grandparents are dead, the family members have scattered to the big cities, traveling a good deal as their professions dictate. Our city residences have refrigerators, gas stoves, electricity, tiled kitchen floors, running water. Our storerooms—even if space and current food rationing regulations permitted us to be more lavish—would seem pitifully understocked to my grandparents and would display such shamefully standardized items as canned foods, ready-ground flour or store-bought *ghee*. Few of us are orthodox in our religious observance. Many of us are Westernized and have broken just about all caste restrictions. All of us have adjusted to the hours, necessities, conveniences and the forfeit of traditional ways enforced by urban living.

But those early years are not without significance, for most of village India (about three quarters of the population) still uses oil and kerosene lamps for lighting. Wood, charcoal and cow dung are still burned for fuel, and water is still fetched from the village well. In the villages, the ancient religious, social and family traditions are most strongly maintained, and as always, life is governed by what food the land can provide.

In a small way, the contrasts between the two not extraordinary households of Allahabad and Mangalore illustrate at least a part of the inexhaustible diversity of India, the overwhelming complexity of its cultural, religious and historical heritage, its imperviousness to generalization, the intractable individuality that plagues anyone attempting to write about any aspect of the country as a whole. It is for these reasons rather than its size that it has acquired that tired sobriquet, "the vast subcontinent." In fact it is about one third the size of the United States, but equally, its territory would cover all of Europe up to the Russian border. However, it is older, and in terms of civilization and ways of living, more profoundly complicated than either.

Over the 5,000 years of its recorded history, and even before, so one gathers from its legends and great epics, India has been invaded by armies, traders, immigrants from all over the world. Some of the conquests are famous —the Aryans during the second millennium B.C., the Greeks, led by Alexander the Great in 326 B.C., the Moghuls in the 16th Century, the British in the 18th and 19th Centuries—but these were interspersed with more obscure and more exotic incursions of Bactrians, Mongols, Scythians, Parthians, Kushans, Huns, Arabs, Turks, Afghans, Portuguese and Dutch. And throughout this tumultuous succession of invaders there remained pockets of tribal and aboriginal life in the more daunting mountain country and in the less accessible inland areas.

With a rather splendidly cavalier disdain of military defeat, India, broadly speaking, lost the battle but won the war, accepting all comers, adopting some of their ways, modifying others, almost imperceptibly persuading people who came as foreign conquerors to stay as Indian nationals—an indefinable but immediately perceptible transmutation that has nothing to do with passports or voting rights. They "became" Indian, in the process changing their own customs and outlook somewhat, changing India's life, habits and thinking somewhat.

Equally in matters of religion—an exceedingly important, even crucial aspect of Indian life—the country displays a profusion of faiths, practices and observances unequaled, I imagine, anywhere else. The home of Hinduism, Buddhism and the religions of the Jains and Sikhs, India also has a large population of Muslims, and contains as well different sects of Christians, one of the oldest settlements of Jews in the world, Zoroastrians, animists and a number of minor faiths. All of these have contributed their own manners, ways and attitudes to the rich texture of Indian life and living.

It is a point of some astonishment to me that after all these centuries of foreign contact, India and most of Southeast Asia should still be screened from the Western world by such a formidable barrier of fantasy, half truths, misconceptions and sheer ignorance. Even the food—one of the first and most immediate contacts a traveler makes with a foreign country—remains virtually unexplored, and a great and varied cuisine evolved from indigenous sources and outside cultures seems to have been reduced in Western minds (those that consider the matter at all) to the comprehensive and meaningless category "curry." To most of them curry is simply a floury, yellow cream sauce that can be used indiscriminately with meat or fish or chicken, and served with rice—and, of course, with Major Grey's chutney. The term curry actually is an Anglicization of the word *kari* in Tamil (a language spoken in South India), which does, indeed, mean "sauce." *Kari* could, perhaps, be more accurately described as the combination of seasonings with which meat or fish or vegetables are cooked to produce a stewlike dish. No Indian cook would ever use a prepared curry powder, because each dish must have its own distinctive *masala*. A large section of the country rarely eats rice, and

Opposite: The southwestern coast of India is a postcard paradise of coconut palms and beautiful beaches, where the Arabian Sea yields the country's richest seafood treasure. The Kerala fishermen shown here are spreading their nets to dry. Their catch includes shrimp, prawns and fish for the region's superb curries and other seafood dishes.

Two extremes of Indian life are represented by the simple goatherds squatting on the banks of Maota Lake, north of Jaipur, and the Amber Palace looming beyond them. The opulent palace, built in the 17th Century, is now abandoned.

as for Major Grey, he is unknown in India, though the appeal of chutney is apparently universal as a catchy verse suggests.

Rank Injustice
All things chickeney and mutt'ny
Taste better far when served with chutney
This is the mystery eternal:
Why didn't Major Grey make colonel?
—*John F. Mackay*

Any Indian who cares about good food would view with scorn someone who would *buy* his chutney ready-made. (Plenty of city dwellers do, of course, though the trade names they know are not Major Grey, but that doesn't prevent chefs from maintaining their supercilious attitude about such lazy habits and unexacting taste.)

There is one aspect of Indian cooking that should be explained in advance to the casual foreign visitor. Regional and religious food habits die very hard here, and as a result there is no major body of dishes and techniques of cooking that one can combine to call a "national cuisine." In a Southern city like Bombay, for example, with its huge and very mixed population, you are able to tell at once, from the food eaten in a private home, what part of the country your host's ancestors came from, what religion they observe, and probably how extensively they have traveled and the degree of their familiarity with foreign ways as well. Apart from the Mahar-

ashtrians who form the central core of the citizenry of Bombay, their state capital, there are large numbers of Gujaratis (from the state of Gujarat immediately north of Maharashtra). There are people from Kerala and Madras, the far southwest and southeast coastal regions, North Indians from Uttar Pradesh, and Goans, many of them Christians, from the small enclave south of Bombay that was ruled for three and a half centuries by the Portuguese. There are also Pathans, from the Muslim tribes of the northwest Himalayan frontier, and Parsis or Zoroastrians, who fled from Muslim persecution in Persia 1,200 years ago to seek sanctuary in India. They settled in the Bombay area, and so did Jains, Sikhs and many smaller groups from all over India. In their homes you would find the distinctive food and cooking of their ancestral province and their ethnic community. Only in some "modern" Indian homes would the meal be likely to include dishes from a variety of regions.

Anyone who wishes to sample the best Indian dishes should not hope to find them in restaurants. Indians are not by custom or choice restaurantgoers. They prefer to entertain and be entertained at home. It is in private houses that you find the best cooking, the most varied dishes, the great and special body of "family recipes," and the individual formalities about the serving of food that are naturally impossible to maintain in public eating places.

The major Indian cities have hotels and restaurants to cater to international and special Indian tastes, but considering their size—Calcutta nearly five million, Bombay about four million, Delhi three million, Madras two million —the number of restaurants is remarkably small. With a few exceptions

At the community well in Karavli, in North India, village women fill their brass and earthenware *lotas* with the day's supply of water. India is still predominantly rural, and for these women and most of their fellow citizens running water and other modern conveniences are unknown.

—mostly the restaurants serving *tandoori* food, which requires a special kind of cylindrical clay oven sunk in the ground—the food in public eating places is likely to be undistinguished. Many second-class hotel dining rooms settle for what Indians disparagingly call "railway curry," meaning the kind of meals you are served in dining cars that attempt to suit every taste and succeed in pleasing none.

In the cities and villages, however, certain foods are customarily bought in bazaars, in small food shops and from street vendors whose specialized expertise cannot be duplicated at home. Families of sweetmakers, *halvais*, whose art is handed from father to son, have evolved regional specialties that are greatly prized and bought to celebrate any auspicious occasion. In general, the reason one buys such sweets is that the time and labor involved in preparing them are too great to make it worthwhile for the average housewife to cook at home the relatively small quantity her family might need. To make the sweet known as *halva sohan*, for example, you have to soak whole wheat for three or four days until the grain swells. Then the wet wheat is ground, and a milky liquid is squeezed out and saved to be cooked with *ghee* and sugar and flavoring until it has the correct fudgelike consistency. Finally the whole sweet is topped with silver leaf, which is exceedingly fragile and difficult to apply smoothly. It contributes nothing to the taste, but is necessary for a properly festive and luxurious appearance. Similarly, many of the milk sweets require tedious hours of simmering the milk, skimming it constantly, to collect the thick, creamy "condensed milk" used in their preparation.

Besides such sweets, there are a number of salty between-meal snacks that are covered by the generic name *chat* and are always bought, because they somehow never taste as good when they are made at home. Among these are some as simple as roasted chick-peas or puffed rice, and some more complicated mixtures such as *bhelpuri (Recipe Index),* a delicious sweet-salt-sour combination of cereals, fried lentils, chopped vegetables, herbs and chutney, which is sold in Bombay at heavily patronized, gaily striped wooden stalls on the city's beaches. Another of these snacks is *panipuri,* a tiny puff of dough, fried and expertly filled with tamarind water, which you have to eat on the spot, in one mouthful to keep from squirting the liquid all over your clothes. And there is *chana-jora-garam,* another spicy, savory concoction that vendors in Lucknow sell from great baskets they carry on their heads. As they walk along the streets they sing special songs of their own composition describing the virtues of their particular varieties in the most persuasive way to attract customers. One such lyric runs:

> *Chana-jora-garam!*
> Brother, I have come from a long, long distance
> To bring you this unimaginably tasty
> *Chana-jora-garam.*
> I use the most excellent and secret *masala*—
> You can know, because all kinds of famous people
> Eat my *chana-jora-garam.*

Even the most transient visitor to India will quickly notice certain all-pervasive customs and traditions with respect to food. He will sense the immense importance placed on hospitality, the deep individual and national concern with the basic production of food, and the essential and intimate part that the offering of food plays in virtually any "occasion," religious or secular, ordinary or exalted. In any Indian village, regardless of how poor or famine-stricken the area, the unshakable Indian tradition of offering food and drink to anybody who enters your house must be maintained—even if it consists of only a sip of precious water and a handful of roasted chick-peas, even if this token means a genuine hardship for the family, and even if the visitor has only stopped by (as once happened to me) to ask the way to the nearest post office. In more prosperous homes graciousness to a guest reaches almost embarrassing proportions. Food and attention will be lavished on him, he will be fussed at and cajoled into eating second, third and fourth helpings, and his hostess will still feel that he hasn't eaten enough. (An elderly friend of mine had, through all the years of her marriage, only one recurring nightmare, which she found quite as distressing as the more familiar dream horrors of falling off cliffs. Twenty unexpected guests arrived at her house—and there wasn't enough food to go around.)

Even on train journeys, as long as you are not traveling in first-class grandeur, you are certain to be invited to share the food your traveling companions have, in the usual Indian way, brought with them. If you happen to have brought your own snacks or a full meal, you will be expected to return the courtesy. As a habit, it has not only its own charm, but also the added interest of plunging you immediately into conversation with strangers, into the typically Indian exchange of information of the most personal and the most general sort. Are you married? Are you happy? How old are you?

What work do you do and do you enjoy it? What is your mother-in-law like? What do you think of India's economic situation? Children? You must, you *must* try this sweet, it's a specialty of our community. Where is your home? And invariably, unless you are a foreigner or clearly a city dweller: How are the crops? What are the chances of a good harvest in your district?

The pervasive Indian concern about local and national agriculture is hardly surprising. Throughout its immense geographic range, from the eternal snows of the Himalayas to the deserts of Rajasthan, from the steamy delta country of southern Bengal to the dry heat and cold of the central plateau and the northern plains, from the cool forested hills of Assam to the moist, intensively cultivated peninsula of the far South, India is primarily an agricultural country. And one peculiar climatic factor, the monsoon, makes the difference to Indian farmers between relative success and outright failure for the year, between the possibility of food security and the prospect, painfully familiar to Indians, of famine.

A former finance minister of the government of India once opened his budget speech with the remark that the entire economy of India is an annual gamble on the monsoon. To an overwhelming extent the wealth, productivity and the crucial matter of feeding a population of over 500 million Indians (growing by 12 million a year) depend on the prompt arrival, the proper distribution and the quantity of the rains of high summer. Recent irrigation schemes, dam projects, tube wells, and the introduction of improved seeds and fertilizers are helping to increase the yield and lessen the total dependence of Indian agriculture on the chancy functioning of the monsoon. But the magnitude of the problem—the feeding of one out of every six people on earth from a land that would scarcely cover the area between New York and Chicago—remains India's most formidable barrier to rapid development and progress. It is only natural that most of India awaits the breaking of the monsoon in June with prayers and temple offerings, and (equally important to a successful harvest) that the timely end of the rains should be hailed with thanksgiving, devotions and celebrations.

So strongly does the vital matter of food production loom in the Indian consciousness that some symbol of it is inextricably involved in the performance of any Indian ceremony. At every family occasion—the birth of a child, the betrothal of a daughter, the religious confirmation of a son—or on festival days, or when good fortune has come to a family, people *must* be invited to a meal, and if for some reason that is impossible, food and sweets must be sent to appropriate friends and relatives. For an event as important as a marriage, the heads of all the families in the community are informed, and (in the days before staple foods were rationed) could come to dinner bringing as many members of their own families as they saw fit. But countless smaller occasions as well—a visit to a temple, a success in business, the passing of a school examination—all require the serving or the gift of food as the chief auspicious offering. The religious significance of such offerings is also deep in Indian thought. The ancient Sanskrit scriptures state, with unequivocal directness, "Annam Brahma" (Food is God), and add that, like God, food maintains all beings, all life. It follows, of course, that food must be treated with equal reverence, and even today in many Indian homes a token offering of food is made to the deity before every meal.

Opposite: India's most celebrated landmark, the Taj Mahal, stands in the fertile plain of the Ganges. The rich alluvial soil around the architectural masterpiece is divided into plots and irrigated to produce potatoes and *methi*—a leafy green herb *(foreground)*. Beyond the partially dried-up Jumna River lies a watermelon patch, where vines are covered with dried grass to protect them from the December frost.

30

Indian cookery varies so widely from region to region, and from one cook to the next, that even the best-known traditional dishes have many variations. Moreover, some ingredients used by Indian cooks are not available in the United States. The recipes in this book therefore have been selected to present the dishes that are most practical for American cooks. Although some modifications were necessary, every effort has been made to preserve the authentic character of Indian food.

Jhinga Kari
SHRIMP CURRY

To serve 4 to 6

1 pound jumbo shrimp (10 to 15 to the pound)
1 tablespoon distilled white or cider vinegar
2 teaspoons salt
1 cup peeled, coarsely chopped fresh coconut *(page 134)*
¼ cup coriander seeds
1¼ cups warm water
5 tablespoons vegetable oil
1 tablespoon scraped, finely chopped fresh ginger root
1 tablespoon finely chopped garlic
½ cup finely chopped onions
1 teaspoon turmeric
½ teaspoon ground cumin
¼ teaspoon ground hot red pepper
¼ teaspoon freshly ground black pepper
3 tablespoons finely chopped fresh coriander *(cilantro)*

Carefully shell the shrimp, leaving the last segment of the shell and the tail attached to each shrimp. With a small, sharp knife, devein the shrimp by making a shallow incision down the backs and lifting out the black or white intestinal vein with the point of the knife. Wash the shrimp under cold running water and pat them dry with paper towels. In a small bowl combine the shrimp with the vinegar and salt, and toss thoroughly. Turning occasionally, marinate the shrimp at room temperature for 15 to 20 minutes.

Combine the coconut, coriander seeds and water in the jar of an electric blender and blend at high speed for 1 minute. Turn off the machine, scrape down the sides of the jar with a rubber spatula and continue blending until the mixture is reduced to a purée.

Pour the purée into a fine sieve lined with a double thickness of dampened cheesecloth and set over a deep bowl. With a large spoon, press down hard on the coconut mixture to extract as much liquid as possible. Then gather the ends of the cheesecloth together and wring it vigorously to squeeze out any remaining liquid. Discard the pulp and set the coconut milk aside. (There should be about 1½ cups of the milk.)

In a heavy 8- to 10-inch skillet, heat 3 tablespoons of the vegetable oil over moderate heat until a drop of water flicked into it splutters instantly. Drain the shrimp and reserve the marinade. Drop the shrimp into the skillet, cover tightly, and cook for 30 seconds, then turn the shrimp over, cover again, and cook for 30 seconds, or until the shrimp are pink and firm but not brown. With a slotted spoon, return the shrimp to the marinade.

Pour the remaining 2 tablespoons of oil into the skillet, heat it, and add the ginger root. Stirring constantly, fry for 30 seconds, add the garlic, and continue stirring and frying for 1 minute. Still stirring, add the onions and fry for 7 to 8 minutes, until they are soft and golden brown. Add the turmeric, cumin, red pepper and black pepper, and stir for 1 minute. Then pour the shrimp marinade into the skillet and bring it to a boil immediately, scraping in any brown particles clinging to the bottom and sides of the pan.

Return the shrimp to the skillet, turning them about to coat them evenly. Pour in the reserved coconut milk and, stirring constantly, bring to a boil over high heat. Reduce the heat to moderate, sprinkle the top with 2 tablespoons of coriander, cover, and cook for 3 minutes. Taste for seasoning.

To serve, transfer the shrimp to a serving dish and pour the sauce remaining in the pan over them. Sprinkle the shrimp with the remaining tablespoon of coriander and serve at once with boiled rice and a chutney.

FRESH CHUTNEY: No Indian curry is complete unless it is accompanied by at least a dab of the homemade relish known as a fresh chutney. These are not preserved chutneys; rather they are made daily from the fruits, vegetables and herbs at hand. The flavor is sometimes tempered through cooking or marinating, but most fresh chutneys are a simple mixture of raw foods, ground or finely cut, and blended with seasonings. Recipes for three of the chutneys shown on the cover follow; for the others, see the Recipe Index.

Dhanya Chatni
FRESH CORIANDER CHUTNEY

Combine the lemon juice, water and ½ cup of the coriander in the jar of an electric blender, and blend at high speed for 30 seconds, or until the mixture is reduced to a purée. Turn the machine off and scrape down the sides of the jar with a rubber spatula. Then add another ½ cup of coriander, blend for 30 seconds, and stop the machine again. Repeat until all of the coriander has been puréed.

Add the coconut, onions, ginger, chili, sugar, salt and pepper, and blend again. When the mixture is perfectly smooth, taste and add more sugar or salt if desired.

Serve immediately. If the chutney is not to be used at once, cover it tightly with aluminum foil or plastic wrap, and refrigerate it. (The chutney may be kept in the refrigerator for about 1 week.)

To make about 2 cups

¼ cup fresh lemon juice
¼ cup water
¼ pound fresh coriander stems and leaves *(cilantro),* thoroughly washed and coarsely chopped, about 2 cups tightly packed
¼ cup peeled, finely chopped fresh coconut *(page 134)*
¼ cup finely chopped onions
2 tablespoons scraped, finely chopped fresh ginger root
2 teaspoons chopped fresh hot red or green chili *(caution: see page 39)*
1 teaspoon sugar
1 teaspoon salt
¼ teaspoon freshly ground black pepper

Imli Chatni
TAMARIND CHUTNEY

Place the tamarind pulp in a small bowl and pour the boiling water over it. Stirring and mashing occasionally with a spoon, let the tamarind soak for 1 hour, or until the pulp separates and dissolves in the water. Rub the tamarind through a fine sieve set over a bowl, pressing down hard with the back of a spoon before discarding the seeds and fibers. Or purée it through a food mill.

Add the ginger, lemon juice, jaggery (or brown sugar and molasses) and the salt to the purée, and stir together vigorously. Taste for seasoning. Serve at once or cover tightly and store in the refrigerator for up to 2 days.

Just before serving, pour the chutney into a small bowl and sprinkle the top with coriander.

To make about 1 cup

¼ cup tightly packed dried tamarind pulp (about 2 ounces)
1 cup boiling water
1 tablespoon scraped, finely chopped fresh ginger root
1 tablespoon fresh lemon juice
1 teaspoon crumbled imported Indian jaggery, or substitute dark brown sugar combined with dark molasses *(page 196)*
1 teaspoon salt
2 tablespoons finely chopped fresh coriander *(cilantro)*

Corom Chatni
FRESH MANGO CHUTNEY WITH HOT CHILI

Wash the mango under cold running water and pat it completely dry with paper towels. Without removing the skin, cut the flesh of the mango away from the large seed inside. Discard the seed and cut the flesh of the mango into paper-thin slices.

Place the mango in a serving bowl, add the chili, coriander, salt and red pepper, and toss gently with a spoon until the ingredients are thoroughly mixed. Let the chutney marinate in the refrigerator for 1 to 2 hours before serving. (Tightly covered and refrigerated, it can be kept for 1 day.)

To make about 1 cup

1 medium-sized firm but underripe mango (about 1 pound)
1 fresh hot red or green chili, stemmed, slit in half lengthwise, seeded, and cut into paper-thin rings *(caution: see page 39)*
1 tablespoon finely chopped fresh coriander
1 tablespoon salt
⅛ teaspoon ground hot red pepper

II

Where Spices Are the Variety of Life

The richly embossed silver dishes at left are appropriate for serving an elegant *murgi kari (bottom of picture)*, a curry made with the choicest pieces of chicken, and saffron rice, shown at the top. The rice gets its color from saffron threads, which come from crocus blossoms. It takes 75,000 of the blossoms to make one pound of saffron.

If you were hiring a cook," I once asked an Indian friend who is a gastronome of some eminence, "what dish would you ask him to prepare as a test of his ability?"

Without a trace of hesitation, she answered *murg masalam*—a chicken preparation in which the *masala,* or spicing, is particularly tricky. This, she went on, would demonstrate his command of cooking techniques—the control of the fire, the judgment of precisely when the *masala* has been absorbed by the meat, the timing to ensure that the sauce is neither too liquid nor too thick. Above all, it would show whether he had the feel for spicing, whether, in her phrase, "his hands are right for grinding."

The variety, the combinations and the uses of spices are the major factors that distinguish Indian cooking from any other cuisine in the world. In preparing *murg masalam (Recipe Index),* for example, the cook would need coriander and cumin seed, cinnamon, cloves, black pepper, cardamom, ginger, red chili, garlic and onion. This is not, by Indian standards, an unusually long or intricate list, but the proportions and the balance of the spices in the *masala* are of paramount importance. Besides—and this is where the expertise of the cook will be truly tested—they must be so judiciously mixed and so subtly introduced that there is no suggestion of overspicing, and so carefully timed in the cooking that not a trace of the "raw" spice emerges in either the texture or the taste of the dish.

Some time after the conversation with my gastronomic friend, I asked my mother the same question—what dish would *she* choose as a test of a cook's ability, and her reply was equally prompt. True to my grandmother's training and her own sense of heritage, she named a Kashmiri specialty, *roghan josh (Recipe Index)*. Her reasons for choosing this masterpiece of lamb preparations again centered on the spicing, although the dish would test a cook's familiarity with special Kashmiri cooking methods as well. To produce *roghan josh* according to her recipe the cook would have to pound, rather than grind, some of the spices—coriander seed, root ginger and dried red chilies. Keeping these separate, he would also have to make a mixture of powdered aromatic spices called *garam masala (Recipe Index)*—cloves, cinnamon, cardamom, fennel, mace, cumin seed, turmeric and nutmeg.

Equally important, the cook would have to know the precise order and the exact moment in the cooking process when each of the individual spices and the *garam masala* should be added to the meat. (The correct order is first the coriander, then the ginger, then the *garam masala,* then the chilies.)

In the final stage of preparing *roghan josh,* the fresh (as distinguished from the dry or powdered) spices would be introduced—finely chopped green ginger, coriander leaf and green chili. Throughout the whole process of preparing the *roghan josh* the cook would judge his spicing with an eye for the color and aroma of the dish as well as its flavor. The timing and amounts would depend on the individual flair of the cook, and, irritatingly enough, this is one reason why it is so difficult to get a coherent recipe from an expert. He will tell you to cook the dish until it "looks right," or to gauge the seasoning by the "right smell." The familiar phrase in recipes "season to taste," has a peculiarly individual meaning in India. It refers strictly to *your* taste rather than to that of some omniscient, arbitrary outside authority. You should have sufficient trust in your own palate and enough of a sense of adventure to improvise—but, as in Indian music, to improvise within the rules.

The character and importance of spices have been recognized in India from the earliest times. Sanskrit writings of 3,000 years ago describe many of the best-known spices, stressing their value as food preservatives—an important consideration in the Indian climate—and attaching special emphasis to their purported medicinal properties. The ancient Sanskrit treatise on *Ayurveda* —the Hindu science of medicine—listed pepper as an ingredient in medicines to cure digestive ailments. It also recommended chilies for digestive ailments and paralysis. Turmeric was to be applied externally as a paste for itches and skin diseases and as a depilatory. Ginger was suggested as a remedy for liver complaints, flatulence, anemia and rheumatism. Cardamom was acclaimed for a whole range of medicinal uses—to combat halitosis, nausea, headaches, fevers, coughs, colds, piles and eye diseases. Coriander was prescribed for constipation, insomnia and childbearing, while whole cloves were recommended for fevers, dyspepsia, toning up the heart, brain ailments, spleen, liver, kidney, stomach and intestinal disorders.

Through the ages the lure of spice riches drew explorers and traders to India's shores. Far back in history, what is now the Malabar Coast of Kerala ranked as one of the Old World's most important trading centers. Phoenician sailors of King Solomon's empire navigated the Arabian Sea to Malabar to purchase spices. Greeks and Romans from the West and Chinese from the East made their way there for the same purpose. Along trade routes of antiquity caravans of as many as 4,000 camels laden with spices and the rich merchandise of the East laboriously plodded from Goa and Calicut to ports on

Vasco da Gama, the Portuguese explorer who opened the first sea route to India's spice riches in 1498, was acclaimed in this 17th Century Portuguese history book. The title "Dom Vasco da Gama" was conferred on him for his navigational exploits. The numeral VI refers to the fact that in 1524 he became the sixth Viceroy of India.

the Persian Gulf and the Mediterranean. From there the cargoes were trans-shipped to marketplaces in Rome and Athens and sold for enormous prices. In the 13th Century Marco Polo, returning to Venice from Cathay by way of India, reported an abundance of pepper, ginger and cinnamon on the Malabar Coast. Later, as tales of the great spice treasures of India and the East multiplied, a period of unparalleled drama in world history unfolded. The great events in this drama—Christopher Columbus' voyage to America, Vasco da Gama's discovery of the sea route round the Cape of Good Hope to Asia, and the first circumnavigation of the world by Magellan—all might, without stretching historical fact and motivation to unreasonable lengths, be ascribed to the value and importance of spices.

Each of these giants in the annals of adventure, exploration and the expansion of mankind's horizons set out on his unimaginably hazardous journey with the purpose of finding a new route to India and the Spice Islands—Java, Sumatra, the Moluccas and Celebes. Each hoped to capture for his country the command of an immensely lucrative spice trade, and each, almost incidentally, changed the whole world's concept of itself. Together these explorers heralded the end of global geographic ignorance, began the charting of new continents, and eventually relegated the mighty Mediterranean—the "Center of the Earth" and a vital highway of international commerce—to the status of a landlocked backwater. And all as a part of the search for spices.

The great dream of an ocean route from Europe to the riches of the Orient did not become a reality until Vasco da Gama arrived at Calicut on India's Malabar Coast in 1498. This event signaled an extraordinary chapter of naval history, in which men faced piracy and violent death, made enormous fortunes, and negotiated unprecedented trade agreements between European royalty and Asian princes. The first such letter, sent by the splendid Zamorin (ruler) of Calicut to the King of Portugal, was inscribed on a palm leaf with an iron stylus. "Vasco da Gama, a gentleman of your household, came to my country, whereat I was pleased. My country is rich in cinnamon, cloves, ginger, pepper and precious stones. That which I ask you in exchange is gold, silver, corals and scarlet cloth."

From that moment on, after bitter sea battles, Portugal wrested the domination of the enormously lucrative spice trade from the Arab mariners and merchants who for centuries had controlled the shipping in the Indian Ocean, the Arabian Sea and the Red Sea. They had channeled their cargoes of spices through Egypt and the Levant to be sold in Europe at incredible prices—a pound of ginger, for instance, sold in England for as much as a full-grown sheep. And even now, there is still, in Dutch usage, a phrase for anything outrageously expensive—"It's as costly as pepper!"

Over the centuries, the three functions of spices in Indian cooking—medicinal, preservative and seasoning—became separated, and in present-day cooking only the concern with flavor remains important, though traces of the old uses, their origins half forgotten, still continue. Lentils or peas, for example, will almost certainly be cooked with ginger, asafetida, mint or dill, which are supposed to counteract flatulence, and the legend still persists that highly spiced food is a virtual necessity for good health as it stimulates the liver, which is apt to become sluggish in a tropical climate.

In pursuing the search for appropriate flavor no Indian cook will admit to hard and fast rules for the use of spices, but a few obvious principles do emerge from even the most cursory exploration of Indian cooking. Common sense would tell you that certain spices—turmeric, coriander, cumin, pepper —are too strong, too sharp or too bitter to be used in sweets, although spices that *are* used in sweets—cardamom, saffron, cinnamon—frequently form part of the flavoring of savory dishes too. And then, *garam masala* is seldom used (I have come across it only in some Bengali recipes) for fish or vegetables or any preparation in which its strongly pungent taste would overpower the more delicate nature of the main ingredients. Turmeric is very rarely found in dry vegetable dishes *(bhujiyas)* that require a short cooking time; it needs a sauce to mellow its rather acrid taste. In some dishes, the very popular lamb *korma*, for example, the spice combination (poppy seeds, ground cinnamon sticks, cardamom and cloves) is as important for the rich texture it gives to the sauce as for its flavor. In others, it is the aroma of a particular spice that takes precedence. When one of the more elaborate North Indian *pulaus* (pilafs) is served, tradition calls for the room to be filled with the fragrance of saffron before the guests begin to eat.

Sometimes spices are used primarily to please the eye, to give the "right" color to a dish. A magnificently strong and versatile Kerala fish curry ("curry" is used here in its proper sense of a highly seasoned stew with plenty of sauce) achieves its characteristic bright red color through the use of powdered chilies and a South Indian fruit called *kokum*, which is described in Sanskrit literature as resembling, in color and texture, the mouth of a beautiful woman—though not, presumably, in taste, which is exceedingly acid. Similarly the "green curries" of lamb or chicken or liver require fresh coriander leaves and green chilies, while turmeric is sometimes used to give a festive yellow color to rice.

Besides these fairly flexible principles of spicing in Indian food, there are one or two other generalizations that can safely be made. On the whole, the North uses more dry spices than the South, and pounds them to make a powder rather than grinding them with a liquid to make a paste. In fact there are groups of women, professional spice pounders, who go from house to house in the North, carrying their cumbersome equipment with them. Usually they work in threes, setting up a heavy wooden trough and manipulating their tall, brass-bound wooden poles with astonishing precision and dexterity. They will pound a month's supply of spices for you—chilies, coriander, turmeric, whatever—each one separately, to be kept in air-tight jars and mixed into *masalas* as you require them.

Generally speaking, the South prefers fresh or green spices, which cannot be stored. These spices are ground with water, lime juice, coconut milk or vinegar to make "wet" *masalas*, which vary in consistency according to the amount of liquid used. The contrasting use of spices reflects a basic difference between the main staple foods of the North and South. The rice eaters of the South number many more liquid dishes in their cooking repertoire. To counteract the dryness of plain boiled rice, sauce is necessary and a wet *masala* blends more smoothly and more evenly in a sauce. The North produces an immense variety of dishes in which the sauce is reduced to a bare minimum, or doesn't exist at all. Here, where bread is used as a utensil for pick-

How to Handle Hot Chilies

Hot chilies are as essential to many Indian dishes as they are to the food of Latin America. The recipes in this book have been carefully adjusted to suit American tastes, while preserving the essential character of each dish. No recipe uses more than three chilies; most use only one. If you like their flavor, increase the chilies to your taste.

However many you use, chilies require special handling. Their volatile oils can make your skin tingle and your eyes burn. Wear rubber gloves, and be careful not to touch your face or eyes while working with the chilies.

To prepare chilies, first rinse them clean in cold water. (Hot water may make fumes rise from dried chilies, and even the fumes might irritate your nose and eyes.) Working under cold running water, pull out the stem of each chili. Indian cooks sometimes leave the seeds (which are the hottest parts of chilies) intact in the pods. When the chilies are to be seeded, break or cut the pods in half and brush out the seeds with your fingers. In most cases the ribs inside are thin and may be left intact, but if they seem thick and fleshy, cut them out with a small, sharp knife. Follow the instructions included in the recipes for slicing, chopping or grinding chilies.

Opposite: Itinerant spice grinders prepare turmeric and chilies for a household in Udaipur. The woman at left pounds the turmeric into small pieces with a mortar and pestle, and the other women then pulverize the pieces to powder with a grinding stone called a *chakki*. These professional spice grinders earn about 55 cents a day. On the wall above them is a painting of Ganesha, the Hindu god of good fortune.

Fresh spices are dispensed at this busy stall in the Crawford Market, Bombay's largest produce center. The customer—a member of Bombay's Bohora Muslim community—is purchasing some green coriander, which is seen in the foreground as well as in the basket at left. Above the boy's head at the left are ginger and garlic. The baskets on the shelves to the right of the clerk hold chilies and more garlic.

ing up other foods (remember you are eating with your fingers), drier foods are much easier to manage. But because spices should never taste "raw," and there is no sauce here to mellow them, a *masala* is frequently lightly cooked in *ghee* before the main ingredients of the dish are added.

Beyond these very general observations, as an Indian cook you are on your own. Only time, experience and experimentation can teach you and give you the necessary confidence. One thing you will quickly discover is that (as elsewhere) no two culinary experts agree; even the best Indian cooks will argue endlessly over the inclusion or exclusion of particular spices and herbs. This point was brought home to me once when a cooking expert whose experience and judgment I had every reason to trust showed me (and allowed me to taste) a good, serviceable, simple way to prepare *garam masala* that called for 15 grams (½ ounce) of dried and powdered cardamom and 30 grams each of cloves, cinnamon and peppercorns.

Not long after that, a cousin of mine came to tea, and I asked her opinion of what seemed to me a remarkably useful and unfussy recipe. She looked at me as though I had lost my wits. "Pepper?" she said. *"Pepper?* But everybody knows you can't use pepper in *garam masala*. It catches the throat." (An unpardonable sin in spicing—a *masala* may sting your palate, but on no account must it "catch the throat," for that can only mean that the spices have not been allowed to mellow in the cooking. With *garam masala* this is a special hazard because the *masala* is often added to a dish in the final phase of preparation so that the aroma will not be lost. Pepper, on such an occasion, would not have time to mellow, would remain raw to the taste, and consequently would be disastrous to the dish.)

40

My cousin, too, was brought up in our grandmother's household in Allahabad, and later received an even more exhaustive and meticulous training from her mother-in-law—a not unusual procedure in India, and the source of some truly inspired cooking. She proceeded to give me her own—or rather, her mother-in-law's—recipe for *garam masala,* and insisted on listing the weights and ingredients by their Indian names. She felt she couldn't be accurate enough if she used Western measurements, for the proportions of the spices are supremely important, and she didn't know the English names for some of the spices—in one case, at least, neither do I. Here is her list:

½ *seer* of *zira* (cumin seed). One *seer* is a little over 2 pounds

1 *pau* (8 ounces) of *saunf* (fennel)

1 *pau* of *bari ilaychi* (these are the big, very strong, slightly bitter cardamoms that are used only in cooking)

1 *chittak* (2 ounces) of *choti ilaychi* (the smaller, sweeter cardamoms that Indians often eat with betel nut or in a *paan* as a digestive after a meal)

1 *chittak* of *laung* (cloves)

1 *chittak* of *dalchini* (cinnamon)

1 *chittak* of *badiani khatai* (a small dark-brown dried flower)

1 *tola* (⅖ ounce) *javitri* (mace)

½ *tola* of *kesar* (saffron)

2 *jaiphal* (whole nutmeg)

My cousin went on to explain that there is a particular and important routine to be observed in mixing these spices. First, they must all be lightly roasted in a dry pan, and the cook should allow for the fact that some spices

Dried and powdered spices for every need are featured at another stall in the Crawford Market. The bins on either side in the foreground are filled with chilies. Garlic, coriander seeds and turmeric are in the boxes immediately in front of the clerk, while tamarind is piled to the right of him. The glass cases behind him hold aniseed, turmeric powder, mustard, cumin seed, bay leaf, pepper, cardamom and other spices.

41

How and When to Substitute Spices

Indians use spices lavishly and cook with an astonishing variety of them. Most spices, such as the cumin, cardamom and turmeric commonly included in the recipes in this book, are available at well-stocked supermarkets. Such unfamiliar spices as fresh ginger root or black mustard seeds can be found at Oriental stores like those listed on page 197. Avoid making substitutions; the entire character of a dish may change. It is always best to use the traditional form of a spice; whole spices tend to retain flavor longer than ground ones and the two forms are not of equal pungency. However, if you must, substitute equal quantities of ground spices for whole ones (or the reverse). In such a case, taste the finished dish carefully and correct the seasoning by adding more if necessary.

cook more quickly than others. The cumin seed and fennel take only a little while. (How long, exactly? "Well, naturally, you can tell at once from the change in smell. The color begins to get a bit darker, too." I figured it at three or four minutes in a medium-hot pan.) The two kinds of cardamom and the nutmeg, first peeled and coarsely crushed to release their flavor, take four or five minutes, and the cloves, cinnamon and *badiani khatai* about seven minutes. Consequently each group has to be cooked separately, then mixed with the saffron (which isn't cooked at all), and then the whole lot is pounded together into a fine powder. If this *garam masala* is kept in an airtight container, it can stay fresh for six months and prove sufficient for the needs of a family of, say, 10 people.

Of course, my cousin remarked, there are some people who prefer to omit the saffron from the recipe because of its inordinately high price—almost as high as gold—or to substitute a variety cheaper than the true Kashmiri saffron. But anyone who really cared about decent eating would consider such senseless penny pinching an insult to the palate. Much better to save on something else—liquor, for instance, which ruins the taste of good food.

My cousin's confidence in her *garam masala* would probably not have been shaken, though she would certainly have had to argue its merits, if she had met yet another excellent cook whom I consulted. His recipe included only the small cardamoms (for their superior aroma), as well as ginger, cloves, coriander seed, turmeric, red chilies, dried garlic and cumin seed. He made a rather recondite distinction between the small, dark and bitter-sharp cumin and the big, light and sweetish seed. These are never used together, and for his *garam masala*, he preferred the gentler ones. I can guess my cousin's reaction. Ginger? Turmeric? Red chilies? Imagine how such aggressive spices would "catch the throat"!

She might, however, make allowances for his eccentricities because she would assume, quite correctly, that he was a Southerner. His inclusion of garlic would have told her that. It is seldom used in North Indian Hindu cooking, and never by Kashmiris, who consider it at best inflaming to the baser passions, and at worst *jhuta*, or unclean. Moreover, before he added his *garam masala* to a dish he would grind it, in the Southern way, with fresh

When an Indian cook grinds liquid and seasonings together, the result is a "wet" *masala*. The ingredients shown here (from right, clockwise on the metal tray) include red chilies, ginger, poppy seeds, coriander seeds, onion and garlic. A pan above them holds water; at top is grated coconut.

green chilies and chopped onions browned in coconut oil, to make a paste.

Nevertheless, in one form or another, with innumerable variations dictated by personal taste or local custom, some form of prepared *garam masala* can be found in most Indian kitchens. Besides this there are a few other *masalas* —or rather some of the most commonly used mixtures of spices—that can be enlarged or embellished according to the *masala* requirements for a particular dish, but meanwhile can be kept (in air-tight containers, of course) for three to six months. Of these, perhaps the simplest and the basis for hundreds of meat preparations is one that calls for coriander seed, red chilies, turmeric and cumin seed. (You may want to hold down the amount of chili if you prefer your food quite bland.) These ingredients are simply dry-cooked a few minutes and then pounded to a powder.

There are many other *masalas,* for *pulaus* and chicken dishes, and finally, there is another combination of spices called *chaunk,* which is not exactly a *masala* and has two separate uses. It is a mixture of about a half teaspoon each of whole mustard seed, cumin, and a medium-sized, finely chopped onion (or garlic in the South). The *chaunk* is always browned in *ghee* or oil until the mustard seeds begin to pop. Sometimes this is done right at the beginning of the preparation of many sauceless vegetable dishes, or some *pulaus.* Sometimes it is done at the very end, as a last flourish to the taste. In such potentially bland dishes as *raytas* (cold mixtures of curds and cooked or raw vegetables) or *dals* (thick or thin purées of the many kinds of lentils), the final addition of the *chaunk* is considered especially important.

In the end, as any Indian cook will tell you, the real standard of good spicing is not *which* spices you use (a matter of individual taste or regional custom), but *how* you use them. The classic test applies decisively in India as anywhere else—the proof of the pudding. A dish is well-cooked when the spices blend into the gravy and the meat. You should be unaware of spices as separate ingredients. They should never taste raw, should never "catch your throat," and should never be so intrusive that the essential character of the dish is lost. But as in any art, the personality and special vision of the artist are vital factors, and in Indian cooking, it is through spicing that you express your individuality and your special talent as a cook.

With her right hand the cook adds whole seasonings and water; with her left she pounds the oversized Indian pestle into a flat circular mortar to turn the combination into a smooth "wet" *masala.* The flat edge around the bowl of the mortar catches any spattering of spices or liquid.

The still life shows a
selection of leading Indian
spices. Black and white
pepper come from the same
berry. The nutmeg tree
provides mace and nutmeg.

1 Green pepper berries
2 Fruit of nutmeg tree
3 Mace
4 Nutmeg
5 Green cardamom pods
6 Dried cardamom pods
7 Dried cloves
8 Green cloves
9 Black and white pepper

The Roots and Berries
That Season India's Food

India is a land of spices, where pepper, cardamom, ginger, turmeric and chilies grow in profusion. The plants and vines that produce these zesty berries, roots and seeds require hot weather and a heavy rainfall for their growth, and India's monsoon climate perfectly fills the bill. More than two million Indian acres are devoted to the production of spices, most of them to chilies, pepper, turmeric and ginger (which, as seen below, must be peeled before it can be used). Indian cooks use these spices in an endless variety of combinations. In preparing this book and the accompanying Recipe Booklet, for example, more than 100 recipes were tested. No two of these recipes used exactly the same spice combination.

A Popular Spice with a Wide Variety of Uses

On the spice shelf in almost any Indian kitchen you will find a jar of turmeric, a slightly bitter spice that Indian cooks use in curries, pickles, and other highly seasoned dishes. As seen above, turmeric is the rhizome (underground stem) of a small plant. Before it can be used, it must be boiled, dried and ground to a fine yellow powder *(opposite)*. The versatile rhizome is valued in India not only for its culinary uses; it serves also as a dye, a coloring for paint, an ingredient in medicines used to treat skin disorders and a cosmetic for pretty Indian women.

At a spice mill in Bombay, a workman *(background)* dumps turmeric into a machine that grinds the rhizomes to a fine powder. The mill can convert two tons of turmeric a day.

The King of All the Spices

Pepper is not to be sneezed at; it is India's most important spice crop and is sometimes called "the king of spices." Men have fought and died for it, Alaric the Goth demanded it as ransom when he besieged Rome in 408 A.D., and English tenants in the Middle Ages were forced to pay part of their rent in this commodity. The spice grows on a tropical vine—mainly in the state of Kerala in Southwest India. Black pepper is the whole berry, picked while it is still green *(left)*, then spread out in the sun on straw mats *(below)* to dry. (White pepper is the core of the ripened berry.) When the berries have dried for a couple of days in the sun, the grower sells them to a wholesaler, who dries them further, grades them according to size, and packages them to be sold in Indian markets or shipped overseas. So highly valued is pepper for its pungent flavor and aroma that in a recent year 24,000 tons were exported.

Using a tried and tested method, Indian women in a field near New Delhi hurl drying chilies into the air to let the wind blow away the straw and sand. Some of these spices are so hot that they will literally sear the mouth and lips of people who are not used to eating them. On the following pages a farm woman near Madurai, in South India, picks out rotten pods from a field strewn with drying chilies, and turns over the good pods to let both sides dry in the sun.

MASALAS: Spices are the key to Indian cooking. Though some foods, such as fried okra with cumin (recipe, opposite), employ only two or three spices, most dishes are made with the elaborate combinations of freshly ground seasonings called masalas. The masalas vary widely and each is designed for a special purpose. Garam masala, for example, is a basic blend of dried spices to be used alone or with other seasonings. (See page 55 for a typical recipe.) Other masalas, each devised to suit a particular dish, combine spices with herbs and may be ground with water, vinegar or another liquid to make a paste or "wet masala." In some cases nuts, coconut, even onion or garlic may be added. The flavors may be balanced to create a harmonious blend, or a single flavor may be emphasized as in a "cardamom masala" or a "coriander masala." To release its flavors, a masala is usually cooked—separately or with other ingredients—before the appropriate meat, fish or other food is added to the pan.

The traditional Indian cook uses various grinding stones as well as mortars and pestles to prepare dry and wet masalas. A more modern and less arduous technique, used in this book, is to grind the seasonings in an electric blender. To ensure a fine grind and avoid overheating the blender, other liquids from the recipe, such as yoghurt and coconut milk, are sometimes blended with the masala.

Murg Ilaychi

CHICKEN CARDAMOM

To serve 6 to 8

MASALA

1 cup unflavored yoghurt
The seeds of 12 cardamom pods
  or 1 teaspoon cardamom seeds
2 tablespoons scraped, finely chopped
  fresh ginger root
1 tablespoon finely chopped garlic
1 teaspoon fennel seeds
½ teaspoon ground hot red pepper

CHICKENS

2 chickens, 2½ to 3 pounds each
4 teaspoons salt
½ teaspoon saffron threads
3 tablespoons boiling water
½ cup *ghee (page 54)*
A 3-inch piece of cinnamon stick
2 whole cloves
2 cups finely chopped onions
½ cup cold water

First prepare the *masala* in the following fashion: Combine the yoghurt, cardamom, ginger, garlic, fennel and red pepper in the jar of an electric blender and blend at high speed for 30 seconds. Turn off the machine, scrape down the sides of the jar with a rubber spatula, and blend again until the spices are pulverized and the *masala* reduced to a smooth purée.

Pat the chickens completely dry inside and out with paper towels and truss them securely. Rub the salt firmly into the skin of both birds and place them in a large shallow baking dish. With your hands or a rubber spatula, spread the skin of each bird with the *masala*. Marinate at room temperature for at least 1 hour, or in the refrigerator for at least 2 hours.

Meanwhile, place the saffron threads in a small bowl or cup, pour in 3 tablespoons of boiling water, and let them soak for at least 10 minutes.

In a heavy casserole large enough to hold the chickens side by side, heat the *ghee* over moderate heat until a drop of water flicked into it splutters instantly. Add the cinnamon and cloves and cook, stirring, until they are evenly coated with *ghee*. Add the onions and, stirring constantly, fry for 7 or 8 minutes, until they are soft and a delicate gold color. Watch for any sign of burning and regulate the heat accordingly.

Place the birds in the casserole, pour in all the *masala,* and add the saffron and its soaking liquid. Turning the chickens frequently, cook over moderate heat for about 10 minutes, or until the birds color lightly without really browning and the *ghee* separates from the *masala* and rises to the surface. Stir in the ½ cup of cold water and bring to a boil over high heat.

Immediately reduce the heat to low. Cover the casserole with a piece of aluminum foil, crimping it at the edges to hold it securely, and set the lid firmly in place. Cook for 30 to 35 minutes, or until the chickens are tender but

Pungent lemony cardamom seeds, next to saffron the world's most precious spice, lend their name and flavor to chicken cardamom.

not falling apart. Remove the casserole from the heat and let the chickens rest, covered, for 15 to 20 minutes before serving.

To serve, transfer the chickens to a deep serving platter. Discard the cinnamon stick and cloves, and moisten the birds with the sauce remaining in the casserole.

Sabzi Bhindi

FRIED OKRA WITH CUMIN

Wash the fresh okra under cold running water, and with a small, sharp knife, scrape the skin lightly to remove any surface fuzz. (Frozen okra needs only to be defrosted and drained.) Pat dry with paper towels.

In a heavy 10- to 12-inch skillet, heat the *ghee* over moderate heat until a drop of water flicked into it splutters instantly. Add the onions and salt, and stir for 7 or 8 minutes, or until they are golden brown. Watch carefully for any sign of burning and regulate the heat accordingly. Add the okra, cumin and pepper, and continue to fry, lifting and turning the vegetables constantly, for 25 minutes, or until the okra is tender and most of the liquid in the pan has evaporated. (Unlike fresh okra, frozen okra will be somewhat sticky at the end of the cooking time.) Serve at once from a heated bowl.

To serve 4

3 tablespoons *ghee (page 54)*
1 medium-sized onion, peeled, cut in half lengthwise, then sliced lengthwise into paper-thin slivers
1 teaspoon salt
1 pound whole fresh okra, or 2 ten-ounce packages frozen okra, thoroughly defrosted
1 tablespoon ground cumin
¼ teaspoon freshly ground black pepper

Ghee

INDIAN BUTTER OIL

To make about 1½ cups

1 pound unsalted butter, divided
into ¼-pound pieces

In a heavy 4- to 5-quart saucepan, heat the butter over moderate heat, turning it about with a spoon to melt it slowly and completely without letting it brown. Then increase the heat and bring the butter to a boil. When the surface is completely covered with a white foam, stir the butter gently and immediately reduce the heat to the lowest possible point. Simmer uncovered and undisturbed for 45 minutes, or until the milk solids on the bottom of the pan are a golden brown and the butter on top is transparent.

Slowly pour the clear liquid *ghee* into a large bowl, straining it through a fine sieve lined with a linen towel or 4 layers of dampened cheesecloth. If there are any solids (no matter how small) left in the *ghee*, strain it again to prevent it from becoming rancid later. The *ghee* must be perfectly clear.

Pour the *ghee* into a jar or crock, cover tightly, and store in the refrigerator or at room temperature until ready to use. *Ghee* will solidify when it is chilled, and for those recipes that require liquid *ghee* it should be melted but not browned over low heat unless otherwise indicated. It may be safely kept at room temperature for 2 or 3 months.

NOTE: Cooking the butter evaporates its water content and separates the pure fat from the milk solids—to create a substance that resembles clarified butter. However, cooking the butter over low heat for a relatively long period not only clarifies it but also gives it a distinctive nutlike flavor produced by no other method. There are no traditional substitutes for *ghee*, but if you are willing to settle for less than the real thing, you may when pressed for time use simple clarified butter in the amounts indicated for the *ghee*. To make it, cut unsalted butter into small bits and, in a small saucepan or skillet, melt it slowly over low heat. Let the butter rest for a minute off the heat, then skim off the foam. Spoon the clear butter into a bowl. Discard the milky solids at the bottom of the pan. A quarter-pound stick of butter (8 tablespoons) yields 5 or 6 tablespoons of clarified butter.

Dam Alu

DEEP-FRIED NEW POTATOES STEAMED WITH SPICES AND YOGHURT

To serve 6

2 pounds new potatoes, each about
1½ inches in diameter, scrubbed
but not peeled
Vegetable oil
1 tablespoon finely chopped fresh
ginger root
1 fresh hot red or green chili, about
3 inches long, stemmed and seeded
(*caution: see page 39*), and cut
crosswise into paper-thin slices
1 teaspoon salt
¼ teaspoon ground hot red pepper
1½ teaspoons *garam masala (page
56)*
½ teaspoon ground cumin
½ teaspoon turmeric
3 tablespoons finely chopped fresh
coriander (*cilantro*)
1 cup yoghurt
¼ cup water

Drop the potatoes into enough boiling water to cover them completely, and boil briskly, uncovered, for 10 minutes. Then drain and peel them.

Pour 2 cups of vegetable oil into a 10-inch *karhai (page 151)* or 12-inch *wok,* or pour 2 to 3 inches of oil into a deep fryer. Heat the oil until it reaches a temperature of 350° on a deep-frying thermometer. In 2 or 3 batches, deep-fry the potatoes for about 2 minutes, or until golden brown on all sides. As they brown, transfer them to paper towels and make five or six ½-inch-deep pricks in each potato with a small skewer or toothpick.

In a heavy 2- to 3-quart saucepan with a tightly fitting lid, heat 3 tablespoons of vegetable oil over moderate heat until a light haze forms above it. Add the ginger and fresh chili, and fry until they are coated with oil. Stirring constantly, add the salt, ground red pepper, 1 teaspoon of the *garam masala,* the cumin, turmeric and fresh coriander. Stir in the yoghurt and water, and bring to a boil. Add the potatoes, turn them about with a spoon to coat them on all sides, and reduce the heat to the lowest possible point. Cover the pan with a sheet of foil and crimp the edges to secure the foil firmly. Set the lid on top and simmer for 20 minutes. Remove the pan from the heat and let the potatoes rest for about 20 minutes before uncovering them.

To serve, mound the potatoes on a heated platter, pour the sauce over them and sprinkle the top with the remaining ½ teaspoon of *garam masala.*

Kesar Chaval
SAFFRON RICE

Pour the rice into a sieve or colander set in a large pot of cold water, and rub the grains lightly between your fingers to remove all surface starch. Changing the water 4 or 5 times, wash the rice until the water remains absolutely clear. Drain the rice thoroughly. Place the saffron in a small bowl, pour in 3 tablespoons of the boiling water, and soak them for 10 minutes or so.

Meanwhile, in a heavy 3- to 4-quart casserole with a tightly fitting lid, heat the *ghee* over moderate heat until a drop of water flicked into it splutters instantly. Add the cinnamon and cloves and, when they are coated with *ghee,* add the onions. Lifting and turning the ingredients constantly, fry them for 7 or 8 minutes, or until the onions are soft and golden brown. Watch carefully for any sign of burning and regulate the heat accordingly. Add the rice and stir for about 5 minutes, until all of the liquid in the pan has evaporated and the grains are a delicate golden color. Again stirring constantly, add the remaining 4 cups of boiling water, the jaggery (or brown sugar and molasses), salt and cardamom seeds, and bring to a boil over high heat. Add the saffron and its soaking water, stir gently, then reduce the heat to the lowest possible point. Cover tightly and cook for 25 minutes, or until the rice is tender and has absorbed all the liquid. Fluff the rice with a fork and serve at once, mounded on a heated platter or in a large bowl.

Murgi Kari
CHICKEN CURRY

Pat the chicken pieces dry with paper towels and sprinkle them with 2 teaspoons of the salt. In a heavy 10- to 12-inch skillet, heat the oil over high heat until a drop of water flicked into it splutters instantly. Add the chicken and fry for 3 or 4 minutes, turning the pieces about with a spoon until they are white and somewhat firm. Transfer the chicken to a plate.

Add the onions, garlic and ginger to the oil remaining in the skillet and, stirring constantly, fry for 7 or 8 minutes, or until the onions are soft and golden brown. Reduce the heat to low, add the cumin, turmeric, ground coriander, red pepper, fennel and 1 tablespoon of the water, and, stirring constantly, fry for a minute or so. Stir in the tomatoes, 1 tablespoon of the fresh coriander, the yoghurt and the remaining teaspoon of salt.

Increase the heat to moderate and add the chicken and any juices that have accumulated in the plate. Pour in the remaining water. Bring to a boil, meanwhile turning the chicken about in the sauce to coat the pieces evenly. Sprinkle the top with the *garam masala* and the remaining tablespoon of fresh coriander, reduce the heat to low, cover tightly, and simmer for 20 minutes, or until the chicken is tender but not falling apart.

To serve, arrange the chicken attractively on a heated platter, pour the sauce remaining in the skillet over it, and sprinkle with the lemon juice.

To serve 6 to 8

2 cups imported *basumati* rice or other uncooked long-grain white rice
1 teaspoon saffron threads
3 tablespoons plus 4 cups boiling water
6 tablespoons *ghee (opposite)*
A 2-inch piece stick cinnamon
4 whole cloves
1 cup finely chopped onions
1 tablespoon crumbled imported jaggery, or substitute dark-brown sugar combined with dark molasses *(page 196)*
2 teaspoons salt
The seeds of 3 cardamom pods or ¼ teaspoon cardamom seeds

To serve 4 to 6

2 to 2½ pounds skinned chicken legs and thighs and boned, skinned, split chicken breasts
3 teaspoons salt
½ cup vegetable oil
1½ cups finely chopped onions
1 tablespoon finely chopped garlic
1½ teaspoons scraped, finely chopped fresh ginger root
1 teaspoon ground cumin
1 teaspoon turmeric
1 teaspoon ground coriander
1 teaspoon ground hot red pepper
¼ teaspoon ground fennel, or fennel seeds pulverized with a mortar and pestle
½ cup water
1 cup finely chopped fresh tomatoes, or substitute 1 cup chopped, drained, canned tomatoes
2 tablespoons finely chopped fresh coriander
½ cup unflavored yoghurt
1 teaspoon *garam masala (page 56)*
1 tablespoon fresh lemon juice

Garam masala is made by grinding or pounding dried spices together. Though it is probably the prototype of the spice blend known in the West as "curry powder," a *garam masala* is made at home and every cook has her own ideas about which spices should be included and in what quantity. A basic version shown at right in a *prath* combines *(from top right, clockwise)* whole black peppercorns, cumin seeds, cardamom pods, coriander seeds, whole cloves and stick cinnamon. These spices are roasted in the oven. Then the cinnamon is crushed, the cardamom pods are broken open and the seeds are stripped from them *(opposite)* to be mixed with the other spices. In the recipe below, the spices are then ground in an electric blender.

To make about 1½ cups

5 three-inch pieces cinnamon stick
1 cup whole cardamom pods,
    preferably green cardamoms
½ cup whole cloves
½ cup whole cumin seeds
¼ cup whole coriander seeds
½ cup whole black peppercorns

Garam Masala
GROUND SPICE MIXTURE

Preheat the oven to 200°. Spread the cinnamon, cardamom, cloves, cumin, coriander and peppercorns in one layer in a jelly-roll pan or large shallow roasting pan. Roast on the bottom shelf of the oven for 30 minutes, stirring and turning the mixture two or three times with a large spoon. Do not let the spices brown or burn.

Break open the cardamom pods between your fingers or place them one at a time on a flat surface and press down on the pod with the ball of your thumb to snap it open. Pull the pod away from the seeds inside and discard it. Set the seeds aside.

Place the roasted cinnamon sticks between the two layers of a folded linen towel and pound them with a rolling pin or a kitchen mallet until they are finely crushed.

Combine the cardamom seeds, crushed cinnamon, cloves, cumin seeds, coriander seeds and peppercorns in a small pan or bowl and stir them together until they are well mixed.

Grind the spices a cup or so at a time by pouring them into the jar of an electric blender and blending at high speed for 2 or 3 minutes, until they are completely pulverized and become a smooth powder. If the machine clogs and stops, turn it off, stir the spices once or twice, then continue blending. As each cupful of spices is ground, transfer it to a jar or bottle with a tightly fitting lid.

Garam masala may be stored at room temperature in an airtight container, and will retain its full flavor for 5 or 6 months.

Roghan Josh
CURRIED LAMB

Place the lamb in a large shallow baking dish and sprinkle it evenly with the red pepper and salt. Combine the yoghurt, the chopped ginger root and the dissolved asafetida (if you are using it), and when they are well mixed pour them over the lamb, turning the pieces of meat about with a large spoon to coat them well on all sides.

Cover the dish tightly with aluminum foil or plastic wrap and marinate the lamb at room temperature for at least 1 hour or in the refrigerator for at least 2 hours.

In a heavy 10- to 12-inch skillet, heat the *ghee* over moderate heat until a drop of water flicked into it splutters instantly. Stir in a liberal grinding of black pepper and the turmeric, then add the lamb and its marinade and, turning and stirring the meat constantly, bring to a boil over high heat. Cover the skillet tightly, reduce the heat to the lowest possible point, and simmer undisturbed for 1 hour.

Sprinkle the lamb with coriander and pour ½ cup of the water down the sides of the pan. Then cover again and simmer for 15 minutes longer. Stir in ¼ cup of the water, cover, and cook for 15 minutes; then stir in the remaining ¼ cup of water, cover, and cook for about 10 minutes, or until the lamb is tender and shows no resistance when pierced with the point of a small, sharp knife. Taste for seasoning.

To serve, mound the lamb on a deep heated platter, moisten the meat with the liquid remaining in the skillet, and sprinkle the top with *garam masala (opposite)* and a pinch of nutmeg.

To serve 4

2 pounds lean boneless lamb, preferably leg or shoulder, sliced 1 inch thick and cut into 2-by-1-inch pieces
¼ teaspoon ground hot red pepper
1 teaspoon salt
1 cup unflavored yoghurt
1 tablespoon scraped, finely chopped fresh ginger root
¼ teaspoon asafetida (if available) dissolved in 1 tablespoon hot water
¼ cup *ghee (page 54)*
Freshly ground black pepper
½ teaspoon turmeric
2 tablespoons finely chopped fresh coriander
1 cup water
½ teaspoon *garam masala (opposite)*
A pinch of ground nutmeg, preferably freshly grated

III

An Extraordinary Vegetarian Cuisine

Meatless cooking can be rich and flavorful, as the acclaimed vegetarian treat *mattar pannir*, shown opposite, proves. Cubes of white homemade cheese and fresh garden peas are lavished with spices, then simmered to tenderness in savory gravy *(Recipe Index)*.

I f the diet is pure the mind will be pure," wrote Manu, the great Hindu lawgiver, "and if the mind is pure the intellect will be pure." Purity of mind and spirit is a cardinal Hindu virtue, ranking in importance with self-control, detachment and nonviolence. For many millions of Indians the purity of the mind and spirit demands a diet of such rigid vegetarianism that in addition to meat, fish and fowl, eggs are also forbidden. To some, even such blood-colored vegetables as beets and tomatoes are omitted from the categories of acceptable foods. Others refuse to eat root vegetables because the process of pulling, say, potatoes or carrots from the ground might cause the death of earthworms or grubs, and even such indirect taking of life is considered sinful. One result of this deeply held tradition is that India has produced one of the most varied and imaginative vegetarian cuisines in the world.

This has not always been the case. The early Sanskrit writings, dating from about 1200 B.C., make it quite clear that meat was commonly eaten at that time and that beef was a special luxury. The customary feast of welcome for an honored guest was supposed to include a fatted calf.

Today beef eating and the slaughter of cattle are such touchy subjects to orthodox Hindus in India that they have enshrined the "sacred cow" symbol in the English language and in the minds of foreigners. At home, it has occasioned debates in parliament, protests, riots, the siege of government offices and floods of letters to the press.

Religious zealots and political opportunists are somewhat embarrassed to find that the revered Vedas, the ancient scriptures, do not support their passionate insistence that the cow has always been sacred to Hindus, and its slaughter a religious offense. Yet as one noted scholar has said: "The ancients were not strict vegetarians in any sense of the term and ate meat freely not excluding beef. In fact the Ahimsa (reverence for life) doctrine had yet to make its influence felt in the direction of vegetarianism and the only question that is legitimate is, *when* this meat-eating was stopped and not when it started, so common it appears to be at this time."

It was a strange combination of influences—characteristic of India's tendency to jumble up the most arcane and the most commonplace matters in its peculiar amalgam of daily living—that was probably responsible for the growing respect for the cow and the eventual spread of vegetarianism in general. Gradually, *ahimsa,* the prime virtue in Buddhist teachings but a novel concept for India at the time (Fifth Century B.C.), began to gain popular acceptance among Indians. An additional factor was the blossoming of a religious cult centered on Lord Krishna, who grew up under the care of a milkmaid and whose closest companions were cowherds. As time passed he became deified, giving by extension a sort of deification to the cows with which popular imagination associated him. The rise of the influence of the Jain religion with its emphasis on the sanctity of all life—even insect and microscopic life—added to the general distaste for meat eating. And then there was just plain economic common sense—not only was the cow a gentle, harmless creature, but the value of milk and milk products and the use of cattle as beasts of burden and for work in the fields were far more important to agrarian Indians than the inclusion of beef in their diet.

By the Fifth Century B.C. Hindu scriptures prohibited meat and even honey for students (possibly in the interests of achieving a "pure intellect"). One Sanskrit verse stated flatly and rather ominously, "If people eat animals in this world, the animals will eat them in the other world." However, it was among Brahmins, traditionally the caste of priests and scholars, that the doctrinal strictures against meat eating came to be most rigorously enforced. Members of the other castes sometimes accepted vegetarianism either through religious persuasion or from economic necessity, but they remained considerably more flexible in their eating habits.

But nothing is simple in India. Vegetarianism, like almost everything else, is subject to qualifications and exceptions. The Saraswats, a particular Brahmin subcaste, claim a special dispensation to be allowed to eat fish. (Many of them live on the southwest coast where seafood is abundant, cheap and delicious, but that fortuitous convenience is never mentioned in theological discussions.) A number of Brahmins in Bengal also eat fish, probably through historic necessity, but they call it the "fruit of the sea" to take the curse off it as a nonvegetarian food. Kashmiri Brahmins will eat lamb and fish, but not chicken or eggs, while countless non-Brahmin families all over India remain strict vegetarians.

Taking the country as a whole, I think it is fair to say—to the extent that one can make *any* generalization about India—that the South is responsible for the true understanding, the refinement and the adventurousness of vegetarian cooking in India. Of course, the South is blessed with an overwhelming variety and profusion of vegetables and fruit, but there are historic and economic reasons as well for its vegetarianism.

With the Muslim invasions of the country beginning in the Eighth Century, all of North and Central India, where the Moghuls held their strongest power and founded their great cities, was introduced to new patterns of living, new manners and tastes, and a new cuisine in which meat was of immense importance. The South, for the most part, remained vegetarian, partly in defense of its religious traditions, partly because it was less affected by Moghul rule, partly from a chronic disdain for the lax, easily swayed, luxury-loving and unorthodox North—and mostly because it is a less affluent and more densely populated region.

The cooking of the South and the South-Central states of India contains several quite distinct regional cuisines, each with its special characteristics, styles and refinements. Madras concentrates on its versatility with grains and lentils; Maharashtra is perhaps the most sophisticated in its combinations of ingredients and the diverse and almost finicky modulations of its tastes; Gujarat has the blandest food; Marwari cooking is the richest; Kerala, like Goa, has to be put in an entirely different classification. There, the daily fare of most of the people follows the general nature of the Madras cuisine, but the cooking of the region is best known for the superb seafood dishes along the southwest coastal strip, and for the equally noteworthy nonvegetarian preparations that the large community of Christians in the area has added to the overall wealth of Indian food.

My first real introduction to India's vast vegetarian cuisine—or rather, to the vegetarian way of life of which the cuisine is only a part—occurred in the South. It came when I returned to India after several years of English boarding schools and went to stay with my South Indian grandmother. Much had changed in her small world since I had last seen her. My grandfather had retired from his medical practice, all her sons were scattered in foreign countries or other parts of India, and my grandparents lived with their only daughter and her husband. But so strong was tradition in that house and (I found to my surprise) in me, that I always thought of it as my grandmother's household, where she reigned uncontested—of course, behind the proper façade of always seeming to defer to the men in the family.

The reverence for life, fundamental to the whole concept of vegetarianism, was brought home to me soon after my arrival. The tall, shuttered doors of my second-floor bedroom, opening onto a narrow balcony over the garden, were nearly always kept open to allow the wind from the Arabian Sea to blow in. And with it, the pigeons. They used to perch on the beams, cooing and quarreling and making a quite distracting racket. When I mentioned this to my grandmother, she agreed unconcernedly that the pigeons were a bit noisy, but explained that it couldn't be helped because, after all, they did nest in the rafters. I asked her if this wasn't sometimes inconvenient, but she said, "Not at all. They deserve the shelter as much as we do." And then she added, by way of a warning not to disturb them, "You might have been a pigeon in your last birth." A chastening thought.

It was hardly surprising that vegetarianism, as one aspect of orthodox Brahmin living, was the rule in her house as it is in many millions of Indian homes. To my grandmother and to other Indian cooks it would seem silly or unnecessary to emphasize that a vegetarian cuisine is designed to give full honor to the vegetables, cereals and "pulses" (protein-rich lentils, peas, beans) that it uses, by exploring their possibilities and heightening their essential nature. But I have found that foreigners often judge a vegetarian meal by how closely it can approximate a nonvegetarian meal. Can, for instance, a vegetable-and-nut cutlet be made to look and taste like meat? Is a vegetarian meal "hearty"? Is it nutritionally well-balanced? Does it look appetizing? Is it going to have the pallid air of dishes of boiled Brussels sprouts and potatoes (remember, I'd been in England for some years), without the comforting presence of roast beef to make it a *real* meal?

In a way, a whole shift of perspective is needed to understand and accept the dominant fact that Indian vegetarians aren't trying to make a meatless meal look, taste, smell or feel like a meal with meat. In fact, their objective is diametrically opposite. For them a vegetarian meal should be quite manifestly and triumphantly *vegetarian*. It can be (and is) hearty, appetizing, nutritionally well-balanced, satisfying, and still have a special flair and distinction of its own even though all meat, fish, fowl and eggs are excluded.

The extra dimension of ethical observance need not, perhaps, concern outsiders. To my grandmother, however, it was the heart of the matter. As a good Brahmin her standards of "purity" in food were uncompromising and were given extra authority by her deep concern for the life of all living creatures. Luckily this concern extended to more mundane expressions such as giving her family absolutely superb—though purely vegetarian—food.

To my other, North Indian, grandmother, the Southern contempt for elegance would have bordered on the shocking—the dismaying absence of ceremony in the preparing and serving of a meal, the preference for banana leaves and small disposable earthenware bowls above proper metal *thalis* and *katoris*, the niggardly use of *ghee* (a symbol of lavishness in the North)—all this would have seemed embarrassingly lacking in refinement. All the same, it was in that bare, utilitarian dining room, with its stone floor and white-washed walls providing an austere contrast to the hibiscus and bougainvillea tumbling about outside the windows (and the fussing pigeons fluttering up to my bedroom above), that my Southern grandmother produced some of the best and most surprising meals of my life, and it was there I was provided with a basic education in the vegetarian cuisine.

The first thing I discovered was that breakfast was the most interesting meal. It has remained my favorite in South India ever since. My grandmother still organized her family's day by the traditional meal hours, and breakfast was served—always by her, personally, though servants could help in the kitchen—at about 10:30. Coffee, freshly roasted and ground, of course, and some selection of whatever tropical fruit was in season had already taken care of any early morning pangs of hunger. Everyone in the family, my grandfather, cousins, my aunt, my mother, my sister and I, would be present. Only my uncle who worked in a Western-style office and kept different hours was missing. We all sat on reed mats on the floor, each with an individual low "table" of plain scrubbed wood on which the fresh banana leaf and the little earthenware bowls (thrown away after each meal) were set.

For so many years at school in England, breakfast, to me, had meant a gray, gelatinous mess called porridge, sometimes with watery scrambled eggs, bread and butter, and tea. My grandmother's idea of suitable breakfast dishes came as an extraordinary revelation of subtle and piquant tastes, and crisp or feathery or spongy textures. Her range was enormous, and it was hard to decide which of her breakfast preparations were the most delectable. One rule, however, was inviolable for them all—they had to be served fresh and steaming hot, directly from the kitchen *chula* to the table. I can still see her tiny, tidy figure, her brightly colored sari draped in the South Indian way. Barefoot, she moved noiselessly between the kitchen and the dining room with such economy of movement that she never appeared to be hurrying, yet she made certain that every helping was fresh and hot. It required a great many trips back and forth, and her sense of style demanded that this rigorous service be both rapid and unobtrusive.

Out of her extensive repertoire, three breakfast dishes have remained my favorites over the years: *idlis, dosas (Recipe Index)* and *hoppers.* I suppose they can all be described as rice cakes of one sort or another, made from rice flour with additions of varying amounts of ground lentils, but that makes them sound hopelessly dull and gives only the facts and none of the truth. It is rather like saying that croissants, brioches and pumpernickel are all breads. Each preparation has its distinct personality, texture and appearance, and just as a Western cook might be judged on his light hand with pastry, so a good South Indian cook is rated by the perfection of consistency, flavor and appearance he can give to each rice cake. My grandmother was supreme.

At this point, I think it necessary to explain briefly the particular importance and the versatility that rice and lentils have acquired in the South Indian vegetarian diet. Westerners, if they think of rice as a significant item in their meals at all, are likely to think of it as a simple, unvarying grain, boiled as an accompaniment to a meat dish, or cooked as some form of *risotto, paella* or rice pudding. In vegetarian India rice is viewed with much greater respect. For instance, an Indian housewife will specify the *kind* of rice she wants to buy for a particular dish—either the long-grain *basumati* or the Dehra Dun rice for *pulaus;* the round-grain varieties for sweets; polished rice for some dishes; partly husked and parboiled rice for many South Indian meals and semiglutinous rice for other occasions. Besides all these varieties, there is pressed rice, beaten rice, puffed rice and, finally, the all-important ground rice or rice flour.

With lentils, similarly, Indians are endlessly choosy. The country grows dozens of varieties—green-husked, black-husked, yellow, red, small, large, round, heart-shaped, flat, sprouted, dried, and on and on—and each is used in particular ways for individual preparations that require the special characteristics of *that* one kind of lentil above any other. While rice provides the bulk requirements for any South Indian meal, lentils are the major source of protein in a vegetarian diet. It is easy, then, to understand the attention that both have been given in South Indian cooking, and to appreciate the imagination and ingenuity that have produced such marvelously diverse dishes out of seemingly monotonous or pedestrian ingredients.

Consider, for example, my grandmother's breakfast dishes. Her *idlis* were fat, round little cakes, grayish white in color, spongy and slightly moist in consistency—*never* heavy, soggy or dry. Their texture was entirely smooth, without a trace of graininess, and the taste, disarmingly simple, slightly salty and hauntingly sour, gave no indication of the amount of trouble and expertise it took to produce this casual, charming flavor. In fact, she had to start work on an everyday breakfast the night before. First, she soaked the rice for half an hour, then she strained it, dried it and ground it. After that

Continued on page 69

Tender Care for India's Most Important Vegetarian Crop

For millions of vegetarians in India—especially those who live in the South and East—rice is the heart of every meal. When they dine, a mound of boiled rice appears at the center of the *thali* and they take a dab of it with almost every mouthful of food. They also eat rice steamed or fried, cook it with lentils and other vegetables, and combine it with sugar, almonds, pistachio nuts, dried and fresh fruits to produce delicate desserts. So important is rice in India that one fourth of all the country's cultivated land is devoted to its production. Here, as in other parts of the world, the grain is raised with special care. First, it is sown in muddy plots; then when the shoots are one to two feet tall (usually about a month after they are planted), special walled plots are flooded *(above)*. The rice is carefully transplanted to these paddies by hand *(opposite page)* and left there to grow until ready for harvesting three to six months later.

Indian agriculture still is a primitive business. Plows are simple iron-tipped sticks; crops are reaped with hand sickles and threshed by plodding animals. On the opposite page, near Madurai, South India, farm workers laboriously bring in the sheaves from a newly harvested rice field. Below, left, in another part of India (the village of Salajanga, near the east coast), tethered bullocks wheel in a tight circle, ponderously threshing rice as a farmer piles the stalks under their hooves.

India produces more than a thousand varieties of rice. In the market at Kottayam, in Kerala, two of these varieties—red and white—as well as puffed rice *(center rear)* are displayed. Red rice gets its color from the bran wrapping left around the kernel. Puffed rice is an ingredient of the popular snack, *bhelpuri (Recipe Index)*.

In rural South India a farm woman brings a bundle of cattle fodder to a market where she will sell it for 15 cents a pound.

she prepared the lentils; the particular sort of lentil that goes into the *idli* dough is called *urad*. Small and black-husked, it had to be soaked for an hour, then ground until it was light and frothy before being mixed with the rice. The *urad* acted as a kind of leaven, and the dough had to be allowed to stand overnight in order to rise properly.

The next morning my grandmother would form the dough into small cakes and set it in the big metal steam cooker that was an essential item in her kitchen. Then she cooked it for 5 or 10 minutes. These instructions may seem simple enough, but unfortunately this is a most deceptive impression. The really perfect *idli* requires some extra dimension of skill and timing, a lucky knack in keeping plenty of air in the mixture, an educated hand to keep the dough from collapsing, an experienced judgment to know just how much the mixture is going to have to rise in order to achieve the right shape for the *idli*.

Eventually the *idlis* would be served, two at a time, too hot to touch, and with them would come the particular chutney my grandmother had decided on for the day, and some kind of *sambar (Recipe Index)*—a sort of lentil purée cooked with vegetables and dried and green spices. Chutneys occupy a position of such importance in the food of almost any part of India, and offer such an astonishing diversity of flavors, such a limitless list of ingredients, that a whole book could be written about their uses, possibilities and significance. They range in taste from the kinds of sweet fruit chutneys that might easily be described as jams or preserves, through the very sharp, hot, spicy, sour varieties that have not even a remote equivalent in the West.

There were two that pleased me most, both quite popular in South India. One was grated fresh coconut ground with red chilies, ginger and onion, and given a sour sweetness with tamarind. The other was a fresh-tasting paste with mint, coriander leaves and lime juice as its predominant tastes.

And that, along with buttermilk or curds, would be the meal—as many *idlis* as you could eat, one of an infinite number of chutneys, and a *sambar* sometimes quite uncomplicated, using only one kind of lentil *(tur*, for instance, which is heavy, bright yellow in color and has a high protein content), and cooked with only one vegetable—say, onion—and the appropriate *masala*. Or there might be a relatively elaborate *sambar* requiring several kinds of lentils and chick-peas, and including such vegetables as okra, eggplant, tomatoes and a variety of long beans that we call drumsticks, which have a rather fibrous casing filled with a very delicate, creamy "marrow." Simple as it sounds, such a meal is remarkably satisfying, combining bland and vivid tastes, pleasing both the eye and the palate with its contrasts of color and texture—yellow, green, white, russet, gray, against the shiny surface of the banana leaf—smooth, grainy, mealy, liquid, creamy textures as you sample each item in varying juxtapositions.

For a change of pace—my grandmother never served the same breakfast twice in a row—there would be *dosas* in place of *idlis*. The ingredients are virtually the same, but there is no similarity in texture, flavor and appearance. For *dosas* the rice-and-lentil-flour mixture, duly fermented overnight, is thinned to a batter, and then comes the tricky part. Like most traditional South Indian kitchens, my grandmother's had a special *"dosa* stone," flat, quite ordinary looking, which was heated, lightly oiled and used as a grid-

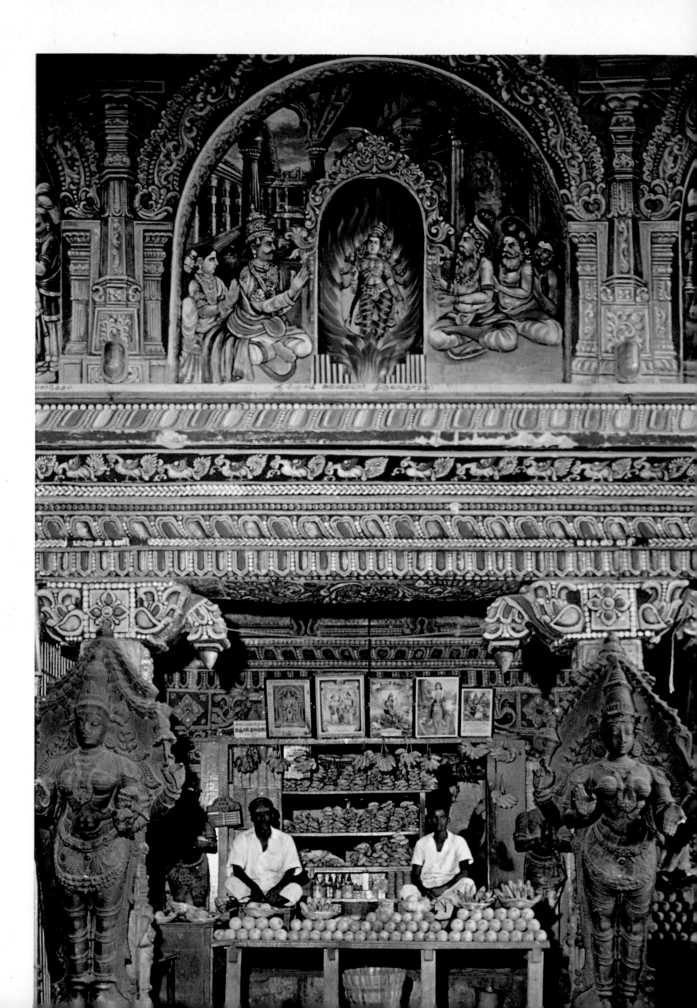

dle. She would never have considered using a more sophisticated griddle —it would have had a will of its own, and wouldn't have allowed her the latitude to determine the character of that day's *dosas* according to her mood.

The *dosas* sometimes appeared before us looking like ordinary pancakes —the same shape and texture but with their own peculiarly attractive, slightly sour taste. Other times they would be folded like an omelet and filled with curried vegetables, golden brown in color and feathery light. The refinement in *dosas* that most delighted me was the "paper *dosa*"—literally as thin and as crisp as paper—which flaked into waferlike fragments at a touch.

But the ultimate achievement of her "breakfast dishes" was, I think, the *hopper* (also known as *appam*). Like the *dosa*, this is, essentially, a pancake. However, it needs—unquestionably must have—its own inviolable pan, a shallow, two-handled iron pan called a *chatty*, which is used for nothing else and is treated rather in the manner that a meticulous Western cook might cosset his omelet pan. To cook the ideal *hopper* (same mixture as for a *dosa*), it is the technique, especially the wristwork, that is all-important. You spoon the thin batter into the heated, greased pan, and then at precisely the right moment, you pick up the pan by the handles and give it a rapid, accurate twist so that the batter swirls up to the edge of the pan, retreats to the base, leaving on the sides only enough slowly trickling, quickly cooking batter to make a wide, crisp border, like the starched lace of a Victorian doily.

When breakfast was over at my grandmother's house, everybody went about his individual concerns—household chores; studies; in my mother's case, social work; for other members of the family, perhaps, solitude or meditation. Most of us took at least a brief afternoon siesta, and met again, as a family, about 5 o'clock. It would have been teatime in the North. In the South it's coffeetime. But with the coffee comes an assortment from a most extensive repertoire of afternoon dishes, all of them, again, using cereals and lentils, spiced, enlivened by fresh herbs, by a squeeze of lime, a scattering of grated coconut or an unusual chutney. It is a very different concept of teatime from the usual Western, ladylike offering of tiny sandwiches and cake.

In my grandmother's house, in the afternoon, we were served a quite substantial meal (in the living room if there were guests, otherwise, as usual, in the dining room). It was a pleasant time of day: The midday heat was over, the reed blinds had been raised from the windows to let in the fading gold of the late afternoon light, the shuttered doors stood wide, opening onto verandas bordered with the cool, luxuriant green of plants—crotons—in big terra cotta pots and something we called elephant-ear because of its huge, fan-shaped leaves.

For some reason servants were permitted to help with the serving of the afternoon meal—perhaps because there was no particular urgency for most of the dishes to be steaming hot or absolutely fresh from the kitchen. One of these dishes, *chiura (Recipe Index)*, is made from pressed rice, deep-fried for just a minute or two in very hot oil. It is very crisp, and flaky, a warm yellow in color, and rich with cashew nuts and peanuts. It can be made in fairly large quantities in advance and kept for about a week in an airtight container until it is needed. The same is true of *murukkus*, something like—very distantly like—fat, oversized pretzels. These were so popular that my grandmother had a special wooden gadget through which she squeezed the

Opposite: Millions of Hindus in India are vegetarians, and in their temples even the offerings to the gods are vegetarian. The bananas and coconuts are on sale at a stall in the corridor of the Great Temple of Madurai in South India, which is a dual shrine to the goddess Minakshi and to Sundaresvar—as Shiva, the god of destruction, is known in South India. The stall—one of six in the temple corridor—also offers *paan*, betel nuts, incense sticks, camphor, red powder and white sandalwood paste for ceremonial use, to worshipers on their way to the shrines. The statues flanking the table are of Shiva's wife Shakti. The one overhead is of Minakshi herself.

murukku dough to ensure the right thickness and shape. But the right brittleness and the peppery, slightly coconutty taste were a matter for her own art and skill.

Other variations on the same general theme of cereal-and-lentil dough, though differently spiced and differently shaped, were the thin, crisp little curls of *saive* or the tiny, light bubbles of chick-pea dough called *bonda*. *Uppama (Recipe Index),* another favorite, provided a contrast of both appearance and texture. It isn't made from a dough or batter; instead, it is fluffy, the cereal grains separate, like rice, and there are as many variations as there are imaginative cooks. In its simplest form, it is based on semolina or farina, flavored with a couple of kinds of lentils, with onions, green chilies, ginger, mustard seed and coriander leaves. In its fancier forms, it contains, as well, nuts and vegetables, sprouted green lentils, coconut and more elaborate spicing. It can be made with pressed rice or tapioca. It can be bland enough to be invalids' food or rich enough for a party dish, and it is usually served with a wedge of fresh lime and chutney.

Along with any one of these preparations the afternoon meal would include a number of what I can only describe as "snacks"—small, salty and spiced, designed to give just a moment's excitement to the palate, not nourishment in any serious way, more of an embellishment, an interesting and delightful flourish. The many kinds of *wada* are an example. These particular ones were little doughnut-shaped nonsenses, usually made from a combination of lentil flours, sometimes from potato, sago, peanut flour or chick-pea flour, sometimes served soaked in spiced curds, sometimes dry with a chutney. In any form, they should, quite literally, melt in your mouth.

If all this seems to add up to an overpoweringly starchy meal, remember that it was always accompanied with fruit. And fruit, in South India, is another story altogether. There are, for example, passionate regional loyalties about mangoes. When they are in season, from about April until the monsoon breaks—anywhere from the middle to the end of June—the emotional provincial and individual arguments flare up about the merits of, say, the plump, golden Alphonso over the slender green Langra or either one over the peach-shaped, rose and yellow Romani. The other fruits don't seem to elicit the same sort of intense commitment, but they all form an essential part of the South Indian diet and an important substitute for sweets, which seldom appear on a South Indian menu except at festival times when sweets are a required part of the auspicious fare. And the dizzying profusion of fruits for which the South is celebrated makes them far from a monotonous substitute for desserts in the Western sense.

At least a couple of the dozens of varieties of bananas are always in season, and then, according to the time of year, we were also offered papaya, ripe jackfruit or pineapple, cut in small cubes and speared with toothpicks. And there would be *chickus* (a cross between a fig and a russet apple), jumlums (a small purple fruit), guavas and *nongus* (an especially delicious palmyra fruit), served whole, or sweet limes, oranges, tangerines, pomelos, peeled and segmented, and sometimes pieces of fresh sugar cane. In the Nilgiris, the spine of mountains that runs down the central part of southernmost India, grow some very good varieties of what Indians are apt to describe as "European fruits"—apples, pears, peaches, strawberries and so on. But I never remember any of those appearing on my grandmother's table.

Southerners like to eat rice three times a day—more often if they can afford it—and in my grandmother's household, where the evening meal was the main one, she frequently served us three large helpings of rice, each with its special accompanying dishes, of course, and to my amazement, it never became boring or predictable. Naturally, the rice was not always plain boiled —in fact, a South Indian friend of mine once listed for me 25 different kinds of rice dishes, *not* counting sweets or preparations made from mixed rice and lentils (for instance, the breakfast dishes). My grandmother's repertoire ranged from a marvelously pungent tamarind rice, through the sour excitement of lime rice, the calm, snowy beauty of coconut rice, rice cooked with different vegetables or nuts, to *tayiryatam*—rice mixed with spiced curds, served cold. Any one of them might appear as one of the "courses" in an evening meal. Sometimes, as a special treat—a small indulgence to my childhood fondness for sweets—she would cook a wonderfully fragrant and delicate sweet rice, using unrefined brown sugar, hauntingly flavored with saffron, cardamom and nutmeg, rich with cashew nuts, raisins and coconut—inconceivably remote from the gluey, milky "rice puddings" that were the plague of my English boarding-school days.

Inevitably, the evening meal at my grandmother's house would include a vegetable curry, perhaps an *aviyal (Recipe Index)*. It is hard for anyone who hasn't sampled the textures and flavors of South Indian vegetables and spicing to understand how enticing this can be. Apart from such familiar vegetables as potatoes, eggplant and green beans, an *aviyal* also contains a number of South Indian specialties: drumsticks, jackfruit seeds (with something of the half-crisp, half-mealy consistency of chestnuts, and even a slight similarity of taste), cooking bananas, bitter gourd, slices of green coconut and green mango. The *masala* should be vivid enough to give sparkle to the vegetables, but not so strong that their character is obscured.

Besides one of the dozens of kinds of vegetable curry, we would certainly be served a leafy vegetable and a "dry" root vegetable or a banana. And then there was a selection of oil pickles—mango, lime, bitter orange, chili. My grandmother's particular brilliance was demonstrated in her green peppercorn pickle, a pickle of quite arresting exhilaration and a sharpness that made you want (very happily) to sneeze. She also had an expert way with banana chips, which were made from green cooking bananas and were as crisp and salty as potato chips. Both of these last items were an extra flourish, just something to titillate your appetite.

The second two helpings of rice were usually less elaborately appointed, one perhaps with *Mysore rasam*, a thin, fiery-hot, lentil consommé, the final one with curds, entirely bland, designed to clear your palate of all the strong, pungent, hot, sour tastes earlier in the meal, and to act as a digestive. Throughout the meal, up to the last stage, there would be relays of fresh, crackly *pappadams*, parchment-thin disks of peppery lentil flour that had been fried in very hot oil.

The meals served in my grandmother's house represented the everyday vegetarian fare of a moderately well-to-do Hindu household in South India. My grandmother was an accomplished cook, but on occasion vegetarian meals can be more elegant and elaborate than those that she regularly served.

I remember one time when I was invited to dinner by a distant relative

Overleaf: Vegetarians in India need not suffer from monotony in their diet; the variety of edible plants the country produces is almost limitless. Those shown on the next two pages were all grown in India and bought in Bombay markets. They are also available in markets in the North. Besides the easily recognizable fruits and vegetables, they include papaya with a wedge removed *(center)*, a snake gourd (the long, slender vegetable lying across the rest), a bottle gourd *(center top)* and an unripe jackfruit (the orchid-colored fruit to the left of the bananas).

who lives in Poona, the emotional, though not the geographic center of the huge state of Maharashtra. It was a festive meal for it celebrated her daughter's betrothal (properly arranged by the elders in the family) and all the relations, however remotely connected, were invited.

Our hostess and her family lived in a Western-style house, unpretentiously but comfortably furnished, but except for the flowers everywhere—in vases, bowls, strung over doorways, hung as garlands over pictures of gods or saints —it was curiously lacking (to the Western eye) in ornaments, art objects, bric-a-brac. On the threshold as we entered the house, however, and on the floor at each doorway within the house, were most beautifully executed *rangolis,* the traditional designs created with colored powders for auspicious events in the household.

The guests were met at the door with the usual Indian greeting, the *namaskar,* of folded hands, and in the sitting room, as is usual in Indian gatherings of this sort, the women sat together on one side of the room, the men on the other, and the bride-to-be, surrounded by her elders, remained silent, her sari decorously pulled over her head. Her only duty was to touch the feet of the senior members of the family as they blessed her and wished her good fortune and good health. No one ever wishes you happiness in India. This is supposed to be in your own hands, of your own making.

Very soon dinner was served, and everybody—from long habit—gave the *thali* on which his food was served a very sharp-eyed scrutiny. In a really good Maharashtrian meal, the arrangement of the items on the *thali* is of immense importance. Unlike the more casual attitude of the far South, to Maharashtrians the appearance of the meal is a very telling point in favor (or to the eternal detriment) of the hostess.

Around each *thali* was another, less elaborate *rangoli,* also perfectly executed. Well, she had passed the first test. Next came the examination of the order in which the food was placed.

Starting at the top of the *thali* and moving down the left-hand rim was a tiny hill of coarse salt, then a wedge of Indian lime (with a character and flavor unlike the Western ones), a fresh chutney, an *achar* (oil pickle), a *rayta* (cooked or raw vegetables or fruit in spiced curds, *Recipe Index),* a *cachumbar* (chopped raw vegetables flavored with fresh green herbs), two fried things, in this case rice wafers and *pakoras,* which can be any vegetable, spiced, coated with chick-pea batter, and fried. And a very crisp *pappadam.*

This was the occasion when I learned that the correct compliment to a Maharashtrian hostess on a particularly fancy or carefully planned meal is: "How wonderfully varied the left-hand side of the *thali* is." This remark, odd as it sounds, would prove to her that you are a discerning, knowledgeable and appreciative guest.

I think I should explain here why the "left-hand side of the *thali*" is considered a crucial test of a good Maharashtrian cook. This is where the "accessories" of the meal best display her imagination, originality and thoughtfulness in the juxtapositions of taste. Maharashtrians are particularly proud of their astonishing range and diversity of chutneys, *achars,* brine pickles and *cachumbars,* and these are the foods served on the left-hand side of the *thali.* Yet, Maharashtrians are as appalled by the showy lavishness of a North Indian party meal as they are by the deliberately offhand manners of the far South. They prefer instead to mark a special occasion with their own brand of restrained elaboration.

Accordingly, at the dinner in Poona, we were served only two kinds of chutney—more would have been vulgarly ostentatious. One was a sweet-sour chutney made with unripe mangoes and raisins, slightly sharpened with ginger and garlic, given its acidity with vinegar, and softened with sugar (continents apart in taste from Major Grey's, although the ingredients sound similar). As a contrast in texture—very important to Maharashtrians—there was a "dry" chutney of pumpkin rind and green chilies, fried crisp in a little oil with sesame seeds and salt.

Our hostess served us only one *achar* made from *anvla,* a gooseberrylike fruit, and everyone appreciated the fact that this had been carefully selected above such other *achars* as mango, lime or chili, so that neither of the chutney tastes or ingredients would be duplicated. And because this was a festive dinner, she had added a *marumba* made from figs, really a rich and fragrant fruit preserve in a thick syrup, delicately flavored with aromatic spices such as cardamom powder, cinnamon and saffron, with a hint of lime juice to keep it from being cloyingly sweet.

Cachumbars and *raytas* are both exceedingly simple in principle, so here the guests judged our hostess by how enterprising she had been in her shopping, and how daring in her combinations of tastes. She passed this test with flying colors, for she had produced an extraordinary mixture of green ginger, melon and orange for a taste as fresh as spring; however, she had mixed in some peanuts because their flavor and mealy texture heightened and added a touch of surprise to the fruit. Her *rayta* was equally unusual: boiled seaweed, still holding the tang of the ocean—although Poona is inland, up in the Western hills—set in a creamy background of curds.

Only after the knowing guests had given the "left-hand side of the *thali*" a quick but thorough survey did they turn their attention to the "main" or substantial part of the meal. All of us noticed at once that the neat, round mold of rice was placed, correctly, just below the center of the *thali*. This is another vital point of Maharashtrian etiquette in the arrangement of food. The rice should never be slap in the middle of the *thali*—such blatant symmetry would be unsubtle. It should certainly *never* be the haphazard mountain of rice ladled out in the far South. And over the rice mold was poured just enough of the golden lentil purée called *tur dal* to look like icing on a cake.

Down the right-hand edge of the *thali*, again conforming to strict protocol in placing, there was a vegetable curry, and one "dry" vegetable preparation. In even the fanciest Maharashtrian meal there will still be only two vegetable dishes on the right-hand side of the *thali*, but the appreciative guest is certain to watch for the unusual or expensive items his hostess has served within this limitation. We, for example, had one of the many Indian kinds of spinach (for one dish must be a leafy vegetable), cooked with pistachios, which not only are expensive, but also give that unexpected touch of fantasy to something as prosaic as spinach.

The "dry" vegetable was, to me, at least, the most interesting item of the whole meal. India, with its countless varieties of bananas, uses a number of them as vegetables rather than desserts, and this particular dish consisted of one of the small yellow and black bananas stuffed with a most elegantly balanced sweet-sour mixture of coconut, tamarind juice, sugar and spices, and

In the hands of imaginative Hindu cooks, vegetarian meals can be nutritious, varied and elegantly presented. On this *thali* is a dinner prepared in Maharashtra for the feast day of the god Ganesha. All the dishes are meat-free: the main ingredients are lentils, potatoes, chick-peas, wheat, rice, coconut, yams and yoghurt. Even the decorative design (called a *rangoli)* around the *thali* is vegetarian, the colorful pattern having been fashioned with beans, rice, lentils, chick-peas and wheat.

then baked. It was an elusive and delicate taste that vanished almost before you could savor it.

Next to the vegetables on the *thali* were set a *katori* filled with a curry made of sprouted grain cooked in coconut milk, and finally one of plain buttermilk. But—and this was a sure indication that we were at a festive meal—there was also a sweet preparation on the right-hand side of the *thali*. Usually a sweet, when it is served at all, is some kind of milk-based preparation, but if you find, as we did, that there are *jalebis* (pretzel-like deep-fried sweets) on your *thali*, then you know that this is a really special occasion. They are thought to be so difficult to make well that most people play safe and buy them from professional sweetmakers, though they will say, with admiration of a particularly expert or dedicated cook, "She *even* makes her own *jalebis!*"

The perfect *jalebi* (*Recipe Index*) should be a loose convolution of fragile, hollow curls (made from a batter of wheat and chick-pea flour, oil and curds), a warm orange gold in color, and by some magic, holding a fragrantly flavored syrup within each curl. The outside should be crisp and infinitely light, and though its surface glistens with syrup, it should be only slightly sticky to the touch. And as important as anything else for the *jalebi* connoisseur, it must be fresh—after even a couple of hours a *jalebi* begins to lose its proper texture, its delicacy and its charm. (A friend of mine has a phrase of all-inclusive contempt for any really inept housewife: "She runs the kind of house where you *expect* to be served stale *jalebis*.")

For the actual eating of the meal, once the essential, preliminary (though unobtrusive) assessment of the arrangement and decoration of the *thali* and its setting is accomplished, we, the guests, each evolved an orchestration of our own. Each of us added different amounts and combinations of the various items to the rice, eating—with our fingers, of course—some things separately, others in mixtures of our own devising. The good Maharashtrian cook should, therefore, always plan her meal with all these possibilities of texture and taste in mind. The individual dishes or the combinations should never offend or astonish your palate. They should, instead, interest and perhaps gently surprise you. Ideally, they should all delight you also.

In a way, that one meal explained something of the basic nature and principles of Maharashtrian cooking. It is an unemphatic cuisine and would probably seem uncharacteristically mild to foreigners who expect all Indian food to be scaldingly hot or strongly overspiced. It concentrates, instead, on retaining the individual character and texture of each major ingredient and produces its best effects by their juxtaposition. Vegetables are never overcooked. The spicing (compared with the far South) is light. Natural colors are preserved—for instance, turmeric is used only in tiny quantities because its brilliant yellow is apt to overpower almost any other coloring. Even the appearance of the *thali* should maintain this sense of understatement and balance—it should never be too crowded or too sparse. In Maharashtra quantity is not (as it is in the North) a matter of pride to the host or a compliment to the guest; restrained elegance and subtlety are.

After the Poona dinner, leaving early according to the usual Indian custom, we could all, with utter sincerity, pay the ultimate compliment by saying, "How beautifully varied the left-hand side of the *thali* was!"

Jalebis
DEEP-FRIED PRETZEL-SHAPED SWEETS

In a deep bowl, make a smooth batter of the all-purpose and rice flours, baking powder and lukewarm water. Let the batter rest unrefrigerated and uncovered for 12 hours.

Just before frying the *jalebis*, prepare the syrup: Combine the sugar, cold water and cream of tartar in a 3- to 4-quart saucepan. Stir over moderate heat until the sugar dissolves. Increase the heat to high and, timing it from the moment the syrup boils, cook briskly, undisturbed, for 5 minutes. The syrup is done when it reaches a temperature of 220° on a candy thermometer. Remove the pan from the heat, stir in the coloring and the rose water. Pour the syrup into a bowl and set it aside.

Pour 3 cups of vegetable oil into a 10-inch *karhai* or 12-inch *wok (page 151)*, or pour oil into a deep fryer to a depth of 2 to 3 inches. Heat the oil until it reaches a temperature of 350° on a deep-frying thermometer. To make the *jalebis*, spoon 1½ cups of the batter into a pastry bag fitted with a plain tube ³⁄₁₆ inch in diameter. Squeezing it directly into the hot oil, loop a stream of batter back and forth 4 or 5 times to form a sort of pretzel made up of alternating figure 8s and circles, one over the other. Each *jalebi* should be about 3 inches long and 2 inches wide.

In batches of 5 or 6, fry the *jalebis* for 2 minutes, or until golden on both sides. As they brown, transfer them to the syrup for a minute, then place them on a plate. Serve warm or at room temperature.

To make about 5 dozen

JALEBIS
3 cups all-purpose flour
¼ cup rice flour
¼ teaspoon double-acting baking powder
2 cups lukewarm water (110° to 115°)

SYRUP
4 cups sugar
3 cups cold water
⅛ teaspoon cream of tartar
2 teaspoons yellow food coloring
⅛ teaspoon red food coloring
1 teaspoon rose water

Vegetable oil for deep frying

The squiggles and loops of batter being squeezed into hot oil at left represent the first step in cooking one of India's favorite snacks, the pretzel-shaped sweets called *jalebis*. The loops are deep fried in oil and dipped in the bowl of sugar syrup at the rear. *Opposite:* A vendor weighs some of these popular confections for a customer at the ancient city of Fatehpur Sikri. Built by the Grand Moghul, Akbar, in the 16th Century, the city was abandoned shortly thereafter when its water supply proved inadequate. The mosque in the background holds the tomb of Salim Chishti, a Muslim saint.

To serve 4

4 tablespoons *ghee (page 54)*
1 teaspoon black mustard seeds
2 tablespoons *urad dal (page 196)*,
  if available
½ cup finely chopped onions
1 teaspoon scraped, finely chopped
  fresh ginger root
1 teaspoon salt
½ teaspoon freshly ground black
  pepper
1 pound fresh green string beans,
  trimmed and cut crosswise into
  paper-thin rounds
¼ teaspoon ground red pepper
¼ cup finely grated fresh coconut
  (page 134)
2 tablespoons finely chopped fresh
  coriander *(cilantro)*
2 tablespoons fresh lemon juice

To serve 4 to 6

CHEESE
2 quarts milk
½ cup unflavored yoghurt
2 tablespoons fresh strained lemon
  juice
PEAS
5 tablespoons *ghee (page 54)*
2 tablespoons scraped, finely
  chopped fresh ginger root
1 tablespoon finely chopped garlic
1 cup finely chopped onions
1 teaspoon salt
1 teaspoon turmeric
¼ teaspoon ground hot red pepper
1 teaspoon ground coriander
1 tablespoon *garam masala*
  (page 56)
2 cups finely chopped fresh tomatoes
1½ cups fresh green peas (about
  1½ pounds unshelled) or 1 ten-
  ounce package frozen peas,
  thoroughly defrosted
1 teaspoon sugar (optional)
3 tablespoons finely chopped fresh
  coriander *(cilantro)*

Same ki Bhaji
FRIED FRESH GREEN BEANS WITH COCONUT

In a 10-inch *karhai* or heavy skillet, or a 12-inch *wok*, heat the *ghee* over moderate heat until a drop of cold water flicked into it splutters instantly. Add the mustard seeds and *dal* and fry for 3 minutes, until the *dal* browns lightly. (If *dal* is not available, fry the mustard seeds alone for 30 seconds.) Thoroughly stir in the onions, ginger, salt and pepper, and drop in the green beans. Stirring constantly, add the red pepper and fry 5 minutes longer. Add the coconut and coriander, reduce the heat to low, and cover the pan. Stirring occasionally, cook for 10 minutes more, or until the beans are tender. Sprinkle with lemon juice, taste for seasoning, and serve at once.

Mattar Pannir
HOMEMADE CHEESE WITH PEAS

Prepare the cheese in the following fashion: In a heavy 3- to 4-quart saucepan, bring the milk to a boil over high heat. As soon as the foam begins to rise, remove the pan from the heat and gently but thoroughly stir in the yoghurt and lemon juice. The curds will begin to solidify immediately and separate from the liquid whey.

Pour the entire contents of the pan into a large sieve set over a bowl and lined with a double thickness of cheesecloth. Let the curds drain undisturbed until the cloth is cool enough to handle. Then wrap the cloth tightly around the curds and wring it vigorously to squeeze out all the excess liquid. Reserve 1 cup of the whey in the bowl and discard the rest.

Place the cheese, still wrapped in cheesecloth, on a cutting board and set another board or large flat-bottomed skillet on top of it. Weight the top with canned foods, flatirons, heavy pots or the like, weighing in all about 15 pounds, and let it rest in this fashion at room temperature for 6 to 8 hours, or until the cheese is firm and compact. Unwrap the cheese, cut it into ½-inch cubes, cover with wax paper or plastic wrap, and refrigerate until ready to use. (There should be about 1 to 1½ cups of cheese cubes.)

To prepare the cheese and peas, heat the *ghee* in a heavy 10- to 12-inch skillet until a drop of water flicked into it splutters instantly. Add the cheese cubes and fry them for 4 or 5 minutes, turning the cubes about gently but constantly with a slotted spoon until they are golden brown on all sides. As they brown, transfer the cubes of cheese to a plate.

Add the ginger and garlic to the *ghee* remaining in the skillet and, stirring constantly, fry for 30 seconds. Add the onions and salt and, stirring occasionally, continue to fry for 7 or 8 minutes, or until the onions are soft and golden brown. Watch carefully for any signs of burning and regulate the heat accordingly.

Stir in ¼ cup of the reserved whey, then add the turmeric, red pepper, ground coriander and *garam masala*. When they are well blended, stir in the remaining ¾ cup of whey and the tomatoes, and bring to a boil over high heat. Reduce the heat to low and simmer partially covered for 10 minutes, stirring occasionally. Add the peas and taste for seasoning. If the gravy has too acid a flavor add up to 1 teaspoon sugar.

Remove the cover and, stirring occasionally, cook for 3 minutes. Then add the cheese cubes and 1 tablespoon of the fresh coriander, cover the skillet tightly, and simmer over low heat for 10 to 20 minutes, or longer if you are using fresh peas and they are not yet tender.

To serve, transfer the entire contents of the pan to a heated bowl or deep platter and garnish the top with the remaining 2 tablespoons of chopped fresh coriander.

Uppama
FARINA WITH VEGETABLES

In a heavy 3- to 4-quart casserole, heat the vegetable oil over moderate heat until a light haze forms above it. Add the *dal* and stir for a minute or so, then drop in the mustard seeds and, when the oil begins to sputter, add the onions. Stirring constantly, fry for 7 or 8 minutes, until the onions are soft and golden brown. Watch carefully for any signs of burning and regulate the heat accordingly.

Add the hot chili and, stirring constantly, pour in the farina in a slow, thin stream. Still stirring, fry for about 5 minutes, until the farina is lightly browned. Stirring well after each addition, add the tomatoes, carrots, scallions, water and salt. Bring to a boil over high heat, reduce the heat to the lowest possible point, cover tightly, and cook for 10 minutes, or until the farina is thick and the vegetables tender. Taste for seasoning.

To serve, pour the *uppama* into a heated bowl and sprinkle it with the coriander and lemon juice.

To serve 6 to 8

¼ cup vegetable oil
1 tablespoon *urad dal (page 196)*, if available
1 teaspoon black mustard seeds
½ cup finely chopped onions
2 tablespoons seeded, chopped fresh hot green chili *(caution: see page 39)*
1 cup quick-cooking farina
1 cup finely chopped fresh tomatoes
⅓ cup finely diced, scraped carrots
¼ cup coarsely chopped scallions
3 cups water
1 tablespoon salt
1 tablespoon finely chopped fresh coriander *(cilantro)*
1 tablespoon fresh lemon juice

Aviyal
SPICED MIXED VEGETABLES WITH COCONUT

Combine 1 cup of the coconut and the 1 cup water in the jar of an electric blender and blend at high speed for 30 seconds, or until the mixture is reduced to a smooth purée. Stop the machine and scrape down the sides of the jar with a rubber spatula. Add the remaining coconut and blend again until smooth. Set the purée aside.

Prepare the *masala* in the following fashion: In a heavy 2- to 3-quart saucepan, heat the vegetable oil over moderate heat until a light haze forms above it. Add the mustard seeds, ginger and garlic, and fry for 30 seconds. Add the onions and, stirring constantly, continue to fry for 7 or 8 minutes, until they are soft and golden brown. Watch carefully for any signs of burning and regulate the heat accordingly. Stir in the ground coriander, turmeric and ¼ cup of water.

Add the green peppers, carrot, broccoli, string beans and scallions, turning them about with a spoon to coat them evenly with the *masala*. Then stir in the reserved coconut purée, hot chili and salt, and bring to a boil over high heat. Reduce the heat to the lowest possible point, cover tightly, and simmer for 15 minutes, or until the vegetables are tender. Check from time to time to make sure that the mixture is moist. If it seems dry, add up to ¼ cup more water, a tablespoon each time.

Remove the pan from the heat, stir the coriander into the vegetable mixture, cover and let the *aviyal* stand at room temperature for 5 minutes or so. Just before serving, taste for seasoning and pour the entire contents of the pan into a heated bowl.

To serve 4 to 6

2 cups coarsely chopped fresh coconut *(page 134)*
1 cup cold water

MASALA

¼ cup vegetable oil
¼ teaspoon black mustard seeds
A 1-inch piece of fresh ginger root, scraped and crushed slightly
2 medium-sized garlic cloves, peeled and cut partially in half lengthwise
½ cup finely chopped onions
2 tablespoons ground coriander
½ teaspoon turmeric
¼ cup water

VEGETABLES

2 green frying peppers, seeded, deribbed and coarsely chopped
1 large carrot, scraped and cut into ¼-inch-thick rounds
1 broccoli stalk, cut into 1-inch lengths
¼ pound fresh string beans, cut into 2-inch lengths
6 scallions, including 1 inch of the tops, cut into 2-inch lengths
1 fresh hot green chili, seeded and chopped *(caution: see page 39)*
2 teaspoons salt
3 tablespoons finely chopped fresh coriander *(cilantro)*

To make about 12 five-inch round
breads

2 cups whole-wheat flour
3 tablespoons *ghee (page 54)*
½ to 1 cup lukewarm water (110°
to 115°)
Vegetable oil for deep frying

Puris
DEEP-FRIED UNLEAVENED WHOLE-WHEAT BREAD

In a deep bowl, combine the flour and the *ghee*. With your fingertips rub the flour and the fat together until they look like flakes of coarse meal. Make a well in the center, pour ¼ cup of the lukewarm water into it, and with your fingers or a large spoon blend the water into the flour mixture. Stirring vigorously after each addition, pour in up to ¾ cup more of the lukewarm water, adding it a tablespoon or so at a time and using only enough water to form a dough that can be gathered into a firm, compact ball.

On a lightly floured surface, knead the dough by folding it end to end, then pressing it down and pushing it forward several times with the heel of your hand. Repeat for about 7 or 8 minutes, or until the dough becomes smooth and elastic.

Again gather it into a ball, place it in a bowl, and drape a dampened kitchen towel over the top. Let the dough rest for at least 30 minutes. You can safely let the dough stand at room temperature for several hours if it is well covered and the towel lightly moistened from time to time to prevent the dough from drying out.

To shape each *puri,* pinch off about 2 tablespoons of the dough and form it into a slightly flattened ball about 1½ inches in diameter. Place the ball on a lightly floured surface and, with a rolling pin, roll it out from the center to the far edge. Lift the dough, turn it clockwise about 2 inches, and roll it again from the center to the far edge. Repeat—lifting, turning, rolling—until the circle is about 5 inches in diameter. Sprinkle a little flour over and under the ball from time to time to prevent it from sticking. As you proceed, cover the *puris* with a dampened kitchen towel.

Pour 3 cups of vegetable oil into a 10-inch *karhai* or a 12-inch *wok (page 151)*, or fill a deep fryer or 10- to 12-inch skillet or sauté pan with oil to a depth of about 2 inches. Heat the oil until it reaches a temperature of 350° on the thermostat or a deep-frying thermometer.

Place one *puri* at a time in the hot oil. It will begin to puff immediately but unevenly. Fry it for about a minute, meanwhile pressing any flat surfaces deep into the oil with the back of a perforated spoon. Turn the *puri* over and, still pressing it with the spoon, fry for a minute longer, or until it is evenly puffed and golden brown. As they brown, transfer the *puris* to paper towels to drain.

Serve the *puris* while they are still warm.

NOTE: To make *chapatis* or griddle-fried whole-wheat breads, prepare the dough as described above and let it rest for 30 minutes. Two tablespoons at a time, shape the dough into balls and roll each one into a 5-inch round.

Without adding any fat, heat a well-seasoned griddle or 10- to 12-inch cast-iron skillet or a skillet that has a nonstick surface. When a drop of water flicked into the pan splutters instantly, add one of the *chapatis*.

Moving the bread about constantly with your fingers or shaking the pan back and forth constantly to keep the *chapati* from sticking, cook it for a minute or so, until the top begins to darken somewhat. Turn the *chapati* over and cook for 1 minute longer, or until it is lightly browned. Transfer the *chapati* to a serving plate and fry the rest in a similar fashion.

If you like, you may spread each *chapati* with about ¼ teaspoon of *ghee* when you remove it from the griddle. Serve the *chapatis* warm.

To make the *puris (recipe opposite)*, rub the flour and *ghee* between your fingers until they blend, then incorporate enough water to make a firm dough.

Knead the dough Indian style in a flat-bottomed pan or Western style on a floured counter or table for 7 or 8 minutes, until it is smooth and elastic.

To form each *puri*, break off a small piece of dough and roll it between the palms of your hands to make a slightly flattened ball about 1½ inches in diameter.

Sprinkle both *puri* and board with whole-wheat flour to keep them from sticking and roll each ball into a wafer-thin round about 5 inches across.

Deep-fry the *puris* one by one, pushing at them with a spoon so that they puff evenly, then drain and serve warm. *Puris* are a traditional part of an Indian *thali*, or individual serving tray like the one at right.

In these refreshing and saladlike *raytas*, described on pages 88 and 89, yoghurt is combined with fruits or vegetables.

1 Baingan ka Rayta
2 Kheera ka Rayta
3 Alu ka Rayta
4 Pakora ka Rayta
5 Kela ka Rayta
6 Pudine ka Rayta

"RAYTAS" (preceding pages) are refreshing yoghurt mixtures frequently served with Indian meals. A "rayta," like a salad, provides a cooling contrast to the main highly seasoned dishes of a meal. Its base is always yoghurt, mixed with fruits, vegetables, seasonings, even fried chick-pea flour balls, depending on the cook's larder and tastes. Recipes for those "raytas" shown on the previous pages follow.

Baingan ka Rayta
YOGHURT WITH BAKED SPICED EGGPLANT

To serve 4 to 6

1 medium-sized eggplant (about 1 pound)
2 tablespoons vegetable oil
¼ cup finely chopped onions
1 teaspoon salt
1 tablespoon *garam masala (page 56)*
1 small firm, ripe tomato, coarsely chopped
¼ cup finely chopped fresh coriander *(cilantro)*
1 cup unflavored yoghurt

Preheat the oven to 400°. With the point of a sharp knife, make 5 or 6 inch-deep evenly spaced slits in the eggplant and place it in a shallow baking dish. Roast the eggplant in the middle of the oven for 45 minutes, or until it is soft to the touch. Watch carefully for any signs of burning and regulate the heat accordingly. Remove the eggplant from the oven and when it is cool enough to handle, peel it and chop the pulp coarsely.

Meanwhile, in a heavy 8- to 10-inch skillet, heat the vegetable oil over moderate heat until a light haze forms above it. Add the onions and salt and, stirring constantly, cook for 7 or 8 minutes, or until they are soft and golden brown. Watch carefully for any signs of burning, and regulate the heat accordingly. Add the *garam masala*, tomato and coriander, and stir for 1 minute. Still stirring, add the eggplant, and cook for 2 or 3 minutes longer.

Place the yoghurt in a small bowl, add the entire contents of the skillet, and gently but thoroughly toss the ingredients together. Taste for seasoning, cover tightly, and refrigerate for at least 1 hour, or until completely chilled.

Kheera ka Rayta
YOGHURT WITH CUCUMBER AND TOMATO

To serve 4

1 medium-sized cucumber
1 tablespoon finely chopped onions
1 tablespoon salt
1 small, firm ripe tomato, cut crosswise into ½-inch-thick rounds, sliced into ½-inch-wide strips and then into ½-inch cubes
1 tablespoon finely chopped fresh coriander *(cilantro)*
1 cup unflavored yoghurt
1 teaspoon ground cumin, toasted in a small ungreased skillet over low heat for 30 seconds

With a small, sharp knife, peel the cucumber and slice it lengthwise into halves. Scoop out the seeds by running the tip of a teaspoon down the center of each half. Cut the cucumber lengthwise into ⅛-inch-thick slices, then crosswise into ½-inch pieces.

Combine the cucumber, onions and salt in a small bowl, and mix them together thoroughly with a spoon. Let the mixture rest at room temperature for 5 minutes or so, then squeeze the cucumbers gently between your fingers to remove the excess liquid.

Drop the cucumber pieces into a deep bowl, add the tomato and coriander, and toss them together gently but thoroughly. Combine the yoghurt and cumin and pour it over the vegetables, turning them about with a spoon to coat them evenly. Taste for seasoning, cover tightly, and refrigerate for at least 1 hour, or until completely chilled, before serving.

Pudine ka Rayta
YOGHURT WITH MINT, ONION AND HOT CHILI

To serve 3 to 4

3 tablespoons finely cut fresh mint
3 tablespoons finely chopped onions
½ teaspoon finely chopped fresh hot red or green chili *(page 39)*
½ teaspoon salt
⅛ teaspoon ground hot red pepper
1 cup unflavored yoghurt

In a small serving bowl, combine the mint, onions, chili, salt and red pepper. When they are thoroughly blended, stir in the yoghurt. Taste for seasoning, cover tightly, and refrigerate for at least 1 hour, or until completely chilled. Before serving, decorate the *rayta* if you like with fresh whole mint leaves.

Alu ka Rayta
YOGHURT WITH SPICED POTATOES

Drop the potatoes into enough boiling water to cover them completely and boil briskly, uncovered, until they are tender but still show some resistance when pierced with the point of a small, sharp knife. Drain the potatoes in a colander, peel and cut them into ½-inch cubes.

In a heavy 8-inch skillet, heat the vegetable oil over high heat until it starts to smoke. Stir in the mustard and cumin seeds and, when they crackle and begin to burst, immediately add the onions. Stirring constantly, add the chili, coriander and potatoes.

Cook over moderate heat, turning the potatoes frequently with a spoon, until the cubes are well coated with the spice mixture. Remove the skillet from the heat and stir in the salt.

Place the yoghurt in a small serving bowl, add the entire contents of the skillet, and toss gently together. Taste for seasoning, cover tightly, and refrigerate for at least 1 hour, or until completely chilled.

To serve 4 to 6

3 medium-sized firm boiling-type potatoes (about 1 pound), scrubbed but not peeled
2 tablespoons vegetable oil
1 teaspoon black mustard seeds
1 teaspoon cumin seeds
3 tablespoons finely chopped onions
1 teaspoon chopped fresh hot red or green chili *(caution: see page 39)*
1 tablespoon finely chopped fresh coriander *(cilantro)*
½ teaspoon salt
1 cup unflavored yoghurt

Pakora ka Rayta
YOGHURT WITH MINIATURE DEEP-FRIED CHICK-PEA FLOUR BALLS

In a deep bowl make a smooth, thin batter of the ½ cup of chick-pea flour, ½ teaspoon of salt and the water, stirring them together with a spoon or with your fingers.

Pour 2 cups of vegetable oil into a 10-inch *karhai* or 12-inch *wok (page 151)*, or pour oil into a deep fryer to a depth of 2 to 3 inches. Heat until the oil reaches 350° on the thermostat or a deep-frying thermometer.

To shape the *pakoras*, hold a hand grater with openings ¼ inch in diameter above the deep fryer, then pick up a little of the batter with your fingers and press it through the grater into the hot oil. In 30 seconds, or as soon as the *pakoras* are brown, remove them from the oil with a slotted spoon and transfer them to paper towels to drain.

Repeat this process until all the batter is fried. (There should be about ¾ cup of *pakoras*.) Cool the *pakoras* to room temperature before using them.

Just before serving, stir the yoghurt, cumin and ½ teaspoon of salt together in a small serving bowl. Gently fold half of the *pakoras* into the yoghurt mixture, and spread the rest of them on top. Sprinkle with red pepper and coriander.

To serve 4 to 6

CHICK-PEA BALLS *(pakora)*
½ cup *besan* (chick-pea flour)
½ teaspoon salt
¼ cup cold water
Vegetable oil for deep frying

YOGHURT
1 cup unflavored yoghurt, chilled
1 teaspoon ground cumin
½ teaspoon salt
¼ teaspoon ground hot red pepper
2 tablespoons finely chopped fresh coriander *(cilantro)*

Kela ka Rayta
YOGHURT WITH BANANA AND GRATED COCONUT

In a small heavy skillet, heat the *ghee* over moderate heat until a drop of water flicked into it splutters instantly. Drop in the mustard seeds and, when they crackle and begin to burst, add the coconut. Stir for a few seconds, remove the skillet from the heat, and then add about 2 tablespoons of the yoghurt.

Place the remaining yoghurt in a small serving bowl, and stir in the skillet mixture and the salt. Add the banana and coriander, and gently but thoroughly toss all the ingredients together. Taste for seasoning, cover tightly, and refrigerate for 1 hour before serving.

To serve 4

2 tablespoons *ghee (page 54)*
1 teaspoon black mustard seeds
½ cup coarsely grated fresh coconut *(page 134)*
1 cup unflavored yoghurt
1 teaspoon salt
1 medium-sized ripe but firm banana, peeled and cut into ¼-inch-thick rounds
1 teaspoon finely chopped fresh coriander *(cilantro)*

IV

Glittering Festivals and Lavish Feasts

A pretty little Indian girl in Tamil Nadu affectionately pats a young bullock that is all dressed up for South India's Pongal rice harvest festivities. The second day of the festival is set aside for giving thanks to cattle for being faithful beasts of burden and givers of milk. On this occasion, the cattle are bathed and haltered with garlands of rice sheaves, colored wood and paper, and their faces are colored with red powder.

For all the formidable problems that India faces, one lighthearted quality remains triumphantly alive throughout the country: a sense of pageantry. Most Indians are poor and are largely preoccupied with the endless routine of obtaining the necessities for existence. Yet they never miss an opportunity to bring some glamor and color into their lives. Any festival, holiday, family wedding, birth, or even so commonplace an event as a market day is an occasion for varying degrees of self-expressive display. It may be a gesture as inexpensive as making or buying a garland of marigolds or roses, glittering with tinsel, to greet a friend or an honored guest. It may be the exquisite designs of flowers and geometric patterns known as *rangoli,* which women make from colored powder to brighten the thresholds of their houses for auspicious occasions. It may simply be the way a villager puts on his best clothes and sees that his wife is decked out in something colorful for an expedition as prosaic (to Westerners) as going to the polls on election day.

Whatever form it takes, this sense of pageantry is irrepressibly Indian. A small farmer will cheerfully go into debt for his whole life to give his daughter a splashy wedding, including a feast for her husband's family, garlands, sweets and at least some sort of music. A man who earns only 100 rupees a month (about $13) may spend as much as two months' salary for his daughter's wedding sari.

The Indian flair for investing occasions with splendor and panache achieves its fullest expression in the series of festivals that punctuate the year. There are so many festivals that it is almost impossible to keep track of them. Some are regional observances, while others are celebrated throughout the country. Some are inspired by the arrival of harvest seasons, but most are religious in their origin. These festivals are always accompanied by feasting, for the offering of food to a deity or to the neighbors is an essential part of every Indian celebration.

The harvest festivals are devoted to grain; wheat in the North, rice in the South and the East. In the North Indian state of Punjab, the festival of Baisakhi celebrates the wheat harvest with holiday revelry, music and spirited dancing by bearded, turbaned Punjabi men. In the Southern states of Tamil Nadu (formerly Madras), Mysore and Andhra, the three-day rice festival of Pongal is one of the most exuberant events of the year, accompanied by cockfights, oxcart races and a peculiar variety of bullfight in which bare-chested young men try to grab bundles of money that have been tied to the horns of ferocious bulls. On the second day all the cattle in each village are decorated with brightly painted designs, garlands and *tikas*—the red marks that Hindus wear on their foreheads—and led out in procession to the jubilant sound of drums and music.

The traditional Pongal feasts are held in the evenings. The main dishes for these meals are made from the newly harvested rice, which is ceremonially cooked and fed to the cattle in a gesture of veneration before the people are served. One of the favorite dishes is *ven pongal*, a delicate rice and lentil preparation mixed with cashew nuts, and gently spiced with peppercorns, cumin seed and ginger. Another popular specialty is *sarkarai pongal*, in which sweet rice is mixed with fried lentils and cooked with molasses, cashew nuts, large seedless raisins and grated coconut. It is flavored with cardamom and saffron and a pinch of edible camphor—to enhance the aroma of the spices without changing the taste of the dish.

Among the most colorful and exciting harvest festivals is the 10-day celebration of Onam in the state of Kerala in Southern India at the end of August and the beginning of September. Essentially this is a rice harvest observance, but its origins are deeply rooted in the mythology of Kerala.

The festival commemorates the return to earth of Mahabali, Kerala's best-known and best-loved mythical Emperor, whose just and benevolent reign was a time of peace and plenty, Kerala's Golden Age. So popular was Mahabali that the lesser gods became jealous and alarmed. They persuaded Lord Vishnu, the chief deity, to find a way of crippling Mahabali's power. Vishnu appeared as a dwarf before the King and asked for a gift of land, only as much as he could cover in three paces. The King readily agreed, only to see the dwarf miraculously extend himself to gigantic size; with two steps he covered all the earth and all the ocean. Where, he asked, should he take the third step he had been promised? The King unwarily replied that the person of a ruler was a separate domain, beyond the land he ruled. So, for his third step, Lord Vishnu trod on Mahabali's head, pushing him down to the infernal regions. But the outcry of the Malayalis (the people of the Malabar Coast) against this summary deposing of their great ruler was so fervent that eventually Mahabali was given his proper place in the heavens and permitted to return to the earth in invisible form once a year.

At Onam, the Malayalis try to recapture the lost glory of Mahabali's reign, to reaffirm Mahabali's popularity in songs and poems, and to gladden the heart of their visiting Emperor. Early each morning everybody takes an oil bath and perfumes himself with sandalwood paste. The women dress their hair in the formal Malabar style, wound high on one side of the head and encircled with flowers. They wear their special Onam clothes, bright bodices and gauzy white cotton "skirts," ankle length and bordered with gold, which even through two thicknesses are almost transparent and clearly show the lines of the body when the women move through the festival's traditional dances. (Malabar women have never been ashamed of their bodies —for good reason, since they are among the most shapely and graceful women anywhere. Many of them maintain the old custom of wearing nothing above the waist, and still bathe bare-breasted in public village pools.)

The Onam festival is a kaleidoscope of colorful and lively events. Young men show off their strength and skill in displays of a kind of open-palmed boxing. Troupes of classical dancers entertain villagers and townsmen with outdoor dances depicting popular legends of epic heroes. In the evenings young girls perform the hand-clapping dance known as *kaikottikali* around traditional brass lamps glowing on carpets of grass where intricate patterns of flower petals have been traced.

The most enthusiastically celebrated events of the Onam festivities are the great gala boat races held on the network of interconnecting rivers, lagoons and canals that lace all Malabar with inland waterways. For the races splendid ceremonial snake boats are brought out (virtually every waterfront village owns one), ranging in length from 100 to 200 feet, with tall, tapering prows arching out several yards above the water. Moving between the holiday crowds of spectators on the banks, followed by hundreds of small catamarans and country craft (used on ordinary days for transporting rice, copra and other necessities from village to village), the snake boats glide to the race's starting point in resplendent procession with flags flying, music playing and people singing. The village headman sits in each boat, commanding under a scarlet parasol. His chanting of the classic story of Lord Krishna (an incarnation of Vishnu), punctuated by a chorus from the oarsmen, accompanied with cymbals and drums, sets the rhythm for the oars.

The boat race is a competition, and there is a winner, but spectators and oarsmen alike tend to regard it as more of a pageant than a contest, the general air of color and festivity mattering more than the mundane question of who wins. When the race is over, the people go back to their villages, and the women serve the *Onam Sadhya*, the traditional feast that they have prepared. Straw mats are laid out on the verandas before the houses, and banana leaves are spread on top of them to serve as *thalis*.

The men are served first, and the women move quickly and deftly among them, helping them to the various Onam dishes. The food is, of course, eaten with the fingers, and as many as 30 or 40 dishes are served. Like most Indian festival foods, the *Onam Sadhya* gives particular emphasis to sweet dishes. The Kerala women serve cubes of bananas, fried crisp and sweetened with molasses, as well as succulent bananas that have been cut into 3-inch sections and steamed in their skins. They offer a delicate rice preparation called *payasam*, cooked with milk and sugar and aromatic spices, and they bring out a sweet lentil dish called *chirupayaru payasam*, cooked with unrefined brown sugar, then simmered with coconut milk, cardamom and *ghee*.

The profusion of foods at Onam produces many excellent vegetable com-

On a Kerala backwater, oarsmen maneuver a ceremonial boat into position for the start of the annual boat race climaxing the 10-day Onam festival. Some of the oarsmen row from a sitting position, while others stand up and steer the boat with long oars. The boats belong to Kerala villages and are rowed by men from the villages. On the opposite page hometown rooters along the shore cheer the Onam boats on.

binations. The women have prepared a pungent *sambar (Recipe Index),* a mixture of spiced lentils and other vegetables. They serve a dish called *thoran* that combines crisp jackfruit stalks or green bananas with coconut, and a festive *aviyal (Recipe Index)*—a vegetable curry with as many as six vegetables, plus mangoes and bananas.

But the most unusual of the Onam dishes is a wonderfully sweet-sour-sharp ginger curry called *puli ingi,* which is bright red in color and pungent to the taste. Watching a Kerala woman prepare it is a fine lesson in Indian cooking. In her immaculate kitchen—which seems almost spartan by Western standards, with its earthen floor and its rows of brass and copper jars filled with lentils, spices, rice and other cooking staples on the shelves—she first peels some ginger root, chops it and mixes it with thinly sliced coconut. Then she prepares a *masala* of several different red and green chilies. Now, she mixes this *masala* with the chopped ginger and coconut slices and cooks the mixture over a charcoal burner. Finally, she adds a bit of tamarind, to provide a special quality of sourness, and some molasses or unrefined sugar, for a light, but essential sweetness.

By Western standards, *puli ingi* is hot, but some of the other Onam curries are even hotter. One of these is mango curry, made with a *masala* of coconut, red chilies, green chilies, coarse turmeric, ginger, garlic, peppercorns, cumin seeds, coriander seeds, mustard seeds, cloves and cinnamon. Another

94

is *naranga* curry: it is based on citron, and the Kerala ladies season it with as many as 25 dry chilies and six green chilies, which means that it is fiery hot. The people of South India eat these incendiary delicacies without blinking an eye, but the Westerner who may be contemplating a trip to Southern India at Onam (or any other time) should not go unwarned.

I was reminded of this point recently by the experience of an Indian friend who was traveling from India to the United States. She stopped off at the London airport, and while there she met a girl from Andhra in South India. The girl was on her way to the States to join her husband, a graduate student at the University of Pittsburgh. She had been sick for two days at the airport hotel with an upset stomach, brought on, she explained, by the blandness of the food. Everything was like eating chalk, she said. She ordered an omelet for breakfast and complained that it had no taste. My friend asked the waiter to bring a bottle of Tabasco in a hurry, and poured three quarters of it on the omelet. That was better, the girl said, but it still was not hot enough. So my friend asked the waiter for some peppers. He brought a bottle, and she dumped 14 to 16 red-hot South American peppers on top of the omelet. The girl's eyes lit up when she tasted it. "Ah. Bhenji" (sister), she said with relief. "Now I have come to life!"

In contrast with Onam and other harvest celebrations, most of India's festivals are religious observances and are Hindu in origin. Astrology, tradition

A special vegetarian meal served on a banana-leaf *thali (above)* at Kerala's Onam festival features *(top row, left to right):* fried banana chunks, banana wafers, bananas boiled with spices and grated coconut, and vegetables mixed with bananas, yoghurt, coconut and spices. The dark foods next to the bananas at left are mango curry, ginger curry and yam chips spiced with red chilies. In the bottom row are *pappadams* (thin bread wafers) with yoghurt just above them, boiled rice with *sambar* (spiced lentils and vegetables); a milk and rice dish called *palpayasam* and lentils seasoned with chilies.

and a vivid imagination have provided a vast number of holy days—occasions when the sun, the moon or one of the planets is in a bad aspect and must be propitiated, days when one or another of the many deities in the Hindu pantheon must be honored, birthdays of mythological heroes or real historical figures (Buddha or Gandhi, for example), days of fasting, or days of special prayer at particular temples. With sufficient piety and ingenuity a Hindu could make a holiday of almost any day of the year.

In a country as diverse and as complex as India, it is not surprising to find that festival legends vary greatly from one area to another. One of the gayest, most colorful of all Hindu festivals is Holi, a time for frivolity and high spirits. A variety of legends is associated with this festival, although most of them relate in one way or another to the activities of Lord Krishna. Holi is celebrated in early spring all over India, but most uproariously in North India and Bengal, the most elaborate celebration being the one that is held in Mathura (between New Delhi and Agra). According to the legend on which this particular celebration is based, Krishna had an evil uncle who sent an ogress named Holika to burn down Krishna's house. But Krishna turned the tables on Holika, and escaped while she burned to death in the blaze.

On the evening before the Holi festival, bonfires are lit in villages and towns all over North India, symbolizing the incineration of Holika and the triumph of good over evil. Dressed in clean—but not new—clothes, everybody gathers by the fire to sing love songs, enact episodes from Krishna's life, explode fireworks, throw colored water on each other and dab each other with colored powder. Pilgrims from all over India flock to Mathura for the celebration. On Holi day men, women and children pour into the streets in a trick-or-treat mood, carrying squirt cans or bicycle pumps filled with colored water, threatening to douse any passerby unless he pays a small token for immunity. Sometimes they simply douse each other for the fun of it.

Indians are great snack eaters, and on almost any outing, particularly at celebrations such as Holi, they often will eat only one full meal in a day, picking up snacks at street corners or bazaars. This habit of unplanned eating has produced a wonderful range of minor food delights.

As you walk along a dusty Indian street at festival time you will see vendors offering crisp snacks called *wadas* and *bondas*. *Wadas* come in many different varieties; a popular version is made of lentils with onions, green chilies and turmeric. The vendors mold the ingredients into a ball, flatten it and deep-fry it in bubbling *gingili* (sesame) oil. *Bondas*, the size and shape of table-tennis balls, also come in many varieties and are cooked the same way. A favorite *bonda* is prepared by cooking a boiled potato with green chilies, coriander, *kari* leaves, coconut, ginger and salt.

Many snacks are gobbled all over the country, and regardless of their regional origin, you are likely to find some of them wherever you go. Among the most versatile are *pakoras (Recipe Index)*. Indian cooks prepare these simple snacks by dipping bits of vegetables—eggplant cubes, potato slices, spinach leaves, cauliflower flowerets, or green chilies—into a batter of chick-pea flour and deep-frying them in oil. Another favorite Indian snack is *chiura (Recipe Index)*, a mixture of pounded rice, toasted peanuts, lentils and a vermicelli of chick-pea flour, each ingredient deep-fried separately and seasoned with sugar, salt and cayenne pepper. By simply adding onion, fresh coriander and perhaps a chutney, Indian cooks make *bhelpuri (Recipe Index)*, another favorite snack, which is served on small, crisp wafers.

One of the prettiest of all Indian festivals is Divali, which is celebrated throughout India in November. The festival marks the darkest night of the year, when dead souls return to earth and must be shown the way by the lights in the houses. All over India, houses, palaces and government buildings are lighted up.

For most Indians—especially the businessmen—Divali is the beginning of the Hindu New Year, when everyone should buy new clothes, settle past debts, heal old feuds and quarrels—a time when everyone should wish everyone else good fortune. An essential part of this general benevolence is the sending of sweets to neighbors, friends, relatives, business associates, colleagues and superiors in work. Indian sweets are of such an immense variety and include so many regional and community specialties that, even if one were to mention only those preparations that have achieved a nationwide popularity, the list would be all but interminable. In Banaras, the site of the most sacred Temple of Annapurna, different Indian sweets are piled in towers 12 or 15 feet high during Divali, and these are only the "dry" sweets. These "dry," or candylike, sweets, such as *peras* or *barfis (Recipe Index)*, often require as a base a sort of thickened or condensed milk called *mawa*, which is tedious to make, but gives an extraordinary richness and smoothness of tex-

Continued on page 102

A Lively Prelude to a Pachyderm Parade

For every national festival in India, there are scores of colorful local celebrations. One of the liveliest of these is the eight-day rice harvest observance held in Trippunithura, in South India, every fall. This festival revolves around the local temple, which is dedicated to the Hindu god Krishna. As the crowds gather at the temple, clowns wearing monkey and lion masks *(opposite page)* frolic among them. The temple band *(above)* renders an ear-splitting serenade and, as the festivities come to a climax, a troop of elaborately decorated elephants *(following pages)* parades around the temple courtyard carrying a statue of Krishna in their midst.

Overleaf: In the courtyard of the temple of Trippunithura, a troop of elephants with gold-plated headdresses and colorful parasols passes in review. A statue of the god Krishna is sheltered under the small golden parasol. Riders on the elephants' backs stand upright and wave mohair whisks in time to the music of the band.

ture. (Most Indians buy such sweets from professional *halvais*, or sweet-makers; if they make them at home, they usually buy the *mawa* to start with.) The *mawa* is cooked with sugar and various flavorings. Almond *barfi*, for example, is a chewy marzipanlike confection made of ground almonds and milk, while pistachio *barfi* is a brittle confection combining *mawa* with pistachio. Either one can delight a sweet tooth, but the ingredients for the two are sometimes combined to make an even more delicious confection called almond-pistachio *barfi* *(Recipe Index)*.

There are many other dry sweets that do not need *mawa*. *Mysore-pak*, deliciously crisp and crumbly, honeycombed with tiny air holes, has roasted chick-pea flour, shortening and syrup as its main ingredients, as do some of the dozens of kinds of sweets called *laddu*. In one popular version of *laddu*, crunchy little dots of chick-pea flour that have been fried in *ghee* are soaked in sugar syrup and then covered with melon seeds. Another popular dry sweet is *shakar-paras*, small brittle diamonds of pastry dipped in syrup and then cooled so that they have a sweet, glassy coating.

Equally diverse in texture and flavor is the panoply of semiliquid milk sweets known as *khir* *(Recipe Index)*. These are preparations in which rice, or some kinds of lentils, sago, tapioca, vermicelli, date pulp or ground almonds are cooked in milk and sugar, usually with a flavoring of cardamom and saffron, until the mixture thickens. It is then poured into *katoris*, left to cool, sprinkled with nuts, decorated with silver leaf and served cold.

The various *halvas*, another popular Indian sweet, may seem more strange to the foreign palate. Many of the best of these are made from grated vegetables—carrots, beets, pumpkin, potato—boiled in milk until almost all the liquid is absorbed, then fried in *ghee*, sugar and flavorings. These should be a little drier than the *khir*, but still not quite of candylike consistency.

And then there are sweets served in syrup. Bengal produces two of the best —*roshmalai* and *roshgulla* *(Recipe Index)*. Both of these require fresh cottage cheese, kneaded with a little flour to make small, very light, slightly spongy cakes that are cooked in syrup. Another syrup sweet, *balushahi*, which is enjoyed all over India, is a crisp tidbit of white flour, deep-fried in *ghee* and then dipped in a sugar syrup.

For sheer grandeur and spectacle, few festivals in India or elsewhere can equal the 10-day celebration of Dasehra in Mysore in late September and early October. The festival is celebrated all over India, but the most spectacular observance is the Mysore one, held in joyful commemoration of the victory of the good Prince Rama over the army of the demon Ravana and in grateful tribute to the goddess Durga who aided Rama.

Rama was the seventh incarnation of the great god Vishnu. He married the beautiful and virtuous Sita, and was supposed to succeed his father as King of Ayodhya. But fate intervened, and Rama was exiled to the forest. Sita followed him there, and one day while alone, she was kidnapped by a monstrous demon named Ravana. With the help of an army of monkeys —the gods had endowed them with supernatural powers—Rama then set out to save his wife, Sita, engaging the evil demon Ravana in a 10-day campaign and ultimately slaying him.

At festival time, nobles come from all over Mysore to celebrate Rama's triumph, to pay homage to the Maharaja and to place their annual tribute to

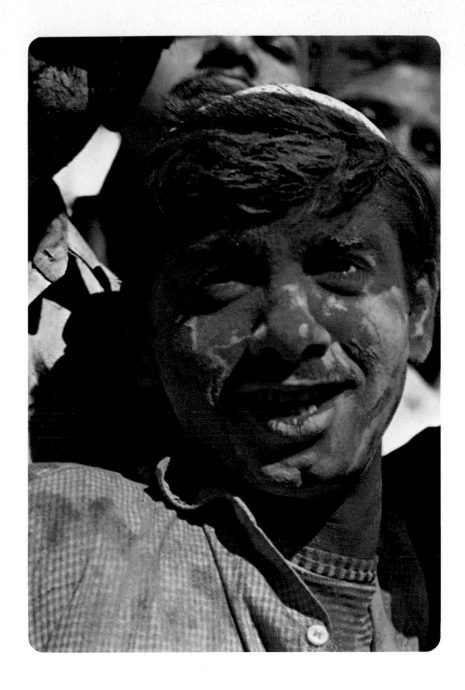

His face, clothes and hair smeared with colored water and powders thrown on him during the Holi festival, a young reveler in Bombay *(left)* good-humoredly awaits a chance to retaliate. The riotous festival, commemorating the triumph of Lord Krishna over the wicked Holika, is marked throughout India by reckless squirting and powder dusting of everyone in sight.

the throne at his feet. In the old days this used to be a sack of gold coins, but the Maharaja—once a powerful ruler—is now merely a figurehead and only the gesture of offering a single coin remains. The Maharaja's response, however, has not changed. He gives each noble a ceremonial *paan* (the traditional perfumed mixture of spices, lime, betel nut and *kattha*, wrapped in betel leaf and covered with silver beaten thinner than onion skin) to signify his approval and blessing.

The first nine days of Dasehra are spent in *puja*, or worship of the deity, and the 10th day is devoted to the celebration of Rama's victory over evil. For nine days the Maharaja spends three to six hours daily worshiping in a palace room as Brahmin priests chant *mantras* (incantations) or read long

One of India's most charming festivals, celebrated throughout the country in the fall, honors the elephant-headed Hindu god, Ganesha. According to legend, Ganesha got his peculiar anatomy when Lord Shiva (one of the three main Hindu gods) cut off the head of a child his wife had fashioned out of chick-pea flour. She was so enraged that he quickly replaced it with the head of an elephant, the first thing that passed his way.

passages from *Durga Purana,* Sanskrit verses recounting the legends of the goddess Durga. During the day the public is not admitted to the palace, but in the evenings 2,500 to 5,000 people crowd into the palace courtyard where they may glimpse the Maharaja.

Dressed in brocade, cloth of gold, cockades and necklaces of precious stones, the Maharaja sits on a throne of carved figwood overlaid with gold and silver. Under an elaborate canopy decorated with a golden, jewel-encrusted peacock carrying an enormous emerald in its beak, he receives his nobles in the great audience hall that is open all along one side to the main palace courtyard. Here his state troops parade, displaying feats of equestrian skill. Acrobats, clowns, sword swallowers, singers and dancers stage a continuous performance. Meanwhile, outside the palace grounds sideshows spring up—groups of traveling players, puppeteers, professional storytellers, and between them all, stalls selling savory snacks, sweets and full meals.

Along with the snacks and sweets that are enjoyed during the Dasehra celebration, those Mysoreans who are observing the full ritual prepare a variety of popular Indian dishes for each of the nine days leading up to Rama's final victory. Every day two or three new dishes are added to the menu, and *all* of the accumulated dishes are cooked each day. The whole affair is rather like the song about the Twelve Days of Christmas and the accumulations of gifts that the lady's true love sent her.

Dasehra begins with the preparation of a *payasam,* a semiliquid sweet with rice as its base, and a staggering array of foods follows. A green vegetable called *thovey* is served. It is spinach, but quite unlike any spinach Westerners have known, because it is highly spiced with a *masala* of turmeric, garlic, onion, green chilies and grated coconut. Another outstanding Dasehra dish, *pachadi,* mixes curds (yoghurt) with ground coconut and is spiced with mustard seeds and red chilies. The growing Dasehra menu includes the highly spiced, lentil-based consommé called *rasam.* A *sambar* appears; cone-shaped dumplings, known as *modak,* stuffed with grated coconut and molasses, are eaten, and the Dasehra diners savor a delicate rice dish called *chitranna,* flavored with lime juice and saffron.

As the celebration progresses, the feast gathers momentum. A different kind of *payasam* is cooked, a very thick one of rice, vermicelli and molasses. Small cakes, called *appams,* are made from a batter of rice flour and unrefined brown sugar, cooked with *ghee.* (According to an old Indian saying, *appams* should be so rich with *ghee* that any gentleman who picks one up will have enough *ghee* left on his fingers to give his moustache a fine gloss.) Besides all these items, each of the dishes from the previous days of Dasehra must be cooked. And so the menu keeps growing in giddy profusion.

On the final day of Dasehra, the end of the mythological 10-day battle culminating in the victory of Rama, Mysore stages the biggest show of all. In the morning the Maharaja goes to the temple to make his obeisance to the deity and to offer the traditional foods: *wadas, payasam,* raw *mung dal* (a yellow lentil) and *paan.* That same evening the festival comes to a climax. The Maharaja, in a golden *howdah,* on a splendidly decorated elephant, rides in state to the sacred *shemi* tree, and cuts off a branch as a symbol of victory over obstacles. It is an incredible procession. The royal elephant is painted with elaborate designs of red and white flowers curling up his legs, his eyes are

elongated with paint, and even his toenails are lacquered. He is bedecked with special elephant jewelry: a massive gold necklace, huge gold earrings, a jeweled plaque for his forehead, glittering gold anklets and gold tips on his tusks. Accompanying the Maharaja's beast are the lesser state elephants ridden by dignitaries of the court, the royal and camel-mounted troops, and the matched black horses of the Maharaja's personal bodyguard with their leopard-skin saddles. The Maharaja and his whole retinue return from the tree in a torchlight procession through the brilliantly lighted capital, watched by thousands of his state's people. And then begins a night of feasting.

By now dozens of dishes have been prepared through the 10 days of Dasehra. Large straw mats are placed on the floor, and the climactic feast is served —*payasam, thovey, rasam, sambar, modak,* banana dishes, *appams, chitranna, jalebi,* chutneys, curries—all of the accumulated festive foods. After the long suspense of King Rama's classic battle and his final triumphant success, everyone can now enjoy a meal of untrammeled extravagance that will live in memory for the rest of the year. And 12 months later, everybody is ready and eager to do it all over again.

Shaped like doughnuts, spaghetti, turnovers and cream puffs, the foods arrayed here on a large *thali* are savory Indian snacks. They were made from a variety of plants, including potatoes, eggplant, sago palm and rice. Among the most popular items are *pakoras* (the disks at upper left) and potato *samosas* (the turnoverlike tidbits at center right).

The Glare and Glitter
of a Spectacular Festival

In New Delhi the 10-day Dasehra festival celebrates the triumph of Prince Rama, an incarnation of the god Vishnu, the embodiment of good, over the wicked monster, Ravana. On the festival's final night, brightly colored effigies of Ravana, his son and his brother (who also fought Rama) are erected in a public park. In Mysore on that same day (where the celebration honors the goddess Durga, who helped Rama overcome Ravana), as the festival draws to a climax *(opposite page)*, the Maharaja rides out of his palace in a golden *howdah* perched atop a brilliantly decorated elephant, accompanied by palace retainers.

The Maharaja and his son ride out to cut a branch off a sacred *shemi* tree, symbolizing good triumphant over evil.

CHAPTER IV RECIPES

To make about 60 small triangular
pastries

PASTRY

3 cups all-purpose flour
1 teaspoon salt
3 tablespoons *ghee (page 54)*
¾ to 1 cup cold water
Potato or lamb filling *(below)*
Vegetable oil for deep frying

POTATO FILLING

2 small boiling-type potatoes (about
  ½ pound)
2 tablespoons vegetable oil
½ teaspoon black mustard seeds
½ cup finely chopped onions
2 teaspoons scraped, finely chopped
  fresh ginger root
1 teaspoon fennel seeds
¼ teaspoon cumin seeds
¼ teaspoon turmeric
½ cup fresh green peas (about ½
  pound unshelled) or ½ cup frozen
  peas, thoroughly defrosted
½ teaspoon salt
1 tablespoon water
1 tablespoon finely chopped fresh
  coriander *(cilantro)*
½ teaspoon *garam masala (page 56)*
⅛ teaspoon ground hot red pepper

Samosas
DEEP-FRIED FILLED PASTRIES

In a deep bowl, combine the flour, salt and *ghee*. With your fingertips, rub the flour and *ghee* together until they look like flakes of coarse meal. Pour ¾ cup of water over the mixture all at once, knead together vigorously and gather the dough into a ball. If the dough crumbles, add up to 4 more tablespoons of water, a tablespoon at a time, until the particles adhere.

On a lightly floured surface, knead the dough by folding it end to end, then pressing it down and pushing it forward several times with the heel of your hand. Repeat for about 10 minutes, or until the dough is smooth and elastic. Again gather it into a ball, brush lightly with *ghee* or vegetable oil and set it in a bowl. Drape a damp kitchen towel over the top to keep the dough moist. (Covered with the towel, it can remain at room temperature for 4 or 5 hours.)

Shape and fill the *samosas* two at a time in the following fashion: Pinch off a small piece of dough and roll it into a ball about 1 inch in diameter. (Keep the remaining dough covered with the towel.) On a lightly floured surface, roll the ball into a circle about 3½ inches in diameter.) With a pastry wheel or small knife, cut the circle in half. Moisten the straight edge with a finger dipped in water. Then shape each semicircle into a cone, fill it with about 1½ teaspoons of the lamb or potato mixture, and moisten and press the top edges closed. (Covered with foil or plastic wrap and refrigerated, the pastries may be kept for 2 or 3 hours before they are fried.)

To deep-fry the pastries, pour 3 cups of vegetable oil into a 10-inch *karhai* or 12-inch *wok (page 151),* or pour 2 to 3 inches of oil into a deep fryer. Heat the oil until it reaches a temperature of 375° on a deep-frying thermometer. Preheat the oven to 200° and line a large shallow baking dish with a double thickness of paper towels.

Deep-fry the *samosas* 4 or 5 at a time for 2 to 3 minutes, or until golden brown on all sides. As they brown, transfer them to the lined baking dish and keep them warm in the oven.

To serve, mound the *samosas* on a heated platter, and accompany them with coriander chutney *(Recipe Index)*, presented separately in a bowl.

POTATO FILLING: Drop the potatoes into enough boiling water to cover them completely and boil briskly, uncovered, until they are tender but still somewhat resistant when pierced with the point of a small, sharp knife. Drain the potatoes in a colander, peel, then cut them into ½-inch cubes. There should be about 2 cups.

In a heavy 10- to 12-inch skillet, heat the vegetable oil over moderate heat until a drop of water flicked into it splutters instantly. Add the mustard seeds and, when they crackle and begin to burst, immediately add the onions and ginger. Stirring almost constantly, fry for 7 or 8 minutes, until the onions are soft and golden brown. Stir in the fennel, cumin and turmeric, then add the potatoes, peas, salt and water.

Reduce the heat to low, cover the skillet tightly, and cook for 5 minutes. Then stir in the coriander and continue to cook, covered, for at least 10 minutes longer, or until the peas are tender. Remove the skillet from the heat

Crisp fried Indian savories include potato *pakoras (top)*, potato-and-lamb-filled *samosas (right)* and eggplant *pakoras (left)*.

and stir in the *garam masala* and red pepper. Taste the filling for seasoning.

Transfer the entire contents of the skillet to a bowl and cool the filling to room temperature before using it.

LAMB FILLING: Place the saffron threads in a small bowl, pour in the water, and let them soak for 10 minutes or so. Meanwhile, in a 10-inch *karhai* or 12-inch *wok (page 151)*, or a heavy 10-inch skillet, heat the vegetable oil over moderate heat until a drop of water flicked into it splutters instantly. Stirring constantly, add the ginger, garlic, onions and salt, and fry for 7 or 8 minutes, until the onions are soft and golden brown. Stir in the lamb, saffron and its soaking water. Still stirring, cook the lamb until all traces of pink disappear. Add the red pepper and *garam masala*, reduce the heat to low and, stirring occasionally, cook uncovered for 20 minutes, until most of the liquid in the pan evaporates and the lamb mixture is thick enough to draw away from the sides of the pan in a solid mass. Watch carefully for any sign of burning and regulate the heat accordingly. When the lamb is done, transfer it to a bowl and let it cool to room temperature before using. Tightly covered and refrigerated, the filling can be kept for 2 days.

LAMB FILLING
½ teaspoon saffron threads
3 tablespoons hot water
¼ cup vegetable oil
1 tablespoon scraped, finely chopped
   fresh ginger root
1 tablespoon finely chopped garlic
½ cup finely chopped onions
1 teaspoon salt
1 pound lean ground lamb
¼ teaspoon ground red pepper
1 teaspoon *garam masala (page 56)*

To serve 6 to 8

6 medium-sized carrots (about 1
   pound), scraped and coarsely
   grated
1 quart milk
1 cup light cream
1 cup jaggery (raw cane sugar), or
   substitute dark-brown sugar
   combined with dark molasses
   (page 196)
½ cup sugar
1½ cups whole blanched almonds
   (about 8 ounces), pulverized in a
   blender or with a nut grinder
¼ cup ghee (page 54)
The seeds of 10 cardamom pods or
   ½ teaspoon cardamom seeds,
   wrapped in a kitchen towel and
   crushed with a rolling pin
¼ cup unsalted pistachios, toasted
¼ cup unsalted, slivered blanched
   almonds, toasted

To serve 6 as a vegetable dish or 8
   to 12 as a snack

1 medium-sized eggplant (about 1
   pound), washed but not peeled,
   cut in half lengthwise, and each
   half sliced crosswise into 12 pieces
1 tablespoon salt
1 cup besan (chick-pea flour)
¼ cup rice flour
1 teaspoon ground cumin
¼ teaspoon ground hot red pepper
¾ cup cold water
Vegetable oil for deep frying

To make about 24 small pieces

4 teaspoons ghee (page 54)
1 quart milk
1 cup sugar
1 cup ground almonds, or 1 cup
   whole or slivered blanched
   almonds, pulverized in a blender
   or with a nut grinder
1 cup unsalted pistachios, pulverized
   in a blender or with a nut grinder
½ teaspoon almond extract

Gajar Halva
SWEET CARROT DESSERT

In a deep heavy 5- to 6-quart saucepan, combine the carrots, milk and cream. Stirring constantly, bring to a boil over high heat. Reduce the heat to moderate and, stirring occasionally, cook for 1 hour, or until the mixture has reduced to about half its original volume and is thick enough to coat a spoon heavily. Stir in the jaggery (or brown sugar and molasses) and the sugar, and continue cooking for 10 minutes. Reduce the heat to the lowest possible point, add the pulverized almonds and the *ghee,* and stir for 10 minutes more, or until the *halva* mixture is thick enough to draw away from the sides and bottom of the pan in a solid mass. Remove the pan from the heat and stir in the cardamom.

With a metal spatula, spread the *halva* on a large heatproof platter, mound it slightly in the center, and decorate the top with pistachios and slivered almonds. Serve warm or at room temperature. In India, *gajar halva* is also sometimes decorated with a special edible silver leaf.

Baingan Pakoras
DEEP-FRIED EGGPLANT

Drop the eggplant into a bowl, sprinkle it with salt, and turn the pieces about with a spoon to coat them evenly. Set aside for at least 30 minutes.

Meanwhile, prepare the batter. Combine the chick-pea flour, rice flour, cumin and red pepper in a deep bowl and, when they are well mixed, pour in the water, stirring constantly.

Pour 3 cups of vegetable oil into a 10-inch *karhai* or 12-inch *wok (page 151)*, or fill a deep fryer with oil to a depth of 2 or 3 inches. Heat the oil until it reaches a temperature of 350° on a deep-frying thermometer.

Squeeze the eggplant pieces gently but firmly to remove as much of their moisture as possible. With tongs or a slotted spoon, dip one piece at a time into the batter and then drop it into the hot oil. Fry the eggplant in batches of 5 or 6 pieces for about 5 minutes, or until golden brown on all sides. As they brown, transfer them to paper towels to drain.

Baingan pakoras are traditionally served as a snack or as part of a meal.

Badam Pistaz Barfi
ALMOND-AND-PISTACHIO CANDY

With a pastry brush, spread 1 teaspoon of the *ghee* on a 7½-inch pie tin.

In a heavy 3- to 4-quart saucepan, bring the milk to a boil over high heat. Reduce the heat to moderate and, stirring frequently, cook for about 35 minutes, or until the milk thickens to the consistency of heavy cream. Add the sugar and stir for 10 minutes. Then add the ground almonds and pistachios and continue stirring 10 minutes longer. Still stirring, add 3 teaspoons of the *ghee* and cook for another 5 or 10 minutes, until the mixture is thick enough to draw away from the sides of the pan in a solid mass.

Remove the pan from the heat and stir in the almond extract. Pour the candy into the pie tin, spreading and smoothing it with a spatula. Let the candy cool for 30 minutes or so, then cut it into about 24 small squares or diamonds. It will harden to the consistency of fudge as it cools further.

Carrots are transformed into a festive dessert called *gajar halva (above)*, elegantly ornamented with nuts and edible silver leaf.

Pakoras

DEEP-FRIED POTATO AND CHICK-PEA FLOUR BALLS

In a deep bowl make a smooth batter of the chick-pea flour, baking soda and water by stirring them together with a spoon or by mixing them with your fingers. Then thoroughly stir in the onion, potato, coriander, cumin, red pepper and salt.

Pour 3 cups of vegetable oil into a 10-inch *karhai* or 12-inch *wok (page 151)*, or pour 2 to 3 inches of oil into a deep fryer. Heat until the oil reaches a temperature of 350° on a deep-frying thermometer. For each *pakora*, scoop up a tablespoonful of the potato and chick-pea flour batter and, with a second spoon, scrape the batter directly into the hot oil. Deep-fry half of the *pakoras* at a time, turning them about occasionally with a slotted spoon for 7 to 8 minutes, or until they are golden brown on all sides.

As they brown, remove the *pakoras* from the oil with a slotted spoon and drain them on paper towels.

Serve the *pakoras* hot or at room temperature. Traditionally they are presented as a snack, but they can also accompany an Indian meal.

To make about 10 one-inch balls

½ cup *besan* (chick-pea flour)
¼ teaspoon baking soda
5 tablespoons cold water
1 small onion, peeled, cut lengthwise in half, and sliced lengthwise into paper-thin slivers
½ cup finely chopped, peeled uncooked potato
3 tablespoons finely chopped fresh coriander *(cilantro)*
½ teaspoon ground cumin
½ teaspoon ground hot red pepper
1 teaspoon salt
Vegetable oil for deep frying

V

A Seafood Paradise in Tropical India

My favorite part of India is the lush green strip of tropical coastline running 700 miles southward from Bombay to Cochin in Kerala. Other areas of the country have more imposing monuments and more sophisticated cities, but ever since I first traveled down this way by steamer more than 20 years ago, nothing has obscured for me the incomparable beauty of this section of India. An almost unnecessary dividend is the diversity, abundance and excellence of fish and seafood found here, a bounty that only the Mediterranean coast, perhaps, can equal.

To the people of India's southwest coast, fish and seafood in general are so inextricably a part of the diet that the idea of managing without them is totally unacceptable, even during the monsoon months when fishing is impossible. Indeed, one of the most fervently celebrated festivals in Bombay is Coconut Day, which falls about the third week of August and marks the end of the "heavy monsoon." Though the rains continue for another month, from Coconut Day onward, the ocean is considered safe enough to allow the fishing boats to go out again, and all the members of the fishing communities gather on the beaches to throw coconuts into the waves in thanksgiving, and to pacify the unpredictable gods and demons of the sea.

The best place to begin to know this part of India and its marvelous seafood is Bombay itself—the city that, after so many intermittent years of living there, I now consider my real home. Bombay is, in fact, an excellent place to begin to know India as a whole. People will tell you that the "real" India is in the villages, which is true in the sense that the vast majority of Indians live there. But it is in the cities—and particularly here in Bombay

On a bamboo rack in Chimbai, a fishing village near Bombay, a day's catch of Bombay duck is hung out to dry in the sun. Once it is dried, Bombay duck is curried, fried or pickled. It is considered a delicacy in this part of India, but it acquires such a strong odor as it dries that some people find it objectionable.

—that you get a sense of the whole Indian experience, the sense of history, of foreign influences, the religious distinctions, the dependence on tradition, as well as the presence and the lack of orthodoxy. India, as you will discover for yourself, has a way of indiscriminately mixing up the august and the absurd, the very new and the immeasurably old, the affluent and the poverty-stricken, the friendly and the reticent, the gay and the sad.

Standing on a Bombay street corner—almost any street corner—you will see walking past you, or entering and leaving shops and houses, women dressed in saris of the distinctive colors and fabrics of their home states. Some will be in Western dresses, some in the narrow trousers and tunics of the North. You will see men in cotton pajamas and *kurtas* (the loose Indian shirts) or in Western sports clothes or business suits. Some will be wearing the white *mundus* (waist-to-ankle sarongs), some in *dhotis* (thin cotton loincloths worn almost anywhere from Gujarat to Bengal), some in the Nehru jackets and narrow trousers of the North. You may well see Indians in the long, white habit of Catholic priests, or in the saffron robes of the *sannyasi*, or Hindu holy men. Often men will be wearing the white hand-spun cotton Gandhi caps; some will have the stiff embroidered skullcaps of the Muslims, or the closely wrapped turbans of the Sikhs, the looser *pagaris* of Hindus, the panache of the Pathan *safar*.

While you are in Bombay, you can sample a variety of fine seafood dishes, in private homes and in restaurants in the Bombay Bay area. Two of my favorites are prawn *patia* and *patrani machli*. There is a story told about certain Indian dishes which, to me, applies best to prawn *patia*. Imagine an Indian fair or festival, where the crowds of people are packed so thickly together that there is scarcely room to place a sliver of bamboo between them. Then imagine that a rogue elephant suddenly appears on the scene. In a second the dense mass of holidaymakers somehow clears a path wide enough for the elephant to make his way through. In a comparable though far less alarming way, no matter how much you may have eaten or how full you may feel, when prawn *patia* is served, you can somehow always make room for it.

In preparing prawn *patia*, Bombay's cooks first select some of the region's truly excellent prawns, and carefully wash and devein them. They marinate the prawns in lemon juice and vinegar for half an hour and cook them with onions, a *masala* and other spices. Then they add the marinade and some puréed tomato to the prawns, and cook the mixture until the prawns turn pink. The result is a superb seafood dish, one whose natural flavor is enhanced by the spices, although the prawns retain the freshness of the sea.

Patrani machli is a much simpler, more delicate preparation. It is really just slices of pomfret—the best of the coastal fishes, whose closest Western equivalent is Dover sole—stuffed with green chutney, wrapped in a banana leaf and steamed or baked. The magic of this dish lies in the elegant quality of the pomfret and the subtlety of the chutney, which must contain, along with the green coriander, garlic, onion and cumin, a little sugar, lime juice and salt. Quite apart from the taste of *patrani machli*, there is something oddly pleasing about the sight of the neatly wrapped packages on your plate. It's like opening charming, unexpected presents at the dinner table.

And then one can't, of course, leave Bombay without at least a word about Bombay duck, which isn't duck at all, but the drier version of a slender, rather bony fish, which is caught in large quantities in local waters and spread out on wide oblong bamboo frames to dry in the sun. Bombay duck may be fried crisp and crumbled over rice as a sort of relish. It may be cooked as a dried-fish curry, or eaten crisp and plain. It is so salty that it needs no other flavoring. Both the taste and smell may indeed be too strong for many palates, but the dish retains its own triumphantly insistent place in the diet of every economic level of the true Bombay population. It accompanies the most frugal meal of the poorest people, and may be added to fancier dishes to lend an emphatic touch of flavoring for more retiring fish.

The best way to see the coastline that lies south of Bombay is to board a small steamer in the city, as I have done on several occasions, and spend four or five days chugging down to the port of Cochin. The steamer stops at small seaside towns whose lovely emerald harbors often are too shallow to allow a steamer passage, and fleets of small boats skim out to load and unload cargo. Lying at anchor in the harbor along the way are the Arab dhows with brightly painted prows that have sailed across the Arabian Sea to trade their dates and gold for Indian cloth and spices, a fugitive reminder of the time, 3,000 years ago when the Phoenician ships came to Kerala to trade for spices, ivory, pearls and peacocks, and the intervening centuries when mariners and merchants from Europe and the Far East came here in search of Kerala's legendary natural wealth.

Even more fascinating are the big, weathered, Indian country craft, with their huge triangular sails, moving gracefully down the coast on the prevailing northeast wind that follows the monsoon. In them live families whose whole life is spent on the ocean and who take to the land reluctantly only for the three months of high summer when the monsoon makes the sea too treacherous for sailing boats. They have a special character, these people, an air of independence, good humor and a sort of exclusivity, as if they belonged to a proud and private club.

In the early morning, from the deck of the steamer, as a country craft sails by, you can catch a quick glimpse of the owner and his family in an ordinary, casual moment in their lives. The wife perhaps squatting by her little charcoal burner, blowing into the fire to bring it to a glow; a couple of small children still asleep, half in and half out of the rough cabin; an older boy mending a strip of sail or a net; the owner at the tiller; another man —probably a relative—relaxing in the bow, eating an orange or a banana, waving or shouting a question or a comment to someone in a passing boat. And in the evening, anchored in another harbor, you hear the sweet, high trills of a bamboo flute from one of the boats, picked up and improved upon by someone on another boat, sometimes overpowered by groups of people singing their special songs, their voices growing gayer and wilder if they are drinking arak, the strong local home-brew distilled from palm beer (for it is an accepted tradition that people who live on the water like to drink). When at last the fires from the evening meal are put out, the people go to sleep, and only the small riding lights rock gently on the water.

Life is hard and demanding on these country craft, but one aspect of it goes a long way toward compensating for the rigors. The food is marvelous. One of the commonest of their dishes, *min vela* curry (literally, fishermen's or boatmen's curry), is so simple, so delicious and so flexible in its formula,

that it has become a sturdy standby in almost every Kerala home. Several different kinds of fish are used—pomfret, mullet and mackerel. The fish are brought to a boil in water with a *masala* of red chili and turmeric paste, a generous amount of tamarind pulp and salt. Finely ground coconut mixed with water is added to the gravy; the mixture is brought to a boil once more, and served. That's all. The delight of this dish depends entirely on the quality and the flavor of the fish, which should be strong enough to hold its own against the abundance of chilies that the boatmen like, and the unexpected sweet-sour piquancy that the tamarind gives to the gravy.

The herring or sardine catch (both of which are prolific, cheap and delicious on this coast) provides an almost equally simple recipe, *makti patichathu*. To prepare it you soak a few pieces of *kudampuli* in water and spread them in a pan. (*Kudampuli* is a better, more succulent variety of *kokum*, the sour, deep-red South Indian fruit that, like tamarind, vinegar, lime or green mango slices, is often used to provide that sharp-sour flavor that the coastal people like in their fish preparations.) On top of the *kudampuli* you spread a layer of fish (herring or sardines). You cook the fish with a thin coating of a *masala* containing plenty of crushed onion, powdered ginger and red chilies. Then you add another layer of fish and another layer of *masala*, until all the ingredients are used up. After this, you add enough salted water to the pan to cook the fish over high heat, and when the fish is done you pour fresh coconut oil over it and serve it.

If the fishermen are feeling especially prosperous they will cook *murasu* curry, which requires pomfret or mullet. These appetizing fish will fetch a good price in the market and are often served in well-to-do households when guests are being entertained. The *masala* for *murasu* curry calls for coriander, turmeric and red chilies, lightly roasted and ground to a fine paste, with a tempering of oil, mustard seed, red onion and *kari* leaves. The fish is cooked in coconut milk with a dash of vinegar.

The coastline in this part of India is scalloped with dazzling white sand beaches, fringed with mop-headed palms, cashew, guava and mango trees. Thousands of fishing communities dot the shore, each with its own impressive and elusive atmosphere. The fishing people in these communities have their own festivals and ceremonies, many of them centering on the moods and the power of the sea. They accept none of the usual Hindu caste distinctions, though technically they belong to the lowest caste, the Sudra, which, absurdly enough, is composed mainly of agricultural workers. In the bazaars, where the women usually do the selling and the bargaining, you can recognize them at once, not only by the way they drape their saris or their *mundus*—tucked up high between their legs to make something like tight shorts, the material sculpted in pleats and clinging to the body—but also by their sharp, irreverent wit and quick banter with any customer. They walk with the commanding assurance of queens.

One fish worth noting here is whitebait. It is generally considered poor man's food in this part of India, and I have known family cooks who refused to buy it in the market because to be seen bargaining for such inexpensive fish would have lowered both a cook's and a family's prestige among the bazaar people. All the same, occasionally one can persuade even the most snobbish cook to buy whitebait (almost surreptitiously) from the

Opposite: An itinerant fish peddler propels his boat across a lagoon in the Kerala Backwaters. He catches *makti* (sardines) in the open sea, then paddles inland through the interior waterways to sell the fish to farm workers who live along the shore. The *makti* are valued for their tastiness and their oil, which is used as a preservative for boat hulls.

117

At a thatched hut along the Kerala Backwaters, a door-to-door fish peddler displays his freshly caught *makti*. His customers usually cook the fish with a *masala* of chilies and turmeric. *Makti* is the most popular fish in this part of India, making up 97,000 of the 235,000 tons of salt-water fish annually caught off Kerala.

fishermen's children who bring baskets of the fish from house to house along the coast to earn a few coppers for themselves. Whitebait makes a marvelous dish, fried crisp with just a little *masala* or in the form of *min tulika*. For this you must prepare three extractions of coconut milk, the first by pressing all the liquid out of fresh grated coconut, and the second and third by pouring some warm water over the dry residue of the first pressing, and repeating the process. The rest of the recipe is fairly straightforward.

You simply sauté sliced onions, ginger, green chilies and *kari* leaves in oil, add the third (weakest) extraction of coconut milk and some salt to the pan, and bring the mixture to a boil. Then you simmer the whitebait in this mixture and, as the liquid evaporates, add the second extract of coconut milk. When the fish is cooked, you pour the first (most concentrated) extract of coconut milk and a little vinegar over the whitebait to make a sauce.

On the second day out of Bombay the coastal steamer stops at the small former Portuguese colony of Goa, an almost theatrical arrangement of hills covered with dense jungles sweeping down to the gilt crescents of beaches where the glittering Mandovi River stretches in a graceful curve to meet the ocean at the capital of Pangim (now called Panaji). Its charm is inescapable, a compact 16th Century port with the sleepy elegance of colonial architecture and acacia-lined boulevards, heightened by the fuss of steamboats, freighters and sailing ships in its harbor. Across the silver and sapphire bay is another peninsula exuberant with jungles and palm groves.

118

Goa, a tiny, luxuriant area 60 by 40 miles, was celebrated in ancient Indian literature for its wealth and beauty. In fact, its name stems from the Sanskrit word for "cow"—the traditional symbol of prosperity. For thousands of years, Goa was ruled by various dynasties of Indian kings and many religions were represented there. But the arrival of the Portuguese began an era that was shatteringly different from anything the community had known.

In 1510 Alfonso d'Albuquerque, who later left his name in America, sailed up the Mandovi River with 23 ships and captured Goa from its current Muslim rulers. After violent hand-to-hand fighting, he knelt down in the public square and dedicated the city to St. Catherine as homage to her feast day. From then on Goa's story was dominated by the Catholic zeal of the conquerors who sparked one of the most brutal and wholesale religious conversions recorded in Asia. It was described by Sir Richard Burton, the 19th Century writer, historian and explorer, as a movement characterized by "fire and steel, the dungeon and rack, the rice-pot and the rupee. . . ."

Those Hindus who could afford to escape left Goa to settle in other parts of India. Others were compelled to remain, and still others stayed from choice. Goa is now roughly half Catholic Christian and half Hindu. Virtually nothing of its past grandeur now remains, except, possibly, Old Goa, one of the strangest and most beautiful legacies of Indian history. The town that was the heavily populated capital of the 16th Century, splendid with palaces, colleges, cathedrals and public plazas, declined as Portuguese power declined, to be devoured by the jungle and to become a sadly lovely reminder of past colonial glory. The ordinary houses of Old Goa, the markets, the evidences of daily life have all vanished. The mud and thatch and plaster of the modest dwellings have all been dissolved by the steamy climate and the annual monsoons, and a century ago Old Goa's citizens fled in panic from epidemics of cholera and malaria. Now only the great public buildings and monuments of stone—the cathedrals, the governor's palace and such—remain, oddly surrounded by thick jungle growths of jackfruit trees, tamarinds and wild vines.

Against the background of this curious heritage, the baroque architecture of Old Goa, the colonial provincialism of Panaji, the simple unchanging ways of the inland villages, modern Goan life presents its special adaptations to its checkered history. In much of its daily living the differences between the habits of the Goan Christians and their Hindu neighbors are very small. It is in their food that the particular nature of the Goan Christian customs is most clearly expressed.

From Goa come countless fish and seafood recipes using both the ocean and the river fish, as well as the many kinds of shellfish that crowd the rocky outcroppings on its shore. One particular variety has become so popular all down the west coast that it is known by the generic name "Goa curry."

This is a very liquid kind of curry, somewhat the consistency of a thick bouillabaisse, made with a mixture of several kinds of fish that are cooked whole (bones and head included), or very coarsely cut into smaller sections. There are many different recipes that have evolved from the original quite simple formula depending on the part of the coastline, the season of the year and the variety of fish obtainable. But the whole exuberant concoction is so delicious that many people I know serve it only for Sunday lunch—knowing

Clams coated with spices, steamed until they pop open, and tossed with grated coconut form this golden, gingery *teesryo*.

that inevitably everyone will eat too much Goa curry and will *have* to take a long siesta afterward.

A fairly representative recipe requires a large quantity of coconut ground into a fine paste with a very hot *masala* of red chilies, turmeric, cumin and coriander. Goans cook the fish in this mixture, adding plenty of onions, tomatoes and water to provide the sauce, and then seasoning it with tamarind, *kari* leaves and green chilies. Of course, the *masala* can be modified or elaborated according to your taste, but the Goans themselves like their famous curry to be almost scarlet with chilies and frighteningly hot.

My own favorite among the bewildering varieties of seafood in Goa is a tiny —about the size of your thumbnail—shellfish that we call *teesryo*. It is something like the very smallest cockle you can imagine, but Goans cook it in coconut milk and lime juice, and sprinkle it with chopped fresh coriander leaves. It is served by itself—like *moules marinière*—in a bowl, with, perhaps, *chapatis* to sop up the juice, and I, for one, can eat—with a greed that far surpasses appetite—at least a hundred at a sitting, leaving a shameful, telltale mountain of shells behind in the bowl.

South of Goa the steamer stops at Calicut where Vasco da Gama first landed in India, and then about 95 miles farther down the coast it comes at last to the enchanting complex of small islands that form the port of Cochin, where the great Portuguese explorer died and was buried. Among its other natural blessings, the Kerala coast at Cochin can claim the best shellfish in India —the shrimp and small crabs are of an unsurpassed delectability. One meal, in particular, enjoyed on a previous visit to Cochin, remains in my memory as the most imaginative and delicious seafood dinner I have ever eaten in India. Possibly the setting had something to do with the delight of that particular meal.

On that visit to Cochin, I had taken my own and my sister's children with me and we were all staying in the Bolgati Palace, a spacious, rambling 18th Century building that had originally been the residence of the Dutch governors of Cochin in the days when they had wrested both the spice trade and the political power from the Portuguese. Set on its own island in the bay of Cochin, surrounded with lawns and gardens down to the water's edge, shaded by giant acacias through which brilliant green flights of chattering parakeets swept and perched all day, the Bolgati Palace is now a government-run guest house where anyone can stay.

In spite of the standard, uninspired, government-issue furniture that has replaced the carved rosewood and brocades of earlier days, the Bolgati Palace retains much of the old, stately atmosphere. The rooms are enormous and high ceilinged, the verandas are floored with very wide, polished teak boards fastened with wooden pegs rather than nails. The walls still carry 18th Century engravings of contemporary Indian scenes. Ming porcelain pieces decorate the modern, serviceable tables and cabinets, and the whole place is filled with haunting memories of bygone governors' parties, of colonial ladies in crinolines sweeping down the staircase to the sound of foreign music and waiting gentlemen in uniforms of blue and gold, with satin breeches and buckled shoes. Now, in unlikely contrast, after sundown, we could see the flares used by the local fishermen on the rocky beaches, and hear the rhythmic drumming of bamboo sticks, which is supposed to attract the fish.

Continued on page 126

121

The Fisherman's Life on the Kerala Coast

Fishing is a way of life on the Kerala coast, where the best seafood in India abounds. Some of these fishermen go out in long boats like the one above with its crew of 13 men, who work together as a team, setting out their long nets and dragging them in. Others, like Kunnal Joseph Verghese *(right)* of the village of Saudi, near Cochin, operate their own small boats. With a four-man crew, including his 21-year-old son Michael and three other boys, Verghese usually sets out at daybreak, steering his boat with a short-handled paddle while the boys row. Shortly after sunrise they set out their nets, pulling them in periodically to check the results. Sometimes they have a good haul of sardines *(opposite)*, although the waters here also yield mackerel, pomfret and small shark. And sometimes they must leap into the water with their paddles, to scare off porpoises that surface to devour their fish and damage their nets.

In the courtyard behind Verghese's house *(opposite page)*, his mother, Mariam, cleans sardines he has brought in from the sea. (Verghese and his family are among Kerala's many Roman Catholics, and therefore bear Christian names.) Meanwhile his wife Katerina prepares a *masala* by pounding chilies, onions and turmeric together. Then she takes the fish into her tiny kitchen *(above)* and cooks them. First, she heats some coconut oil and fries the freshly pounded *masala* in it. Then she adds water and salt and stews the sardines in this liquid mixture.

Like all government guesthouses, the Bolgati Palace had a resident cook and a staff of servants, but no regular menus or set mealtimes. In the usual way, we used to outline our program for the following day to the head bearer (or major domo), and then give our food orders to the cook, who walked over from the kitchen quarters (about five minutes away). He would have to take a small boat to the mainland very early in the morning to get the best pick of fish and vegetables in the market.

For our first evening, because we are all ardent fish and seafood eaters, we asked the cook simply to buy whatever seemed best in the next morning's catch, to cook it in any way he pleased, but to be sure that he gave us more than one variety of seafood. To our satisfaction, when he returned late that morning, he was laden with crabs, prawns and pomfret. Possibly he was stirred by our enthusiasm, possibly intrigued by the unorthodoxy of our request. Certainly he was a very good cook, for we all remembered the meal he produced as the best we had eaten in Kerala.

The cook let us watch as he prepared one of the evening's outstanding dishes, a robust prawn curry, and his deftness and skill better helped us to understand the magic of that meal. First, he cleaned and salted the large orange-colored prawns. Then he proceeded with "a good hand" to choose a fresh *masala* of coriander seeds, red chili, a few black peppercorns and plenty of onion, garlic and coconut, all ground together on a large grinding stone to form a smooth brown paste. An exciting aroma had already permeated the smoke-filled kitchen as we all pressed forward and around the *chula* (stove) to watch the process of cooking. In a bronze copper vessel he poured a quantity of coconut oil and, when it smoked he tossed in a sprig of *kari* leaves and the *masala*, stirring it around with the flair of a man accustomed to continued success. Moments later the prawns were added with a little water and then they were allowed to simmer until they had taken on at first a light pink and then the color of coral.

That evening we dined in a long, formal dining room, the scene of forgotten foreign banquets, where inordinately lofty ceilings were crossed with great teak beams and slow-moving fans. Shuttered doors stood open onto the verandas on three sides, and beyond, the velvet darkness of the rustling garden was broken only by the fishermen's flares and the fitful starlight on the water of the bay.

In this stately setting the three of us sat, grouped with absurd formality at one end of an enormous table while the bearer served us the specialties that the cook had concocted for our dinner. A half-glimpsed flurry of nudging and whispering servants at the pantry door indicated that we were being watched with some degree of curiosity by the lesser servants and kitchen helpers. When dinner was served, we could not help but admire the large prawns the cook had prepared. In the midst of the emphatic spicing that we had watched, they had retained their sea freshness and their special character.

Along with the prawns, we ate some superb stuffed crabs that were seasoned with the very lightest of *masalas*. The cook had sprinkled them with black pepper, red chili powder and a fugitive flavoring of tamarind, and garnished them with fresh coriander. The crabs were caught in the rocks that fringe Bolgati Island, and were served in their shells.

But the most unusual dish, one that none of us had tasted before, was

made with fish roe. To about a cup of mashed fish roe our cook had proceeded to add a "fresh" *masala* of two tablespoons each of finely chopped green chili and ginger, pepper, a few *kari* leaves and salt. On several layers of a green banana leaf he placed portions of this mixture, folding it in the form of an envelope. This he placed over hot ash and baked for half an hour. The result was a remarkably delicate taste and a handsome dish.

Besides all this, the Bolgati Palace cook had produced for us (with some amusement, I suspect, or to see if we were really the stalwart fish fans we claimed to be) a dried-fish curry, made from the reserve supply that all coastal households keep for use during the monsoon, and a fish pickle or preserve called *min pada,* both of which are usually considered too overpoweringly fishy for any but a Kerala palate. But the years of living in Bombay had whetted our appetites for this kind of seafood, and my older niece in particular, who is an excellent cook in her own right and a pickle enthusiast, was so delighted with the *min pada* that she demanded the recipe.

As the cook explained to us later, making *min pada* is a long and tedious process. He always makes sure he is starting with a good variety of fish, like pomfret, which is fairly large and firm in texture. First, he cleans the fish, fillets it and cuts it in slices. Then he covers the slices with salt and sets them aside for 24 hours, turning the slices over every now and then.

While the fish is soaking in the brine, the cook marinates a generous amount of tamarind in vinegar for five or six hours. Then he strains this mixture through a sieve, leaving only the tamarind pulp, which is semiliquid

The setting sun's rays filter through "Chinese nets" installed at Cochin Harbor to dip fish from the ocean. The primitive nets work on the seesaw principle. The flexible poles that support them are tied down at the shore end, and when the poles are released, the nets dip down into the water. The fish swim into the inland Backwaters at high tide. Then when the tide ebbs, fish moving out with it are trapped in the nets.

127

and has been given an extra acidity by the vinegar. Then, as the next step, he prepares a *masala* by grinding red chilies, turmeric and cumin seeds into a thick paste with vinegar.

At this point the cook's work has scarcely begun. Now he takes the fish from the brine, wipes it absolutely dry and coats it with the *masala* paste. Next he pours some of the tamarind vinegar into a widemouthed jar—enough of it to cover the bottom—and then in layers, he spreads a scattering of ginger and garlic slices, then pieces of fish, then more garlic and ginger, another layer of tamarind vinegar, until all the fish is used up and the final layer is composed of whatever is left of the tamarind, ginger, garlic and *masala*.

Once he has finished layering the *min pada,* the cook fills the jar with fresh vinegar, seals it and sets it in the sun every day for about three weeks, shaking it as often as possible. After this the *min pada* is finally ready to be served, always in small quantities, after the fish slices are lightly fried so as to retain the strong hot-sour taste of the *masala* and tamarind and provide only an accompaniment—a startling accent, really—to the meal.

Besides the *min pada* and other seafood dishes there were, of course, vegetables, raw and curried. But I don't remember what they were, for the imaginative flair of the fish preparations, the extremes of delicacy and reckless pungency in the flavors the cook had produced from the bounty of the Kerala coast quite obscured everything else in my memory. As we sat there devouring this truly remarkable meal, we were surrounded by the souvenirs of past Dutch grandeur, and I couldn't help thinking how horrified those distant Dutch colonists would have been by the uninhibited flavors and the explosive spicing of our meal. I felt vaguely sorry for them having to eat their plain, dull meat-and-potatoes kind of food with "salt and pepper to taste."

From Cochin southward stretches the complicated and lovely network of lagoons, canals and rivers, prosaically called the "Backwaters," that winds through the heart of Kerala. This is storybook tropical country. Coconut palms curve over the Backwaters; behind them are banana groves, clumps of jackfruit and mango trees, and the exuberant green of rice fields. An Arab traveler of the 14th Century described his journey through Kerala: "The whole way by land (along the coast) lies under the shade of trees, and in all the space of two months' journey, there is not one span free from cultivation. Everybody has his garden and has the house planted in the middle of it." Scattered along the banks of the Backwaters are clusters of thatched huts, and in the courtyards outside the women stand pounding rice with heavy wooden poles. Sometimes you see them squatting on the ground, their backs arching, arms rising and falling with infinite grace as they beat out coconut husks to make coir fiber—the stiff elastic coconut fiber used in matting. They wear their hair knotted high on the head, decorated with frangipani and jasmine. The little girls in long full skirts and tight, bright bodices walk barefoot in single file along the water's edge on their way to school, books carried on the head, glossy braids decorated with scarlet hibiscus or gardenias. The boys, less sedate, yell out greetings and the inevitable questions —"Where are you coming from?" "Where are you going?"—to men on the passing gondola-shaped boats carrying supplies between people's homes.

In the Backwater lagoons, and on the Cochin quaysides, men fish with large circular nets mounted on wooden frames that they call "Chinese nets," although these nets actually were introduced to India by Portuguese settlers in the 16th Century. For the fresh-water catch, and for the fish that thrive in brackish water, Kerala has innumerable recipes. Among the favorites is *min mappas* with carp as its main ingredient. Kerala cooks prepare the *masala* for this fish dish in two stages—first, they roast some red chilies, coriander, turmeric and peppercorns and grind them with a little water to a smooth paste. Then, they mix mustard seed, sliced red onion, garlic, and whole red chilies (split to release their flavor), and sauté them in oil. Now they add the ground spices to the pan and lightly fry them, and after that pour in the liquid that was used in grinding the spices. When this liquid has evaporated, they add coconut milk, then slices of *kudampuli,* salt and the fish. All this is simmered until the fish is done and then, finally, they pour more coconut milk over the carp and serve it.

The inland villages of Kerala, though quite different from the fishing communities along the coast, have at least one preoccupation in common. Their life, too, is much involved with the water, and fish retains the same importance that it has for the seaside people. In fact, among the villagers, one of the essential talents of a prospective bride, much discussed and analyzed by the elders when a marriage is being arranged, is her dexterity in cleaning and cutting fish, and whether she has "a good hand" with a fish curry. At the wedding itself, the ceremonial preparation of the fish that is to be served to the guests is considered so crucial a matter, to be judged by such implacably critical eyes and such knowing palates, that it cannot safely be left to the women of the family alone—they may well be too overexcited to give it the serene care and the experienced attention it requires. "Respectable ladies" (worthy of respect, that is, for their proved expertise) of the neighborhood are called in to help in all the preliminaries and the cooking of the all-important fish, and to save the family from possible disgrace. In this part of India, the most caustic and disparaging remark about a marriage feast (even if all else is perfect) is, "The fish was without proper honor."

It would be a formidable task to attempt to enumerate the hundreds of fish recipes to be found here in the inland villages, the countless local variations, the family specialties. They range in character from the utterly straightforward, to the most complicated and exacting. For example, here is a baked fish preparation, called *pulicha min,* which uses the whole fish, preferably mackerel or pomfret, with a *masala* of only ground red chilies and caraway seeds. The cook cuts gashes in the fish, and lightly spreads it with salt and the *masala*. She lines a pan with banana leaves that have been rubbed with a little coconut oil. The fish is placed on these leaves, a little vinegar is added, and the fish is covered with more banana leaves, then the pan is covered and set on a low heat, with live coals scattered on the lid.

The variety of gravyless dishes and curries, dried-fish preparations and pickles, shellfish, fresh-water fish, sea fish and variations enjoyed here is enough to exhaust even the most enthusiastic cook—though never the Kerala appetite. A local saying, perhaps, best illustrates the Kerala mystique about fish. The standard remedy that is suggested for any woman who seems disgruntled, out of sorts, peevish, faultfinding is, "Better give her a big fish." Apart from the occupational therapy of cleaning and cutting a big fish, the intense interest in cooking it well and the satisfaction of serving and eating it will certainly banish all ill temper and bad spirits.

To serve 4 to 6

1 fresh coconut, shelled and coarsely
    chopped *(page 134)*
3 tablespoons coriander seeds
2½ cups hot, not boiling, water
¼ cup vegetable oil
12 whole black peppercorns
1 medium-sized garlic clove, peeled
    and flattened slightly with the side
    of a large knife or a kitchen mallet
A 1-inch piece of fresh ginger root,
    scraped and flattened slightly with
    the side of a large knife or a
    kitchen mallet
½ cup finely chopped onions
1 teaspoon salt
½ teaspoon ground coriander
¼ teaspoon ground cumin
¼ teaspoon turmeric
A pinch of ground hot red pepper
4 tablespoons finely chopped fresh
    coriander *(cilantro)*
1 pound lump crab meat, fresh,
    canned or frozen, picked over to
    remove all bits of shell and
    cartilage

To serve 4

4 skinned 8-ounce sole fillets, or
    substitute four 8-ounce flounder
    fillets or other firm white fish
2 tablespoons fresh lemon juice
2 teaspoons salt
½ teaspoon freshly ground black
    pepper
7 tablespoons *ghee (page 54)*
1 medium-sized garlic clove, peeled
    and flattened with the side of a
    large knife
1 tablespoon scraped, finely chopped
    fresh ginger root
¼ cup finely chopped onions
¼ teaspoon ground hot red pepper
¼ teaspoon turmeric
¾ cup finely cut fresh dill

Kurlleachi Kari
CURRIED CRAB MEAT

Combine the coconut meat, coriander seeds and 1 cup of the hot water in the jar of an electric blender. Blend at high speed for 1 minute, then stop the machine and scrape down the sides of the jar with a rubber spatula. Blend again until the coconut and coriander are completely pulverized and the mixture is reduced to a smooth purée.

Line a fine sieve with a double thickness of dampened cheesecloth and set it over a deep bowl. With a rubber spatula, scrape the entire contents of the blender jar into the sieve.

Press down hard on the coconut with a large spoon to extract as much liquid as possible. Then bring together the ends of the cloth enclosing the pulp and wring it vigorously to squeeze out the remaining liquid. There should be 1 to 1¼ cups of coconut milk.

Return the coconut-purée mixture to the blender, add the remaining 1½ cups of hot water, and blend for 30 seconds. Set the cheesecloth-lined sieve over a separate bowl and pour in the coconut mixture. Press down hard on the coconut with the back of a spoon, then wrap it in the cloth and squeeze it vigorously to wring out the remaining liquid. Discard the pulp. There should be about 1 to 1½ cups of the second coconut milk.

In a heavy 2- to 3-quart saucepan, heat the vegetable oil over moderate heat until a light haze forms above it. Add the peppercorns, garlic and ginger, and stir for 30 seconds.

Add the onions and salt and, stirring constantly, fry for 7 or 8 minutes, until the onions are soft and golden brown. Watch carefully for any signs of burning and regulate the heat accordingly. Add the ground coriander, cumin, turmeric and red pepper, and stir for 2 or 3 minutes. Then pour in the second coconut milk, bring to a boil over high heat, and partially cover the pan. Reduce the heat to low and simmer for 10 minutes.

Uncover the pan, raise the heat to high and, stirring constantly, pour in the first coconut milk in a slow, thin stream and add 2 tablespoons of the fresh coriander and the crab meat. Cook briskly for 2 or 3 minutes to heat the crab through, then remove the pan from the heat, sprinkle the remaining fresh coriander over the top, cover the pan tightly, and let the curry steep for 5 minutes.

To serve, ladle the entire contents of the pan into a heated bowl.

Machli ki Tikka
ROLLED FILLETS OF SOLE WITH FRESH-DILL STUFFING

Wash the fillets under cold running water and pat them dry with paper towels. Sprinkle both sides of the fish with the lemon juice, 1 teaspoon of the salt and the black pepper. Then set the fillets aside on a platter and marinate them at room temperature for 10 to 15 minutes.

Meanwhile preheat the oven to 350° and prepare the filling in the following fashion: In a heavy 7- to 8-inch skillet, heat 4 tablespoons of the *ghee* over moderate heat until a drop of water flicked into it splutters instantly. Stirring after each addition, add the garlic, ginger, onions, red pepper, turmeric, dill and remaining teaspoon of salt.

Reduce the heat to low and, stirring constantly, fry for 7 or 8 minutes, until the onions are soft and golden brown. Watch carefully for any signs of burning and regulate the heat accordingly.

Remove the skillet from the heat and taste the filling for seasoning. Place equal portions of the filling on each fillet, spreading it evenly with a spatula or table knife to cover the fish completely. Starting at the narrow end, roll each fillet around the stuffing into a small, thick cylinder. Skewer these rolls with 2 or 3 toothpicks to secure them, if you wish.

In a 10-inch ovenproof skillet or a shallow flameproof casserole just large enough to hold the fillets comfortably side by side, heat the remaining 3 tablespoons of *ghee* over moderate heat. Place the rolled fish in the skillet with the loose, narrow ends of the fillets down and cook uncovered for 5 minutes. Transfer the skillet to the middle shelf of the oven and bake for 12 minutes, or until the rolls are firm when pressed lightly with a finger. Slide the skillet under the broiler for 2 or 3 minutes to brown the fish lightly.

With a slotted spatula, transfer the fish rolls to a heated platter. Quickly bring the liquid remaining in the pan to a boil over high heat and stir until it is well blended. Pour the sauce over the fish and serve at once.

Jhinga ki Tikka
FRIED SHRIMP CAKES

Combine the shrimp, onions, ginger root, fresh coriander, mint, bread crumbs, 1 teaspoon of the salt and a liberal grinding of black pepper in a deep bowl, and turn them about with a spoon until thoroughly mixed. Add the egg and lemon juice, and knead vigorously with both hands, then beat with the spoon until the mixture is smooth. Marinate uncovered at room temperature for 20 to 30 minutes.

Meanwhile, make a smooth, thick batter of the chick-pea flour, ground coriander, red pepper, water and the remaining teaspoon of salt by stirring them together with your fingers or a spoon.

In a heavy 10- to 12-inch skillet, heat the *ghee* over moderate heat until a drop of water flicked into it splutters instantly. Divide the shrimp mixture into 6 equal portions and shape each one into a round, flat cake about 3 inches in diameter and ¾ inch thick.

With a pastry brush or your fingers, spread the batter on both sides of each shrimp cake. Fry the cakes in the hot *ghee* for 5 or 6 minutes on each side, until they are a delicate golden brown.

Transfer the cakes to a heated platter, squeeze a little lemon juice on each one, and serve at once.

Cachumbar
TOMATO, ONION AND GINGER SALAD

In a small serving bowl, combine the tomatoes, onions, coriander, lemon juice, ginger root and salt, and turn them about with a spoon to mix them thoroughly. Sprinkle the top with the chilies, and refrigerate for at least 1 hour, or until thoroughly chilled.

To make 6 three-inch cakes

1 pound uncooked shrimp, shelled, deveined and finely chopped
1 cup finely chopped onions
2 tablespoons scraped, finely chopped fresh ginger root
2 tablespoons finely chopped fresh coriander (*cilantro*)
1 tablespoon finely chopped fresh mint
¼ cup soft fresh crumbs made from homemade-type white bread, pulverized in a blender or shredded with a fork
2 teaspoons salt
Freshly ground black pepper
1 egg
¼ cup fresh lemon juice
¼ cup *besan* (chick-pea flour)
1 teaspoon ground coriander
⅛ teaspoon ground hot red pepper
¼ cup cold water
3 tablespoons *ghee* (*page 54*)
1 lemon, quartered

To serve 3 to 4

2 medium-sized tomatoes, washed, stemmed and coarsely chopped
¼ cup finely chopped onions
¼ cup coarsely chopped fresh coriander (*cilantro*)
3 tablespoons fresh lemon juice
1 tablespoon scraped, finely slivered fresh ginger root
1 teaspoon salt
2 fresh hot green chilies, washed, stemmed, seeded and cut crosswise into paper-thin slices (*caution: see page 39*)

To serve 6 to 8

A whole 4-pound sole or flounder,
 cleaned but with head and tail
 left on, or substitute any other 4-
 pound firm, white whole fish
1 teaspoon salt
2 tablespoons vegetable oil

MASALA

3 tablespoons finely chopped garlic
3 dried hot red chilies, each about
 1½ inches long, washed and
 seeded (caution: see page 39)
A 1-inch cube of fresh ginger root,
 scraped and coarsely chopped
2 tablespoons finely chopped fresh
 coriander (cilantro)
1 tablespoon coriander seeds
1 teaspoon jaggery, or brown sugar
 combined with molasses (page
 196)
1 teaspoon turmeric
½ teaspoon black mustard seeds
½ teaspoon fenugreek seeds
1 tablespoon salt
½ cup fresh lemon juice
½ cup vegetable oil
2 cups finely chopped onions
1 cup finely chopped fresh tomatoes
½ teaspoon garam masala (page 56)

2 tablespoons finely chopped fresh
 coriander (cilantro)

To serve 6

¼ cup vegetable oil
1 tablespoon scraped, finely chopped
 fresh ginger root
2 large onions, peeled, cut
 lengthwise in half, then sliced
 lengthwise into paper-thin slivers
1 teaspoon salt
2 tablespoons ground coriander
1½ teaspoons turmeric
4 dozen small hard-shelled clams,
 washed and thoroughly scrubbed
1 fresh coconut, shelled, peeled and
 coarsely grated (page 134)
1 tablespoon fresh lemon juice
1 tablespoon finely chopped fresh
 coriander (cilantro)
½ teaspoon ground hot red pepper

Pakki Hui Machli
BAKED FISH WITH CORIANDER MASALA

Wash the fish under cold running water and pat it completely dry inside and out with paper towels. Sprinkle 1 teaspoon of salt inside the fish and let it marinate for 15 to 20 minutes.

Preheat the oven to 400°. With a pastry brush, spread the 2 tablespoons of oil evenly over the bottom and sides of a shallow baking-and-serving dish large enough to hold the fish comfortably. Set aside.

To make the *masala*, combine the garlic, chilies, ginger root, 2 tablespoons of fresh coriander, coriander seeds, jaggery, turmeric, mustard seeds, fenugreek seeds, 1 tablespoon of salt and the lemon juice in the jar of an electric blender. Blend at high speed for 30 seconds, then turn off the machine and scrape down the sides of the jar with a rubber spatula. Blend again until the mixture becomes a smooth purée.

In a heavy 8- to 10-inch skillet, heat ½ cup of vegetable oil over moderate heat until a light haze forms above it. Add the onions and, stirring constantly, fry for 7 or 8 minutes, until they are soft and golden brown. Watch carefully for any signs of burning and regulate the heat accordingly.

Add the *masala* and cook, stirring constantly, for about 10 minutes, or until most of the liquid has evaporated and the mixture is thick enough to draw away from the sides of the pan in a solid mass. Stir in the tomatoes and *garam masala* and remove from the heat.

Coat one side of the fish with 1 cup of the *masala* mixture, smoothing and spreading it evenly with a spatula or the back of a spoon. Turn the fish over and place it coated side down in the prepared baking dish. Fill the cavity of the fish with 1½ cups of the *masala*, then close the opening with skewers or by sewing it with heavy thread.

Spread the remaining *masala* over the top of the fish and cover the dish tightly with its lid or with aluminum foil.

Bake in the middle of the oven for about 25 minutes, or until the fish is firm when pressed lightly with a finger. Uncover and slide the fish under the broiler for 1 or 2 minutes to brown it lightly. Sprinkle with 2 tablespoons of fresh coriander and serve the fish at once, directly from its baking dish.

Teesryo
CURRIED STEAMED CLAMS

In a heavy 10- to 12-inch skillet, heat the vegetable oil over moderate heat until a light haze forms above it. Add the ginger and stir for a minute, then drop in the onions. Stirring constantly, fry for 7 or 8 minutes, until they are soft and golden brown. Watch carefully for any signs of burning and regulate the heat accordingly.

Stir in the salt and ground coriander, cook for a minute or so, then stir in the turmeric. When the mixture is well blended, add the clams, turning them about with a spoon to coat them evenly.

Cover the skillet tightly, reduce the heat to low, and steam for 8 to 10 minutes, or until the clams open.

Immediately transfer the entire contents of the skillet to a deep heated platter. Scatter the coconut over the clams and sprinkle them with lemon juice, fresh coriander and red pepper. Serve at once.

Coriander, red chilies and tomato top a baked sole, *pakki hui machli*, served with bean salad, *rajma-chana salat*.

How to Buy, Open and Prepare a Coconut

Before buying a coconut, shake it to make sure it is full of liquid. The fresher the coconut, the more liquid it will have, so select one that is comparatively heavy for its size. (Coconuts without liquid or those with moldy or wet "eyes" are likely to be spoiled.)

TO OPEN THE COCONUT: Preheat the oven to 400°. Puncture 2 of the 3 smooth, dark eyes of the coconut by hammering the tip of an ice pick or screwdriver through them. Drain all the coconut liquid—into a measuring cup if you plan to use it. Indians rarely cook with this liquid though they do drink it chilled.

Bake the empty coconut in the oven for 15 minutes, then transfer it to a chopping board. While the coconut is still hot, split the shell with a sharp blow of a hammer. The shell should fall away from the pieces of meat. If bits of meat still cling to the shell cut them away with a small knife.

TO GRATE COCONUT: Pare off the brown outer skin of the coconut meat with a swivel-type peeler or small, sharp knife. Then grate the meat, piece by piece, with a hand grater.

TO MAKE COCONUT MILK: Without removing the brown skin, cut or break the meat of the coconut into 1-inch pieces and place them in the jar of an electric blender. Add ½ cup of hot, but not boiling, water, cover the jar, and blend at high speed for 1 minute. Stop the machine and scrape down the sides of the jar with a rubber spatula. Continuing to blend uncovered at high speed, pour in an additional 1½ cups of hot water in a slow stream, cover the jar, and blend until the coconut is reduced to a smooth purée.

(To make the coconut milk by hand, grate the unpeeled coconut, piece by piece, into a bowl and stir in 2 cups of hot, not boiling, water.)

Scrape the entire contents of the jar or bowl into a fine sieve lined with a double thickness of dampened cheesecloth and set it over a deep bowl. With a wooden spoon, press down hard on the coconut to extract as much liquid as possible. Bring the ends of the cheesecloth together to enclose the pulp and twist the ends tightly to squeeze out the remaining liquid. There should be 2 to 2½ cups of milk. (This same technique is always used, although the proportion of coconut to water may vary from recipe to recipe.)

In most cases, coconut pulp is discarded after it has been squeezed dry. However, some recipes call for a second milk made by saving the pulp, returning it to the blender and repeating the entire process with 2 additional cups of hot water. The second milk is thin and less flavorful than the first.

Tali Machli

DEEP-FRIED FISH FILLETS

Drop the onion into a small bowl, sprinkle it with 3 teaspoons of the salt, and toss the slices about to coat them well. Set aside.

Rinse the fillets under cold running water and pat them completely dry with paper towels. With a sharp knife, split each fillet in half lengthwise and cut it crosswise into 6 equal pieces. Sprinkle the fish with ½ teaspoon of the salt and set them side by side on a strip of wax paper.

In a deep bowl, make a smooth, thick batter of the chick-pea flour, rice flour, cumin, red pepper, the remaining ½ teaspoon of salt and the 6 tablespoons of water, stirring them together with your fingers or a spoon.

To serve 4 to 6

1 small onion, peeled, cut in half lengthwise, then cut lengthwise into paper-thin slices
4 teaspoons salt
4 eight-ounce sole fillets, skinned, or 4 eight-ounce fillets of other firm white fish
½ cup *besan* (chick-pea flour)
¼ cup rice flour
½ teaspoon ground cumin
½ teaspoon ground hot red pepper
6 tablespoons cold water
Vegetable oil for deep frying
1 fresh hot green chili, about 3 inches long, washed, seeded and chopped *(caution: see page 39)*
1 tablespoon finely chopped fresh coriander *(cilantro)*
¼ teaspoon *garam masala (page 56)*

Drop the fish into the batter, turning the pieces about until they are evenly coated, and again spread them side by side on the wax paper.

Preheat the oven to 250° and line a large baking dish with paper towels. Pour 3 cups of vegetable oil into a 10-inch *karhai* or 12-inch *wok (page 151)*, or pour oil into a deep fryer to a depth of 2 or 3 inches. Heat the oil until it reaches a temperature of 350° on a deep-frying thermometer.

Deep-fry the fish, 4 or 5 pieces at a time, for about 5 minutes, turning them frequently until they are golden on all sides. As they brown, transfer the pieces to the lined baking dish and keep them warm in the oven.

To serve, mound the fish in the center of a heated platter and sprinkle it with chopped chili, coriander and *garam masala*. Rinse the onion slices under cold running water, pat them gently but thoroughly dry with paper towels, and arrange them in a ring around the fish.

Rajma-Chana Salat
MIXED BEAN SALAD

To serve 6 to 8

Drain freshly cooked chick-peas, black-eyed peas and kidney beans in a sieve or colander and cool to room temperature before using them. If you plan to use canned peas and beans, drain them, rinse under cold running water, and pat them dry with paper towels. Combine the garlic and olive oil in a small cup and steep at room temperature for 15 minutes.

To assemble the salad, combine the scallions, coriander, fresh chili, cumin, salt and a few grindings of black pepper in a large bowl. When they are well mixed, stir in the lemon juice. Add the chick-peas, black-eyed peas and kidney beans; toss together gently and sprinkle the olive oil on top.

Stir the beans and peas together again but this time more thoroughly, then push the garlic clove underneath the surface of the beans and cover the bowl tightly with aluminum foil or plastic wrap. Refrigerate the salad for at least 2 hours, or until it is thoroughly chilled. If you like, remove the garlic clove before serving the salad.

NOTE: If you plan to use freshly cooked chick-peas for the salad, start them a day ahead. Wash ¾ cup of chick-peas in a sieve under cold running water, then place them in a bowl or pan, and add enough cold water to cover them by 1 inch. Soak at room temperature for at least 12 hours. Drain the chick-peas and place them in a pan with enough fresh water to cover them by 2 inches. Bring to a boil, reduce the heat, and simmer partially covered for 1½ to 2 hours, until the chick-peas are tender but not mushy.

For 1½ cups of cooked black-eyed peas or kidney beans, start with ¾ cup of the dried variety. They may be soaked overnight in water to cover. Or they may be prepared for cooking with the quick-soak method: Place one or both in a saucepan, add enough water to cover them by 1 inch, bring to a boil and cook briskly for 2 minutes. Remove the pan from the heat and let the peas or beans soak for 1 hour.

When dried peas or beans are soaked for 12 hours or more, they should be drained and the soaking water discarded. If you choose the quick-soak method, you may cook the black-eyed peas or beans in the soaking water. With either technique, add enough fresh water to cover the black-eyed peas or kidney beans by 1 inch, and simmer them for 1 to 1½ hours, until they are tender but still intact.

1½ cups chick-peas, freshly cooked or canned
1½ cups black-eyed peas, freshly cooked or canned
1½ cups red kidney beans, freshly cooked or canned
1 large garlic clove, peeled and flattened with the side of a heavy knife or a mallet
1 tablespoon olive oil
½ cup finely chopped scallions, including 1 inch of the green tops
3 tablespoons finely chopped fresh coriander *(cilantro)*
1 fresh hot green chili, about 3 inches long, washed, seeded and chopped *(caution: see page 39)*
¼ teaspoon ground cumin
½ teaspoon salt
Freshly ground black pepper
3 tablespoons fresh lemon juice

VI

Barbecuing in the Indian Style

India's version of barbecued chicken is the *tandoori murg* at left. Tenderized in yoghurt marinade, seasoned with ginger and garlic, it gets its rich russet color from saffron and a few drops of red dye. In India cooks use cochineal dye; you may get the same effect with food coloring.

Years ago, when I was a child, I went with my mother to spend a couple of months with an aunt who had a large farm in the Punjab, a province in the Northwest of India. The farm is now in Pakistan because the frontier line that was drawn in 1947, separating India from the new Muslim state of Pakistan, severed the Punjab. My aunt's farm in the days when I visited it, grew sugar cane, wheat, corn, cotton and fruit, and she also maintained a herd of cattle. The quantity of milk her cows produced was far too great for the needs of the family, and since she had no refrigeration or electricity, it could not be stored even for a day.

In consequence, every morning the fresh milk for the household would be poured into a separate vessel, and all the rest would be churned for butter and buttermilk to be handed out to the daily procession of village women who came to the farm. Each of these women carried her own jar, and often a baby as well, casually slung across one hip in the Indian way. Each would be given her share of buttermilk, with a dollop of fresh butter on top.

One of my favorite amusements on the farm used to be helping (most ineptly) to churn the milk by pulling alternate ends of the rope twisted around the wooden handle of the churn. To keep a steady, even rhythm, we used to recite aloud an absurd little jingle that traditionally accompanies the churning:

> *Gur-gur, gur-gur, doodh biloyé,*
> *Jathni ki baché royé,*
> *Rothé hai tho roné deo,*
> *Hum ko doodh biloyné deo.*

Gur-gur, gur-gur [this is supposed to be the
noise the churn makes], we are churning milk,
The children of the village people are crying,
If they're crying, let them cry,
Just let me get on with churning the milk.

For most of the village people, the standard daily diet was buttermilk, a preparation of *sag* (leafy greens, only remotely like spinach), with some variety of *tandoori* bread and pickles. In that part of the country virtually every kitchen has a *tandoor*, a special kind of clay oven, unknown in the South, and very rare in most other parts of India. We often ate a similar meal ourselves on the farm, occasionally with the added luxury of lamb kabobs, and always with fresh fruit—usually blood oranges from the orchards. I remember those meals with a strong, if distant, nostalgia for all their stages, but most of all the final taste of the *tandoori roti,* which seemed to me then (and still does) the best kind of bread I had ever eaten.

In the course of the morning, after the milk was churned, the women of the household would assemble in the shade of the huge *nim* tree in front of the kitchen building. There, amid floods of family gossip, continually interrupted by the demands of the children, the arrival of vendors who were dispensing food, glass bangles, or Banaras saris, or perhaps by a visit from a neighbor or simply some passerby with time on her hands, the women sat cleaning the vegetables for the noontime meal, or slicing the carrots, cauliflower and turnips for brine pickles.

Eventually, when everything else was ready, my aunt would vanish into her kitchen, crouch beside her *tandoor,* and start shaping and baking the bread. She was willing to allow the cook to make any other item in the meal, but she insisted that the bread, especially our favorite, *naan,* had to be her personal responsibility.

A *tandoor* is shaped rather like the huge jar in which Ali Baba hid from the Forty Thieves. It is usually sunk neck-deep in the ground or, if built above ground, is heavily insulated on the outside with a thick layer of plaster. The charcoal fire on the flat bottom of the jar should heat the sides of the *tandoor* to a scorching point about halfway up, and to a hot glow for the rest, diminishing, of course, near the neck. To achieve this particular distribution of heat, the *tandoor* has to be lit at least two hours before anything is cooked in it, and longer if it is not frequently used.

Watching an expert like my aunt making *naan* is both a spellbinding and an alarming experience. The dough is made from wheat flour, milk, curds, eggs, melted *ghee,* salt and a little sugar, kneaded very thoroughly, and preferably kept overnight covered with a damp cloth. If this is impossible, it should stand for at least three hours to allow the curds to ferment and make the dough rise. The dough should be absolutely smooth and rather elastic in consistency, and, after more kneading, it is divided into even-sized lumps.

My aunt never used a rolling pin (this was the part that made for such compulsive watching), but dipped her hands in flour, then slapped a lump of dough between her palms with astonishing speed and dexterity until it was more or less oval in shape and thicker around the rim than in the center. Then she scattered chopped onion and poppy seeds on it, and plunged her bare arm into the heated *tandoor* to stick one end of the *naan* to that part of the side that was hot but not scorching. The outward-curving shape of the *tandoor* allowed the major part of the *naan* to hang loose over the heat from the point at which it was attached to the inside. The weight of the dough pulled the *naan* into its characteristic teardrop shape, and its elasticity kept the *naan* from breaking off and falling into the coals.

The process of shaping the *naan* takes only seconds, and the cooking a few minutes. When it is ready to serve, it should be light brown in color, the rim should have swelled a little to become slightly spongy, and the central part should be about as thick as a pancake but more brittle in texture. Eaten alone, or with pickles, or with any variation of the classic *tandoori* meat or chicken preparations, it is one of the most delicious kinds of bread in India.

Tandoori chapatis, almost equally good, are made with the same dough as ordinary *chapatis,* but after the big, thin disks are rolled out on a floured board, they are brushed with melted *ghee,* folded over, again brushed with *ghee,* and rolled out once more. This process is repeated several times so that the *chapati,* after it is baked, will be flakier than the usual kind and crisper on the outside. My aunt used to make another wonderful variety of *tandoori chapati* from corn flour, very brittle, almost biscuity in texture, which we ate spread with homemade butter.

The best-known of the *tandoori* dishes is a chicken preparation for which broilers are skinned, the meat of the breast and legs carefully cut in slits not quite to the bone, sprinkled with salt and lime juice, and marinated for at least 12 hours. The marinade is a mixture of well-beaten curds and a *masala* of ground ginger, garlic, green and red chilies, and sometimes saffron (for the color). If the broilers do not seem tender enough, a piece of green papaya is often added to the *masala.*

The cooking of the chickens in the preheated *tandoor* takes only about 20 minutes. They are speared on long, thin iron spikes that are then placed in the *tandoor,* the tips of the spikes in the glowing (but not flaming) coals, the handles resting against the edge of the neck. The chicken should be about 12 inches above the heat. The spikes are taken out every few minutes so that the birds can be basted with melted *ghee* and the marinade.

Tradition holds that a *tandoor* in regular use improves the flavor of anything cooked in it, for the heated clay itself releases a mellow fragrance that permeates the food. For *tandoori* chicken another important ingredient in the final taste is added by the particular kind of smoke that comes from the dripping of the marinade onto the hot coals.

The *tandoori* chicken, when it is served, should be accompanied by scallions, sliced white radish, wedges of fresh lime, and *achar* (brine pickles). Often there is a *cachumbar* as well—chopped cucumber, tomatoes and onions, sprinkled with coriander leaves and slivers of green chilies—and sometimes a chutney. And, of course, *naan* or some other variety of *tandoori roti* (bread), and buttermilk to drink. The chicken should be a warm red-gold in color, without gravy, but extremely tender (from the curd marinade), and with the spicing and the *tandoor* aroma integrally a part of the meat—it should never, that is, be sharp to the palate on the surface and bland inside, but evenly flavored throughout. The vegetables should always be raw and crisp and served only with salt and a squeeze of lime. The *naan* or *roti*

Using rods long enough to reach to the bottoms of the well-like ovens (*tandoors*) in front of them, cooks in the Moti Mahal Restaurant in Delhi bake breads called *naan (left foreground)* and *tandoori chapatis (center)*, as well as chicken *(right background)*. The patties of dough for the two kinds of bread are slapped flat by hand, then stuck to the sides of the hot *tandoors*. After only a few minutes, they come out crisp and brown. A special marinade gives *tandoori* chicken its vivid color.

should be absolutely fresh, and it should be still hot from the *tandoor*. Altogether, this combination of dishes makes for one of the most popular meals in North India and in many of the cities in other parts of the country. It provides the incentive for some of the rare occasions when Indians (most of whom do not have *tandoors* in their own kitchens) eat out from choice, and many of the best-known urban restaurants in the country have made their reputation on *tandoori* specialties.

It seems extraordinary, considering the nationwide appeal that *tandoori* cooking has acquired, that its basic repertoire consists of only four items: two kinds of bread, chicken and a lamb dish called *boti kabab*. For this dish, cubes of lean lamb are marinated in curds, this time with plenty of onions, a little coriander seed, turmeric and *garam masala* added to the marinade. The meat is skewered onto the same thin iron spikes, held in place by a whole raw onion, and broiled in the *tandoor*. In Bombay, some restaurants offer a *tandoori* grilled fish—a radical departure from traditional *tandoori* menus, which never include fish—to please the coastal palate. But the chicken-*naan* meal remains the favorite, and no one, in my experience, has so far been able to duplicate by other methods the peculiar and delicious flavor that the *tandoor* gives to the food cooked in it, though it does seem odd that the taste of an oven, of all things, should be so important to a style of cooking.

Naan
LEAF-SHAPED BREAD

In a deep bowl, combine the 4 cups of flour, sugar, baking powder, baking soda and salt, and stir with a large spoon or your fingers until well mixed. Make a shallow well in the center, drop in the eggs, and stir them into the flour mixture. Stirring constantly, pour in the milk in a slow, thin stream and continue to stir until all the ingredients are well combined.

Gather the dough into a ball and place it on a smooth, slick surface such as a large baking sheet or jelly-roll pan, or a marble slab if you have one. Knead the dough by pressing it down and pushing it forward several times with the heel of your hand, then folding it back on itself end to end. Repeat for about 10 minutes, or until the dough is smooth and can be gathered into a soft, somewhat sticky ball. Sprinkle a little flour over and under it from time to time as you knead to keep it from sticking to your hands.

Moisten your hands with a teaspoon of *ghee*, gather the dough into a ball, and place it in a bowl. Drape a kitchen towel over the bowl and let the dough rest in a warm, draft-free place for about 3 hours.

Slide two large ungreased baking sheets into the oven and preheat the oven and pans to 450°. Divide the dough into 6 equal portions. Moistening your hands with *ghee* occasionally, flatten and form each portion into a tear-drop-shaped leaf, wide at the base and tapered at the top. Each leaf should be about 6 inches long and 3½ inches across at its widest point, and about ⅜ inch thick. Arrange the bread leaves side by side on the preheated baking sheets and bake them in the middle of the oven for 6 minutes, or until they are firm to the touch. Slide the leaves under the broiler for a minute or so to brown the tops lightly. Serve the *naan* hot or at room temperature.

To make 6

4 cups all-purpose flour
1 tablespoon sugar
1 tablespoon double-acting baking
   powder
¼ teaspoon baking soda
½ teaspoon salt
2 eggs
1 cup milk
4 to 6 teaspoons *ghee (page 54)*

Husaini Kabab
GRILLED SKEWERED LAMB

Place the lamb in a deep bowl and sprinkle it with the cumin, turmeric and salt, turning the cubes about with a spoon to coat them evenly. Add the yoghurt, onions, coriander, ginger and garlic, and toss the ingredients together until thoroughly blended. Marinate the lamb (covered loosely with foil) at room temperature for at least 2 hours or in the refrigerator for 4 to 6 hours.

Light a layer of coals in a charcoal broiler and let them burn until white ash appears on the surface, or preheat the broiler of your kitchen stove to the highest possible point. Remove the lamb from the marinade and string it on 3 or 4 long skewers, pressing the cubes tightly together. If you plan to broil the lamb in the stove, suspend the skewers side by side across the length or width of a large baking pan, preferably lined with an open-meshed rack upon which the bottom of the meat can rest.

Broil about 3 inches from the heat, turning the skewers occasionally, for 10 to 20 minutes, or until the lamb is brown and is done to your taste.

To serve, slide the lamb off the skewers with a knife, mound it attractively on a heated platter, and sprinkle it with *garam masala*. In India, *husaini kabab* is often served with *sas (Recipe Index)*.

To serve 4

2 pounds boneless leg of lamb,
   trimmed of excess fat and cut
   into 1½-inch cubes
1 teaspoon ground cumin
½ teaspoon turmeric
2 teaspoons salt
¼ cup unflavored yoghurt
¼ cup finely chopped onions
2 tablespoons finely chopped fresh
   coriander *(cilantro)*
2 tablespoons scraped, finely
   chopped fresh ginger root
1 teaspoon finely chopped garlic
½ teaspoon *garam masala (page 56)*

1 teaspoon saffron threads
3 tablespoons boiling water
2 chickens, 2½ to 3 pounds each
½ cup fresh lemon juice
4 teaspoons salt
2 teaspoons coriander seeds
1 teaspoon cumin seeds
A 1-inch piece of fresh ginger root,
    scraped and coarsely chopped
2 medium-sized garlic cloves,
    coarsely chopped
1 cup unflavored yoghurt
½ teaspoon red food coloring
¼ teaspoon ground hot red pepper
2 tablespoons *ghee (page 54)*
Salat (opposite)

Tandoori Murg
ROAST CHICKEN WITH YOGHURT MASALA

Drop the saffron threads into a small bowl or cup, pour in the boiling water, and soak for 5 minutes.

Meanwhile, pat the chickens completely dry inside and out with paper towels and truss the birds securely. With a small, sharp knife cut 2 slits about ½ inch deep and 1 inch long in both thighs and breasts of each bird. Mix the lemon juice with the salt and rub them over the chickens, pressing the mixture deeply into the slits. Place the chickens in a large, deep casserole, pour the saffron and its soaking water over them, and let them marinate at room temperature for about 30 minutes.

Sprinkle the coriander and cumin seeds into a small ungreased skillet and, shaking the pan constantly, toast them over moderate heat for a minute or so. Then drop the seeds into the jar of an electric blender, add the ginger, garlic and 2 tablespoons of the yoghurt, and blend at high speed until the mixture is reduced to a smooth paste. With a rubber spatula, scrape the paste into a mixing bowl. Stir in all of the remaining yoghurt, the food coloring and the hot red pepper.

Spread the yoghurt *masala* evenly over the chickens, cover the casserole with a lid or foil, and marinate for 12 hours or overnight at room temperature, or for at least 24 hours in the refrigerator.

Preheat the oven to 400°. Arrange the chickens side by side on a rack in a shallow roasting pan large enough to hold them comfortably. Pour any liquid that has accumulated in the casserole over the chickens and coat each one with 1 tablespoon of the *ghee*. Roast uncovered in the middle of the oven for 15 minutes, then reduce the heat to 350°, and continue roasting the birds undisturbed for 1 hour more. To test each chicken for doneness, pierce the thigh with the point of a small, sharp knife. The juice that runs out should be pale yellow; if it is still tinged with pink, roast the chicken for another 5 to 10 minutes.

Remove the birds from the oven, cut away the trussing strings, and let the chickens rest for 5 minutes or so for easier carving. Just before serving, cut each chicken into 6 or 8 serving pieces and arrange them attractively on top of a platter of *salat (opposite)* or place the whole birds in the center of a large heated platter and garnish the rim with the *salat* ingredients.

OUTDOOR COOKING: In India, *tandoori murg* is roasted in a special clay oven over hot coals. You can get a somewhat similar smoky flavor by roasting the birds in a hooded charcoal grill equipped with a rotating spit.

Following the recipe above, prepare and marinate the chickens without trussing them. About 2 hours before you plan to serve the *tandoori murg*, light a 1- to 2-inch-thick layer of coals in the grill, cover it with the hood, and let the charcoal burn until white ash appears on the surface. This may take as long as an hour.

One at a time, remove the chickens from the marinade and string them lengthwise end to end on the spit. (The birds will be wet and slippery, so it is a good idea to do this in the kitchen over a counter or table.) Anchor the chickens in place on the spit with the sliding prongs. Then tie the drumsticks and wings snugly against the bodies of the birds with short lengths of wire, twisting the ends of the wire tightly to hold them securely.

Fit the spit into place above the coals and plug it in. Baste the chickens

Whole chickens, spitted on an iron spike and roasted over coals, emerge crisp, fragrant and golden red from an Indian *tandoor (left)*. With the recipe for *tandoori murg* opposite, you can get equally tempting results in an oven or on a charcoal grill.

with the *ghee,* cover the grill with the hood, and roast for about 1 hour. Baste the roasting birds 3 or 4 times with a tablespoon or so of the remaining marinade, but do not use the liquid lavishly; it may cause the coals to flame up and burn the chickens. To test for doneness, pierce a thigh with the point of a small knife; the juice that runs out should be pale yellow.

To serve, remove the spit from the grill, unscrew the prongs, and slide the chickens onto a platter. Untwist or cut off the wires. Cut the birds into pieces and serve them on top of a platter of *salat,* or place the chickens in the center of a large platter and garnish the rim with the *salat* ingredients.

Salat

MIXED VEGETABLE SALAD

Spread the slivers of onion evenly over the entire surface of a large serving platter and arrange the tomato slices in a ring around the edge. Arrange the radishes, lemon wedges and chilies decoratively around the tomatoes, and sprinkle the vegetables evenly with the lemon juice, salt and a liberal grinding of black pepper.

Salat is a traditional accompaniment to such *tandoori* meats as *tandoori murg, husaini kabab* or *moghlai kabab.* After the meat is cooked, it is placed on top of the *salat* and is usually sprinkled with a little *garam masala (Recipe Index)* before serving.

To serve 4 to 6

2 large onions, peeled, cut in half lengthwise, then cut lengthwise into paper-thin slivers
2 large firm, ripe tomatoes, washed, stemmed and cut crosswise into ¼-inch-thick slices
24 radishes, trimmed and washed
2 medium-sized lemons, each cut lengthwise into quarters
3 fresh hot green chilies, washed, slit in half lengthwise and seeded *(caution: see page 39)*
¼ cup fresh lemon juice
1 teaspoon salt
Freshly ground black pepper

143

VII

Venerable Specialties of the Minorities

In the extraordinary mosaic of cultures, religions and traditions that go to make up Indian life, certain small ethnic, religious and geographic communities have evolved such distinctive manners, habits and food customs that, although indisputably Indian, they retain a definite identity of their own. Among these uniquely colorful minorities are the Jains, Sikhs, Parsis, Syrian Christians and Goans. Some of these communities, such as the Jains and Sikhs, are offshoots of older, larger religious groups. Others, such as the Parsis and the Syrian Christians, trace their ancestry to a foreign country, while still another—the Goans—acquired their special status 300 years ago as a result of colonization of their homeland by a foreign power—Portugal.

One of the most distinctive of all Indian minorities is the Jains, a sect that came into being as an offshoot of Hinduism in the Sixth Century B.C. by the guru Mahavira. For Mahavira and his followers the vegetarian strictures of the ancient Hindu scriptures did not go far enough. The Jains felt that every organic thing has a soul. Even now, so extreme is their concern for all forms of life that the most orthodox among them wear face masks to prevent them from breathing living microbes and thereby killing them. As they walk along the street, such Jains carry brooms, carefully sweeping the roadway before them and praying to themselves that they will not inadvertently step on ants or other living creatures.

Many Jains refuse to eat any vegetable or tuber that grows in the ground, for fear that in uprooting it they might destroy worms or insects. Thus they forgo root vegetables such as potatoes, onions and beets, and refuse even to eat tomatoes because they appear blood colored. For the most part the Jains

Atop a scaffold at Shravanabelagola in Mysore, members of the Jain sect pour milk over a giant statue of their revered saint, Gommatesvara, as pilgrims pray in the foreground. An extremist vegetarian sect, the Jains come here every 12 years to anoint the statue as a gesture of veneration.

depend on lentils, leafy green vegetables and rice for their sustenance.

Another well-known religious minority in India is the Sikhs, those stalwart, bearded, turbaned men of the Punjab, whose courage and awesome mien have struck terror into the hearts of opposing armies through the ages. The Sikhs are a community of about eight million, founded in the 15th Century by the guru, Nanak, a reformer who combined the teachings of both the Hindus and the Muslims. Primarily an agricultural people, they are settled in the Punjab, along the foothills of the Himalayas. Early in their history, in order to protect themselves against the religious persecution of the Moghul court of Delhi, they established a military fraternity called the Khalsa. The suffix Singh, or "lion," was affixed to their names, and as a part of his initiation into the Khalsa, each Sikh swore to wear the five Ks of the sect. These are:

1. *kes:* the uncut hair
2. *kanga:* the comb worn in the hair
3. *kaccha:* the soldier's shorts that Sikhs wear
4. *kara:* the steel bangle worn on the right wrist
5. *kirpan:* the saber used by Sikhs.

Along with these identifying features, another distinctive mark of the Sikhs is their food. These men are the best farmers in India, producing the country's finest wheat and milk. Many of their special food preparations are made with corn, wheat and sugar, and their dishes are always prepared with pure *ghee,* which gives them a unique fragrance and flavor.

The Syrian Christians, a minority group on the Malabar Coast of Southwest India are a mixture of Syrian settlers and native Indians. The Christian part of their names is believed to date from the time of Thomas Didymus, one of the Twelve Apostles, who came to India as a missionary in 52 A.D.; the Syrian part of the name is thought to have been acquired in 345 A.D. when about 400 souls emigrated to India to escape persecution in Syria. Led by a remarkable merchant prince, Thomas of Canaan, the new arrivals were received with courtesy. They merged with descendants of people converted by St. Thomas (known as Nazranis), gave their name to the community that developed, and became extremely influential in the life of their adopted land. So impressive was the personality of Thomas of Canaan that Ceruman Perumal, the local ruler, appointed him as an advisor on matters concerning the administration of his own state and trade with the outside world. At the feasts held in Perumal's court, Thomas was served his food on a double layer of banana leaves—a privilege that was normally reserved for royalty. In memory of this proud honor, the Syrian Christians even now on ceremonial occasions fold over the ends of the leaves on which their food is presented as a symbolic reminder of the high esteem in which their ancient leader was held in his adopted land.

Like the people of Malabar around them, the Syrian Christians are primarily an agrarian people; many of them still live within a curious, loose feudal arrangement that has gradually become more flexible over the centuries but still retains serfdom of a sort. A Syrian Christian family of my acquaintance in Malabar provides an illustration of how the system works. The family property is not particularly large, but it maintains a considerable number of farm laborers who, through long tradition, owe allegiance to the family

146

and live on the family estate. These people must perform whatever work the family requires of them before they may accept employment from other land-owners, and they are paid in food, shelter, medical care and old-age security.

My friends' house is in a compound surrounded by gardens. It is situated on high ground where tapioca and vegetables are cultivated, and there are co-conut palms, pepper trees, jackfruit, mangoes and papayas here, with thick rows of pineapples fencing off the neighboring property. The rice paddies and the banana plantations are at some distance from the house.

For such families it is a matter of pride to store and eat their own rice. The whole performance of storing, cooking and serving it is of such pivotal im-portance to daily life that it has acquired much of the solemnity and the rigid formality of a ritual. In the center of each house, made entirely of carved wood, is a granary where the newly harvested rice is stored two or three times a year. One entire side panel of the granary is removed to pro-vide entrance space for the gunny sacks full of grain, and this is the only time when anyone other than the senior woman in the household may enter the granary.

At intervals during the year, a two months' supply of rice is removed from the granary for the second major stage in the preparation of the rice, the parboiling. This is the sole occasion when field hands may assist with the compound work, though the whole activity must be supervised by the woman of the house. It is a fantastic sight, the parboiling of this massive quan-tity of rice. Wood fires are lit in enormous stone *chulas* in the courtyard, and staggeringly huge cauldrons of rice and water—12 or 14 feet in diameter—are set on them. When the parboiling is done, the rice is drained in woven bamboo baskets and spread out to dry on bamboo mats. My friends tell me the accepted badge of a prosperous family is a house surrounded by ve-randas wide enough to accommodate the drying rice when the weather is too uncertain to spread the grain outdoors.

The estate workers are paid in parboiled rice, and once the grain is dry, the bulk of it is stored again, this time in a separate section of the granary. Later, relatively small quantities of parboiled rice, enough, say, to supply the compound's needs for two weeks, are removed and the next stage, the husking and winnowing of the grain, begins.

On a visit to my friend's estate, I once arrived on the day of the husking and winnowing of the grain, and watched with fascination as these timeless tasks were performed. The women of the household stood in pairs over wood-en troughs in the courtyard, bare-breasted and barefooted, wearing only sa-ronglike white cotton *mundus* from the waist to the ankle. With marvelously graceful, rhythmic movements, one of the women raised a tall wooden pole as high as her arms would stretch and dropped it into the trough. Her com-panion caught it on the rebound and repeated the movement, and the muffled thuds of the husking, as basic to life as a heartbeat, filled the courtyard until the rice was ready for the winnowing. Then, holding wide woven palm-leaf trays filled with the grain, the women stood with their backs to the wind, gent-ly shaking the trays, allowing the chaff to blow away like a long, irregular stream of smoke.

Because there were not enough women in the household to perform these tasks, extra help from the neighborhood had to be hired, and paid for in rice instead of money. But—and this is one of the curious paradoxes that confuse and enliven Indian life—the hired women were of an "acceptable" status, eligible, that is, to set foot in a "pure" kitchen. Even though the Syrian Christians may well be the oldest Christian community in the world, some of the laws of caste and the attitudes of their pre-Christian Hindu ancestry still prevail in their daily life. My friends view the sanctity of their kitchen and the handling of food much the way that my Brahmin grandmothers used to. The people who would have belonged to the lower Hindu castes, had they not become Christians, are still forbidden from taking part in the ceremonials of preparing and cooking the food for the, so to speak, Brahmin Christians—idiotic as the contradiction in terms may seem.

The routine of the day in the home of my Syrian Christian friends reminds me very much of life in the households of my childhood. The senior woman rises at 5 in the morning, and first wakes one of the servants to clean all the cooking utensils—even though they were washed the night before—to ensure their purity for the new day. Her next essential task is to prepare the early morning "jaggery-coffee" herself. She makes this with unrefined palm sugar (jaggery), boiled in water with powdered coffee (which must be roasted and ground in the house). The coffee is drunk black or with milk, but no solid food may be served until after family prayers. No one may touch any food before washing and cleaning his teeth. In Allahabad, I remember, each of us used to break off a fresh, bitter-tasting fibrous twig from the neem tree, chew one end to soften it, and then use it as a toothbrush. Neem is supposed to have antiseptic and astringent qualities, both supposedly good for the gums. My Syrian Christian friends use charred rice husks powdered with salt instead of toothpaste, and a damp finger instead of a toothbrush.

Between 7:30 and 8 a.m. in my friends' Syrian Christian household, breakfast is served. This consists of *puttu* (steamed rice flour and coconut cakes) and these, again, must be prepared by the woman of the house. A servant may grind the flour and grate the coconut, but the actual mixing of the ingredients with a sprinkling of water and the packing of the batter in hollow bamboo for cooking is exclusively her responsibility. The bamboo is filled with the mixture, then set upright in a narrow-necked copper jar partly filled with water and steamed for four or five minutes. Very carefully the cooked *puttu* must be pushed out of the bamboo container onto a dish, forming a neat, long cylinder, which is then separated into individual cakes and served hot with sweet yellow bananas or with palm treacle and more coffee.

The main meal of the day is lunch, and for it all the members of the family return from work or school or errands. If somebody's office is too far away to permit this, the food will be sent to him in metal containers. No Syrian Christian eats in a restaurant.

The staple food for lunch, as for any other meal, is invariably rice, always plain rice boiled in water, never made into *pulaus* or cooked in broth the North Indian way. With it there is a meat or a fish preparation, either a curry or a sauceless dish, and two or three vegetables. At least one of these vegetables is cooked with plenty of liquid; one is cooked with a good deal of coconut (usually some kind of fleshy vegetable—squash, green tomatoes, cooking bananas, unripe jack fruit, breadfruit), and there will be one leafy or green vegetable. Occasionally, a *dal* is added as a change or an extra flourish, while buttermilk and pickles are daily essentials. There are no desserts.

The serving of a meal has its own accepted ritual, and this, too, is performed by the senior woman. She may be helped by the girls in the family, but not by the servants, who are permitted only to carry into the dining room the earthenware pots in which the various dishes have been cooked. Using ladles made from coconut shells attached to wooden handles, she portions out the rice and accompanying preparations in the shallow metal bowls, about 14 inches in diameter. These bowls take the place of *thalis* and *katoris*, and she refills them as needed from the cooking pots. My friends explained to me that they always prefer to cook and serve in earthenware to avoid any metallic taste in the meal, especially in deference to the fish preparations and the sour-hot flavors that dominate many of their dishes. Even the eating bowls that they use are made of bell metal, which does not affect the taste of the food; or, as they say, doesn't "curl the tongue." It is a relatively recent innovation; in the old days one always ate from banana leaves.

Because the Syrian Christians are not bound by Hindu strictures about eating beef, they have evolved and refined a number of excellent beef dishes, including curries and "dry" preparations. And although their repertoire includes many superb fish and shellfish recipes, any small Syrian Christian village may well pool its financial resources for a special event or festival and buy a calf, slaughter it (a job that, of course, the Hindus in the neighborhood wouldn't touch), and divide the meat among the people.

Beef is so seldom eaten in most of India that, as a rule, cattle are not bred for eating purposes. The quality of the meat is therefore likely to be too poor to allow for dishes such as steak or roast beef. But this drawback has inspired Syrian Christian cooks to produce highly ingenious and imaginative dishes of cubed or minced beef, with spicing and sauces that can effortlessly persuade you to forget that the meat itself is not particularly good.

One of these preparations is called *irachi thoran*, a beef dish with grated coconut. In making it, you first boil the cubed meat with vinegar and salt until it is tender, and then crush it on a grinding stone and shred it to remove any stringiness from the texture. After that, you lightly fry the shredded beef with green and dry *masalas*, pushed to the edges of the pan to clear a space in the center, which is filled with plenty of grated coconut and a *masala* dominated by crushed ginger, garlic and onions. The meat is then spooned over the coconut-*masala* mixture, allowed to steam for a few minutes, then thoroughly stirred and served.

Another beef dish, *irachi piralan*, uses vinegar to tenderize the meat cubes before they are sautéed with sliced onions, potatoes and a wonderfully aromatic *masala*, rich with cinnamon, cloves and cardamom. Several other dry preparations get around the tenderizing problem by slicing the meat very thin or by using minced beef to produce a kind of Indian hamburger cooked with a very simple *masala* of ginger, green chilies and onion.

Apart from their talent with beef cooking, which is unique in India, the Syrian Christians have two other specialties: some flamboyantly spiced duck dishes, and a repertoire of truly noble game recipes. Actually, even the duck preparations can fairly be included in the repertoire of game cooking because most of the recipes call for wild duck. The two notable exceptions are special Christmas treats: duck *mappas* (an extravagantly rich preparation, cooked in *ghee* with coconut, onions and *masala)*, and the festive roast duck (with a stuffing of chopped duck liver, onions, green chilies, ginger and *garam masala)*.

The Syrian Christians also make two magnificent preparations with wild boar. One is a remarkably robust curry with a thick sauce including onions, ginger and a *masala* that is strong enough to hold its own against the gaminess of the meats. Still, it is the light, fantastic touch provided by the addition of slices of fresh young coconut that delights me most. The other unusual recipe is for a wild boar pickle in which the cubes of meat are thickly coated with a *masala* containing plenty of mustard seed and other spices, packed into a stone jar and covered with oil. When the pickle has matured, it takes a pretty unshockable palate to enjoy it by itself. But if eaten with rice or used as a relish in a blander meal, it holds the sudden excitement of —say—seeing one's first tiger in a jungle.

North of Malabar, along the same coast, lies the small former Portuguese colony of Goa, already visited in this book (Chapter 5) for a sampling of its seafood specialties. The Goan Christians (unlike the Syrian Christians) have also produced pork dishes, which makes their cuisine unique in India. These range from the familiar roast suckling pig that composes the standard Christmas dinner, to such an exotic item as baked pork head stuffed with brains, peas, onions, ginger, mint and green chilies, basted with vinegar.

The more usual Goan dishes, however, include some truly delicious and original uses of pork. It is difficult to choose among them, but the two that please me most are pork *baffat* and pork *indad*. The first is a dry curry, cooked in an aromatic *masala* with virtually no gravy, but the thing that makes it surprising and delightful is the addition of sliced radishes near the end of the cooking time. These are the long, white Indian radishes, not as sharp as horseradish or as bland as turnips, but somewhere between the two. It is the contrast between the crisp, clean taste of the radish and the inevitably greasy texture of the pork that gives the dish its distinctive flavor.

Pork *indad* is a true curry, with plenty of gravy, that differs from many of the other pork dishes because of its appealing, offbeat sweet-sour taste. The tamarind, cloves and cinnamon in the *masala* give the meat an almost perfumed flavor, while the sugar and vinegar in the gravy (besides other spices, of course) take the curse off the fattiness and provide the dish with its special character. Another spicy red curry called *sorpotel*, made of meat, liver and pork rind, is an absolute must at any Goan Christian banquet or feast. It is served with the accompaniment of *sannon*—a fluffy white bread of rice and toddy (the sap of the palm tree) that in appearance and texture resembles the *idlis* (rice cakes) of Madras. The taste however is unique, the toddy giving *sannon* a sweet taste and an accent unlike any other wheat cake.

Goa is the only place in India where I have eaten sausages like those found in the West—but even here they are very different in flavor from the Western varieties. The Goans produce pork and liver sausages, as well as several other kinds of highly spiced sausages, the best of which is *chourisam*. The *chourisam* must be marinated for 24 hours in a rather complicated *masala* mixed with vinegar before the sausages are made. The end result, which is sharp, vinegary, garlicky, gingery and very stimulating to the palate, is well worth the time and trouble.

150

Perhaps the most interesting of all Indian minorities are the Parsis, who fled Persia 1,200 years ago to escape religious persecution and settled in the state of Gujarat and in Bombay. A small reminder of their early days of enforced emigration is sometimes seen on the streets of Bombay to this day in the stiff shiny black hats that orthodox Parsi gentlemen wear. This hat, the story goes, is shaped to resemble the hoof of a cow—a symbol of deference to the compassionate Hindus who, so many centuries ago, gave the fugitive Parsi community shelter and a new home.

By now, however, the Parsis are entirely Indian in feeling and loyalty, although they still retain some of their ancient heritage in their religion and food habits. Modern Parsis still adhere strictly to Zoroastrianism. For example, fire is sacred to them, and unlike Hindus, they do not desecrate fire by cremating their dead. Their fire temples, equally remote in ceremony and atmosphere from Hindu temples, are exclusively for Parsis. If you were to visit a Hindu temple, regardless of your religion or nationality, you would be able to wander about anywhere except for the very innermost shrine, but no one who is not a Parsi may enter a Parsi temple.

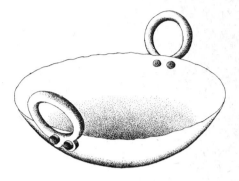

DEEP FRYERS: TWO ORIENTAL VERSIONS
The recipes in this book suggest that the Indian *karhai* above and the Chinese *wok* below be used as deepfrying utensils. The *karhai* is deeper and narrower than the *wok*, but both have rounded bottoms, so that as little as 3 cups of oil will fill them to a depth of 2 or 3 inches for deep frying.

The Parsis adhere to ancient forms in their religious practices, but in their food and in their daily living they have evolved a curious and fascinating compromise between the traditions of their ancestors and those of the country of their adoption. In their living habits they are known to be the most "Westernized" of all Indians—but the food the Parsis serve could never be found on an American or a European table. When a Parsi friend calls to invite me to come to dinner, I'm often told in English (their Indian language is Gujarati, mine is Hindi), "This is informal—come in slacks, no need for a sari. Between 8:30 and 9 o'clock, all right?" For formal occasions, however, it is assumed that everyone will wear Indian clothes.

When I arrive (in slacks) I find a beautifully appointed home. It is Western in the sense that there are sofas, chairs and coffee tables bearing cigarettes, ashtrays, hors d'oeuvre and cocktail napkins, and Western alcoholic drinks will be served. But a more discerning glance around the room shows that the pictures on the walls are all by Indian artists. The furniture is carved Indian rosewood upholstered in Indian fabrics, while the ornaments, ashtrays, plates or bowls holding the hors d'oeuvre or nuts also are all of Indian design. In short, it is an Indian house—of a different tradition.

And when dinner is served, by Indian servants, course by course, not all together on a *thali,* there is no longer any question about where—in which country, that is—you are dining. There are many marvelously exciting, rich items in the Parsi cuisine, but its major distinguishing factors—found virtually nowhere else in India   are the use of kid and of eggs.

The Parsis have produced a version of scrambled eggs, called *ekuri,* that makes ordinary scrambled eggs seem pallid by comparison. Sometimes they add chopped green peppers, onions, green chilies and coriander to the eggs —they vary the *masalas* in innumerable ways—and sometimes they serve the *ekuri* with fried bananas, or mix in slices of green mangoes. Indeed, there are as many varieties of *ekuri* as there are imaginative cooks, and I have yet to eat an *ekuri* that didn't give my palate a mild but delightful shock.

Another favorite Parsi egg dish requires a very thick, heavily spiced purée of tomatoes and onions with a little unrefined brown sugar. The purée is spread in a shallow baking dish, dotted with butter, and sprinkled with chopped coriander leaves. Then, as a Parsi friend of mine expresses it, "you make little dimples" in the purée, break an egg into each dimple, and bake the whole thing until the eggs are done. It is served hot, with very thin *chapatis,* and is far more exciting and interesting to taste than it sounds.

Best of all, in my opinion, is a dish for which you must first prepare a sweet-sour mince of lamb. Again, this is spread in a baking dish and topped with stiffly beaten eggs, which rise like a soufflé in the oven. I think it is the combination of the fluffiness of the eggs and the grainy piquancy of the lamb that gives this particular dish its special delight.

No discussion of Parsi cooking would be complete without mentioning *dhansak* if only because this great dish has become so famous and so popular that many Indians think of Parsi cooking as consisting of very little else. The word *dhan* means "wealth," which gives you some idea of the nature of the dish. The closest thing to it in Western cooking would, I suppose, be a *cassoulet.* The ingredients are entirely different, but the principle is the same. It requires cubes of good, slightly fatty meat, preferably breast of lamb, and slices of tripe, all cooked in a purée of at least three different kinds of lentils and sometimes eight or nine. It also contains a number of vegetables, usually slices of red pumpkin, eggplant, tomatoes, onions, a few leaves of spinach and some leaf coriander.

I once attended the preparation of *dhansak* at the home of a Parsi friend in Bombay—and watched her choose, measure and cube meat, vegetables and the fresh and dry ingredients of the *masala.* While three different lentils—*toovar, chana* and *mung dals*—were cooking with water and salt on a medium fire, my friend proceeded to cut up the fleshy piece of the breast of lamb into large cubes. Then she cut and cleaned the vegetables, the purple of the eggplant vying for prominence with the red pumpkin and the green spinach. Any number of vegetables may be used in this dish, but my friend chose to limit herself to four—pumpkin, eggplant, spinach and tomato. On the grinding stone she blended into a smooth paste a *masala* of fresh ginger, garlic and the dry spices of cloves, peppercorns, cinnamon, cumin, coriander and a very few red chilies, which were not the excessively hot type. The green chilies, fresh coriander and mint were chopped separately and kept aside. In a large copper vessel she melted *ghee* on a medium flame and cooked the onions to a light brown. Next she added the *masala,* fried it a bit, and put in the chopped tomatoes and vegetables, then lowered the flame and cooked them until they were very soft, the mixture resembling a kind of multicolored purée. By this time the lentils had cooked to the required consistency, and, using a round indented wooden ladle placed in the center of the *dal* vessel, she proceeded with a rhythmic rolling of the ladle held within the palms of her hands, to break up the lentils into a sort of coarse purée. To the bland lentils she added the aromatic vegetable and *masala* purée, and blended it together, tossing in the lightly fried cubes of meat, mint, chilies and coriander. When this was done, she topped it off with a cream of crisply fried brown onions. The end result was surprising indeed. Gone were the stunning hues of yellow, purple, green and red. Instead we saw a light brown stew with specks of green coriander and brown onions, but the richest, most forceful and most filling meal I have ever eaten.

The recipes for this chapter are examples of the distinctively different cuisines of the three leading minority groups of India that are discussed in the preceding pages of the text: the Syrian Christians, the Goans and the Parsis.

Vath (Syrian Christian)
ROAST DUCK WITH CASHEW STUFFING

Drop the cashews into a small bowl or pan, pour in 2 cups of boiling water, and soak them for at least 15 minutes.

Wash the duck under cold running water and pat it completely dry inside and out with paper towels. Rub both the breast and neck cavity and the skin with 2 teaspoons of the salt and set the duck aside. Chop the liver, heart and gizzard fine.

Combine the bread, eggs, raisins, coriander, sugar, vinegar and black pepper in a deep bowl, and toss them about gently with a spoon until they are well mixed.

Pulverize the cardamom seeds with a mortar and pestle or drop them into a bowl and crush them fine with the back of a spoon.

In a heavy 10- to 12-inch skillet, heat the vegetable oil over moderate heat until a light haze forms above. Stir in the cumin, anise seeds, onions, garlic, ginger and 1 teaspoon of salt and, stirring frequently, fry for 7 or 8 minutes, until the onions are soft and golden brown. Watch carefully for any signs of burning and regulate the heat accordingly.

Stirring well after each addition, add the chopped duck liver, the heart and the gizzard, the turmeric, cardamom, tomatoes and green chili. Cook the mixture over moderate heat, stirring constantly, for about 3 minutes, until the giblets are lightly browned.

With a rubber spatula, scrape the entire contents of the skillet over the bread-and-egg mixture and turn them about gently with the spatula or a spoon until they are thoroughly combined.

Preheat the oven to 450°. Drain the cashews in a sieve or colander and chop them fine. Stir the nuts and red pepper into the bread mixture.

With a trussing needle or small skewer, gently prick the skin of the duck at about 1-inch intervals all over its surfaces. Spoon the nut-stuffing mixture loosely into the breast and neck cavities, and sew the openings securely with heavy thread.

Truss the bird securely and place it on its side on a rack in a shallow roasting pan. Roast in the middle of the oven for 10 minutes, then turn the duck on its other side and roast 10 minutes longer. Reduce the heat to 350°, turn the duck breast side up and roast for about 1 hour and 40 minutes, basting the bird occasionally with the *ghee*.

To test the bird for doneness, pierce the thigh of the duck with the point of a small, sharp knife. The juice that trickles out should be a clear yellow; if the juice is still slightly tinged with pink, continue roasting the bird for another 5 to 10 minutes.

Transfer the duck to a heated platter and let it rest for about 10 minutes for easier carving.

To serve 4

½ cup unsalted cashew nuts
A 4½- to 5-pound duck
3½ teaspoons salt
The liver, heart and gizzard of the duck
1½ cups bread cubes made from homemade-type white bread, trimmed of all crusts, and cut into ½-inch dice
2 hard-cooked eggs, shelled and cut lengthwise into quarters
1 tablespoon seedless raisins
1 tablespoon finely chopped fresh coriander *(cilantro)*
1 tablespoon sugar
2 tablespoons distilled white vinegar
1 teaspoon coarsely ground black pepper
The seeds of 8 whole cardamom pods or ½ teaspoon cardamom seeds
1 tablespoon vegetable oil
½ teaspoon ground cumin
½ teaspoon anise seeds
1 cup finely chopped onions
1 tablespoon finely chopped garlic
A 1-inch piece of scraped, fresh ginger root, cut into paper-thin slivers
½ teaspoon turmeric
1 cup chopped fresh tomatoes
1 fresh hot green chili, about 3 inches long, washed and cut into ½-inch rounds with the seeds intact *(caution: see page 39)*
½ teaspoon ground hot red pepper
2 tablespoons melted *ghee (page 54)*

To make about 10 filled pancakes

PANCAKES
1 cup all-purpose flour
1/8 teaspoon salt
1 egg
1 cup milk
3 tablespoons *ghee (page 54)*

FILLING
1/4 cup imported jaggery, coarsely
    crumbled, or substitute dark-
    brown sugar combined with dark
    molasses *(page 196)*
1 cup finely grated fresh coconut
    (page 134)
1 teaspoon scraped, very finely
    chopped fresh ginger root
1/2 teaspoon anise seeds

To serve 4

6 eggs
1/4 cup milk
1/2 teaspoon salt
1/4 teaspoon freshly ground black
    pepper
3 tablespoons *ghee (page 54)*
1 teaspoon scraped, finely chopped
    fresh ginger root
3 tablespoons finely chopped onions
3 tablespoons finely chopped fresh
    coriander *(cilantro)*
1/4 teaspoon turmeric
2 teaspoons finely chopped fresh hot
    red or green chili *(caution: see
    page 39)*
1/2 teaspoon ground cumin

Alebele (Goan)
PANCAKES WITH SPICY COCONUT FILLING

Combine the flour, salt, egg and milk in a deep bowl and beat with a whisk or a rotary or electric beater until the ingredients are well blended. Set the batter aside to rest at room temperature for at least 20 minutes.

In a 6- to 7-inch skillet, preferably one with sloping sides, heat 1 teaspoon of the *ghee* over moderate heat until a drop of water flicked into it splutters instantly. With a small ladle, pour about 3 tablespoons of the batter into the pan and immediately tip it back and forth to spread the batter quickly over the entire surface of the pan.

Cook for a minute or so, until the edges begin to brown lightly, then with a spatula turn the pancake over and cook the other side for a minute. Slide the pancake onto a plate and proceed with the rest of the batter, using 1 teaspoon of *ghee* for each cake.

When all the pancakes are cooked, make the stuffing by rubbing the jaggery between the palms of your hands and crumbling it fine into a bowl. The warmth of your hands will slowly melt the molasses covering the individual sugar crystals and enable you to separate them into tiny bits. (The brown sugar and molasses substitute needs only to be placed in the bowl and mashed smooth with the back of a spoon.)

Add the grated coconut, ginger root and anise seeds, and mix with your fingers until all of the jaggery is completely melted and the ingredients are well combined.

Spread a tablespoon of the filling on the lower third of each pancake and roll it up but do not tuck in the ends. Arrange the filled pancakes attractively on a platter and serve at once. If you prefer, you may cover the platter tightly with plastic wrap and set the *alebele* aside at room temperature until ready to serve.

Ekuri (Parsi)
SCRAMBLED EGGS WITH CORIANDER AND GINGER

Break the eggs into a deep bowl and mix them lightly with a whisk or fork. Add the milk, salt and black pepper, and stir until all of the ingredients are well combined. Do not overbeat or allow the egg-and-milk mixture to foam or become frothy.

In a heavy 10-inch skillet, heat the *ghee* over moderate heat until a drop of water flicked into it splutters instantly. Add the ginger and fry for 10 seconds, then add the onions and fry for about 1 minute, until they are soft but not brown.

Stirring constantly, add the chopped coriander and then the turmeric. Pour in the beaten egg mixture and sprinkle the top with the fresh chili. Reduce the heat to the lowest possible point and, stirring constantly with the flat of a table fork or a rubber spatula, cook the eggs until they begin to form soft, creamy curds.

Immediately spread the eggs on a heated serving plate, sprinkle the top with cumin, and serve.

Ekuri (also spelled *akoori*) is traditionally garnished with slices or wedges of fresh tomato and may be further embellished with sprigs or leaves of coriander. It is usually accompanied by plain *parathas (Recipe Index)*.

Even so familiar a dish as scrambled eggs becomes an exotic treat when it is made Indian style. The *ekuri* shown above is spiced with fresh ginger and coriander set off by a sprinkling of hot green chili, then served garnished with tomato wedges and coriander sprigs.

VIII

Northern India, Where Lamb is King

Shahjahani biryani is a
mixture of saffron rice and
lamb, named for the Moghul
Emperor Shah Jahan who
built the Taj Mahal. As
shown here, it is
embellished with leaves of
silver and may be
accompanied by kela ka
rayta—yoghurt with
banana and fresh coconut.

The Moghlai cuisine of North India is the richest and most lavish in the whole country, and its exalted reputation largely stems from the wealth and variety of lamb dishes. It has been said that a really superb North Indian cook can produce a different lamb dish for every day of the year. I have never had occasion to verify this point, but even a cursory enumeration of the different sorts of lamb *kababs,* curries, "dry" (as opposed to "curried") meat preparations, roasts and meat-and-rice dishes of the opulent Moghlai cuisine tends to bear it out.

History, religion and tradition have combined to persuade North Indian cooks to focus their attention and ingenuity on the seemingly endless possibilities of lamb. Pork was ruled out for them because the Muslims, who originated North Indian meat dishes, abhor this meat. Beef was largely absent from the repertoire because the cuisine evolved and developed in a predominantly Hindu country, where, as we have seen, the cow is sacred. Neither geography nor habit encouraged the inclusion of fish or seafood in the diet. And although the Moghlai cuisine included some excellent chicken dishes, they never compared in quality or scope with the supreme Moghlai culinary achievement, the inspired cooking of lamb.

The first Moghul invaders came into North India as early as the Eighth Century—sweeping down through the Khyber Pass—the same route that Alexander the Great had taken a thousand years earlier—into what is now Pakistan. They were Muslims and in the 12th Century they established the Delhi Sultanate, the first Muslim kingdom in India. It was not, however, until 1526 that one of these Muslim rulers, Babur the Moghul—a descendant of Tamerlane and Genghis Khan—successfully invaded the Punjab, and proclaimed himself Emperor of India.

Babur's rule inaugurated a Moghul era of unparalleled splendor (and savagery), when great cities, palaces, mosques and monuments were built in North India. He and his successors came to be known as Grand Moghuls, celebrated for their florid manners and courtesies, the showiness of their hospitality and their delight in material comforts.

An Englishman of the 16th Century, traveling in India during the reign of the greatest of the Moghuls, the Emperor Akbar, recorded an astonished glimpse of some of the accouterments of the royal cities. "The King," he wrote, "hath in Agra and Fatehpur Sikri 100 elephants, 30,000 horses, 1,400 tame deer, 800 concubines and other such store of leopard, tiger, buffaloes, cocks and hawks that it is very strange to see. He keepeth a great Court. Agra and Fatehpur Sikri are very great cities, either of them much greater than London." And all of court life reflected a comparable extravagance, abundance and emphasis on high living.

Before the coming of the Moghul emperors, the great Hindu empires had tended to concentrate their cultural talents on music, dance, literature and some of the world's most impressive sculpture. The genius of the Muslims emerged more forcefully in their imposing architecture (the Taj Mahal built at Agra in the 17th Century is the outstanding example), the charm of their poetry and painting, and the panache and elegance of their living. One aspect of this concern for style and luxury remains in the great cuisine the Moghuls bequeathed to India and Pakistan.

The true magnificence of the Moghlai cuisine was brought home to me some years ago when I attended a Moghlai banquet—perhaps the most memorable meal of my life—in Hyderabad, before India had become as acutely austerity conscious as it is now, and before food rationing made such an elaborate feast impossible.

In those pre-Independence days, Hyderabad was the largest of India's princely states, the fiefdom of a Muslim ruler, His Exalted Highness, the Nizam, with a Muslim aristocracy of Nawabs under his patronage. The party to which I was invited was given by one of the wealthier Nawabs in celebration of his son's marriage. There were hundreds of guests—so many that even in the enormous dining hall of his palace not all of them could be accommodated at one time, and dinner was served in three sittings.

The party began at twilight in the garden, and as the guests arrived, the women were given bracelets made of fresh double jasmines, while the men received boutonnieres of roses bound with silver, and everyone was sprinkled with rose water. The garden was illuminated with colored lights hung in the trees and with Chinese lanterns, but even without this illumination, the colors of the women's clothes would have made a gaudy enough display. The Muslims wore *gharuras,* the full, ankle-length skirts, with short jackets, in brilliant colors—shocking pink, parrot green, sapphire blue—all embroidered with gold and sequins and swathed in gauzy white veils. Some of the orthodox Muslim guests wore *burkhas* over their party clothes—the full length, heavy veils that leave only the eyes of a woman exposed. These women sat and dined behind perforated screens through which they could watch the party without themselves being seen. The Hindu women were in saris of

Opposite: A 16th Century painting from an illuminated biography of Akbar, the greatest of Moghul emperors, shows him being entertained at Dipalpur, Punjab, by his foster brother, Khan Azam. The various flasks and covered dishes below the imperial chair indicate that a royal feast is about to begin. Akbar lived daringly—at the table as well as in battle—and was fond of palm wine laced with opium and spices.

equally vivid colors, with their best jewelry. Most of the men wore the high-collared, long black jackets (many with jeweled buttons) called *achkans* over narrow trousers. Originally this was the correct Muslim court dress, but ultimately it was adopted by all of North India for formal occasions.

The bride and groom sat on a platform on one side of the lawn, screened from the guests and each other by curtains made of long strings of jasmine and tinsel hanging from a narrow wooden frame. As the evening breeze stirred the scented, fragile fall of flowers, the young couple were only partly and intermittently visible to the rest of us. She was wearing a pink *gharara,* her hair sprinkled with tiny silver flakes and decorated with a gold, gem-encrusted plaque, part of the traditional bridal jewelry. The palms of her hands and the soles of her feet carried exquisite designs drawn in henna (a process that takes all day and the skill of an expert). The groom, in an *achkan* with pearl and emerald buttons, wore garlands of flowers, and as guests brought presents to the young couple, he lightly touched each one to signify his acceptance of the gift. It is considered vulgar actually to *take* presents. Someone else is designated to perform the sordid business of receiving them and unobtrusively putting them away among other possessions in the house.

Scattered about the lawn were a number of *takhats* (low wooden platforms for the guests to sit on) covered with Persian carpets with big and small brocade bolsters to serve as back and arm rests. One special, luxurious *takhat* was covered with red brocade embroidered with real gems, for the use of the bridal couple after the party was assembled and the gifts had been offered. On yet another *takhat* sat the *qawali* singers, seven men who performed in turn, clapping out the rhythm and singing the lyrics so artfully and ambiguously that the songs might be purely devotional, addressed to God, or —with just a slight change in their nuance of expression or phrasing—they might be heard as passionate love songs.

Throughout the early part of the evening, to the accompaniment of the *qawali* singers and the exchanges of courtesies and conversation among the guests, uniformed servants, each with a scarlet sash and fez, moved about serving drinks and snacks. At this particular party there were Western liquors and champagne (forbidden to orthodox Muslims), as well as the traditional fruit drinks of the Moghuls—chilled apple, melon, pomegranate and mango juices, always with a squeeze of lime to take the edge off the sweetness. These drinks are called *sharbat,* from which the American "sherbet" derives. The uniformed servants also served *falsa,* a mixture of several fruit juices, teasingly flavored with tamarind and ginger, salt and sugar, with slices of orange, apple and banana, and whole mint leaves floating in it.

Huge silver trays were passed to the guests, bearing bowls of nuts, *bhujiyas,* or slices of vegetables dipped in chick-pea batter and fried crisp, tiny spiced meatballs, small boiled potatoes with a choice of chutneys, one of tamarind, salt and chilies and the other of green mint and coriander, *tikka kababs* (pieces of boned chicken rubbed with a *masala* and grilled), along with many other sharp or salty hors d'oeuvre.

At about 9 o'clock the *muzbi,* a special appetizer for joyous or ceremonial feasts, was served. This is a Moghul dish, described in ancient records; it is a kind of barbecue, cooked outdoors on a charcoal fire built in a pit. The fire was lit at 3 o'clock that afternoon, then covered with an iron grill on

160

Continued on page 164

A Wedding Shower of Fruits and Sweets

Food plays an integral part in ceremonial occasions in India, especially in the series of events leading up to a wedding. When Maharajkumar Bhwani Singh, a Hindu prince of Jaipur, invited his friends to ceremonies at the Jaipur City Palace confirming his engagement to Padmini, Princess of Sirmur, the bride's family sent a traditional gift of fruit and sweets, and the noble guests, in formal attire complete with swords and scarlet turbans, filed by carefully examining the food, which had been arranged on a marble floor in the palace. But the food was not presented for the pleasure of the Prince's guests. It was simply a symbolic gift and, after the engagement ceremony, it was distributed to servants in the City Palace. Later, the wedding itself was held in New Delhi, the bride's hometown. At the beginning of the ceremony, a Hindu Brahmin priest tied the right hands of the bride and groom together with an orange scarf. The priest prepared a fire and ceremonially tossed sandalwood, vermilion paste, rice and butter into the flames. Then the bride and groom walked around the fire seven times together and, as this ritual ended, they fed each other some ceremonial food (overleaf).

At the conclusion of their wedding rites, the demure bride and her new husband, both festooned with marigolds and jasmine, feed each other rice while relatives look on. Later at Jaipur *(opposite)*, 12 retainers carry the bride in a marigold-bedecked palanquin through the main gate of the City Palace, the couple's future home. Behind her, the bridegroom is borne through the gate on an elephant.

which flat, scrubbed stones were placed and heated to the scalding point over smoldering charcoal.

The breast of lamb that was to be barbecued had first been soaked for six hours in a *masala* of garlic, onion, ginger, green chili, turmeric, red chili and a pinch of *garam masala* ground together with curds and a little water. The lamb was then cut into pieces about an inch and a half square, with no bone but plenty of fat. The pieces of meat were dipped in a thin paste of crushed almonds, poppy seeds, sesame seeds and *chironji* (a green seed about the size of a pea with a nutty flavor). The meat was not thickly coated; just enough of the paste was added to lend a fleeting richness to the flavor of the *masala*.

The meat was thrown on the stones, and when it had cooked for two or three minutes, the servants speared the lamb on long, thin iron spikes, pushing four or five pieces onto individual plates that already held a garnish of sliced onion, green chutney and a wedge of lime. The guests were then served as they gathered round the pit fire in groups. Each piece of lamb was succulent and very tender, its flavor enhanced, but not overwhelmed, by the long immersion in the marinade. The taste was that of the lamb itself, with just the added zest of the *masala* and the piquancy of the garnish. It was the most delicious appetizer I had ever eaten.

The dinner itself was served indoors. The guests sat on the floor around small, low tables—about six to a table—on which designs made with flower petals surrounded the dishes of different sweets; an almond *khir* (the milk-based sweet essential for auspicious occasions), a very thick, custardlike egg *halva* and a carrot *halva*, all covered with silver leaf and rich with nuts, especially pistachios. Along one side of the huge room, on a long trestle table decorated with flowers and tinsel, were eight immense platters, each holding an entire roast sheep placed on its back with its legs in the air. The sheep had been bought four months earlier so they could be properly fattened on the Nawab's estate. Before cooking, the meat was slashed with long knife cuts, and each incision was filled with a *masala* of onions, garlic, chilies and ginger. Then the sheep were roasted on a spit over an open fire until the meat was tender. After that, each sheep was stuffed with a *pulau* of rice, raisins, carrots, onions, garlic. Whole roasted chickens and whole hard-boiled eggs were buried in the *pulau*. Finally the entire unwieldy creature was placed in a covered pot (the size of a giant's cauldron) with *ghee*, water, more *masala* and saffron, and baked until both the stuffing and the meat were cooked through, and all the *ghee* and water absorbed. It didn't look very pretty, but the fabulously rich and surprising combinations and contrasts—the strong, garlicky lamb and the blander chicken and eggs, the delicately flavored *pulau* and vegetables, suffused with the aroma of saffron and the sudden, unexpected sweetness from the raisins—all tasted unfamiliar and marvelous.

That, however, was only the showy dish, the one that announced in the most blatant way possible that this was, indeed, a princely banquet. The others, equally delicious, were of a more manageable nature, the sort of food one can serve at a less ostentatious party and cook in smaller quantities. The *biryani (Recipe Index)*, for example, has become such a popular main dish throughout North India that it has developed many different forms, with varying *masalas* and changing ingredients. Expert cooks will argue for hours about the best recipes and insist with patriotic fervor on the virtues of particular local embellishments. Essentially *biryani* is a lamb-and-rice preparation —not a *pulau,* in which the rice takes precedence over the meat or vegetables with which it is cooked. *Biryani* can also be made with chicken or fish, but these are recent variations, and the classic Moghlai dish uses only lamb.

The Moghlai *biryani* is a fine example of the way Indian cooks employ a broad variety of seasonings to enliven a dish and bring out its flavor without destroying its essential character. To prepare the *masala* for it, they grind ginger, red chilies and almonds together. The *masala* is cooked in *ghee* and combined with the meat, and then a second *masala* is prepared. Curd is strained through fine muslin, to bring it to the smoothest consistency. Then the curd is mixed with cloves, cardamom, turmeric, finely chopped green chilies, coriander, mint and a very delicate variety of cumin seed called *shahi zira* (royal cumin). The curd mixture is seasoned with lime juice and then added to the lamb. The rice for the *biryani* is boiled separately and then sprinkled with saffron dissolved in milk. When the lamb and rice have been cooked, the whole dish is arranged in layers on a heavy cooking pot—a layer of rice, then a layer of lamb and then a layer of fried onions, and so on until all the ingredients have been used. Finally the layered *biryani* is covered with milk and *ghee;* the cooking vessel is sealed around the edges with wheat-flour paste, placed in the oven, and baked for an hour.

The end result, fragrant with saffron, and unexpectedly subtle considering the elaborate *masalas,* is decorated with silver leaf to honor both the guests and the dish. Decorative and delicious, it is an elegant blending of two unsophisticated ingredients. Anyone who tends to think of lamb and rice as prosaic foods should try it.

While the basic formula for the *biryani* allows for numerous variations of style and ingredients, it is still relatively inflexible compared with another Muslim specialty served at the Moghlai banquet, the *kabab.* There are dozens of varieties of *kababs* served in India—made from cubed, sliced or minced lamb—broiled, steamed, fried or skewered. Two of the fanciest varieties were served at the Nawab's banquet. One was the *shami kabab,* a deliciously subtle combination of lamb, fruit and nuts, made from minced lamb and chick-peas (about eight parts to one) cooked in water over a slow fire with a *masala* of onions, green ginger, cinnamon, cloves, cardamom, turmeric, coriander and red and green chilies. The other was *nargesi kabab,* featuring a whole hard-boiled egg thickly coated with a layer of spiced, minced lamb, cooked with tomatoes and onions and a *masala* of onions, cumin, fresh coriander, garlic, ginger and *garam masala.* Heavier and less subtle than the *shami kabab,* it teased and delighted the palate with its juxtaposition of crumbly and smooth textures, its sharp and mild tastes. It had, besides, another rather charming distinction: its appearance. The evocative name *nargesi* means narcissus, and when the *kabab* is broken open, the golden yolk of the center with its surrounding rim of white against the earth-brown background is supposed to remind you of that most charming of flowers.

These were only some of the dishes served at the Nawab's banquet. For gourmets there was a *roghan josh,* the wonderfully rich and aromatic lamb curry cooked in *ghee* and spiced with powdered ginger, coriander seed, red chilies, and the all-important *garam masala.*

There was *murg masalam,* one of the best-known chicken dishes in the

Moghlai repertory, spiced chicken, sprinkled with sliced almonds and walnuts. Even the *dal*—so often simply a pedestrian lentil purée—was remarkable on that extraordinary evening.

Throughout the meal members of the Nawab's family, however distantly related, stood in attendance, watching over each group of tables, urging guests to second and third helpings, insisting with florid courtesy that "our humble dwelling" could never provide the luxury and the truly princely food that "you surely enjoy in your own palaces," but imploring them, "just to please and honor us, do have just a little more. . . ." This duty is never assigned to servants, who—though they do eventually bring round silver bowls of warm water, scattered with floating rose petals for the guests to wash their hands—are never permitted to perform the ceremonial distribution of perfumed, silver-covered *paans* that formally ends the meal. That final act of graciousness must also be the duty of family members.

After dinner, when everyone had eaten far too much, came the time for lordly relaxation and "informal" entertainment—which meant the appearance of the dancing girls. Traditionally, of course, no women were permitted to attend this part of the festivities. Their presence, even behind screens, would certainly cramp the style of both the male guests and the dancing girls. Our host, however, was a traveled and sophisticated man, and the ladies were allowed to watch at least the beginning of the proceedings, though it was made quite clear that the men must be given pride of place, and so the women were expected to retire early.

Reclining on *takhats* set against the walls of a large reception room, the men were offered hookahs to smoke and liqueurs (including a fierce local distillation called *asa*) to drink, while the musicians and dancers assembled. The musicians playing the *sarangi*, the harmonium and *tablas* (hand drums) were men, and performing with them were the traditional trio of girls—each with her particular accomplishments—and an elderly, gray-haired woman who was not exactly a chaperone, though her presence was supposed to lend dignity to the occasion. One of these girls always specializes in a kind of dancing that can be as innocent or as seductive as her audience seems to demand. Another enchants the men with song and flirts with them with accompanying hand and head gestures (especially those of the eyes). Still another lovely girl does both, and she is the only one who, so to speak, is available after the performance.

The entertainment began with a solo display by the dancer, designed to please the eye. This was followed by a selection from the singer, sitting coy and still, whose purpose was to delight the ear. During these performances the men showed their enthusiasm for a particularly complicated dance step or an unexpectedly subtle improvisation in a song with the appreciative exclamation, "Va, va!" Then, when the company seemed suitably receptive, the third girl performed to put the men completely at ease and to break whatever ice remained.

She was the only one of the troupe who was permitted to move about among the guests—without touching them, of course, and her skill was judged by how cleverly and gracefully she could evade any clutching hand. She used her veil with almost shameless duplicity, to attract and entice far more than to hide her features. The *ghazals* she sang—brief, flowery, amo-

Opposite: At sunrise on Dal Lake, in the Vale of Kashmir, fishermen pull in their nets and head home after working through the predawn hours. Their catch includes many varieties of fish, the most important of which are two species of carp. They will cook the fish in curries or fry them in oil or *ghee*. Beyond the lake lies a range of the snow-mantled Himalayas.

The Grand Moghul Jahangir, who was Emperor of India from 1605 to 1627, is shown in a contemporary painting accepting food and wine from retainers. The son of the great Akbar, Jahangir was the second in the line of four great Moghul emperors. Although a despot, he is also remembered for his devotion to art and literature. His son Shah Jahan continued the tradition of royal patronage of the arts and built the Taj Mahal. Under Jahangir's grandson Aurangzeb, the empire reached its largest territorial extent.

rous lyrics, in rhyming couplets—sound almost brazen in their English translation, and although they are more oblique in Urdu, the intent is obvious in either language:

> "I am lost now, beloved, now that you look
>   at me with your bewitching eyes."
> "You look toward me, and your glance—
>   your glance is like a knife thrust in my
>   heart and I am helpless."
> "I am made for love, so is it not natural
>   that I should love all [men] around me?"

In turn, all through the night or for as long as they could keep the men interested, the girls continued to perform. Just how it all ended is a matter that no lady is supposed to concern herself with or wish to know.

Closely related to the Moghlai cuisine featured at this sumptuous banquet is the cooking of the Hindu Kashmiri of North India, those Hindus who left the Kashmir Valley 300 or 400 years ago to settle—for the most part —in North India. The Hindu Kashmiri preoccupation with lamb dishes has come about through a geographic accident. The Kashmiri Brahmins have been meat eaters since ancient Vedic times when meat was an accepted part of the diet of all Indians, even of the Brahmins. However, in their isolated Valley of Kashmir they were cut off by the formidable barrier of the Himalayas from the vagaries of religious strictures and popular shifts of sentiment and habit that made vegetarians of Hindus elsewhere in India. The Kashmiri Brahmins, although pious Hindus in other matters, continued to eat meat even after they had emigrated to other parts of North India. They excluded chicken and pork from their diet, although the reason they gave for this exclusion was not religious. It was simply because they considered both chickens and pigs "dirty feeders" and consequently a health hazard. The Kashmiri Brahmins were—and still are—quite willing to eat wild boar, jungle fowl or any of the game birds. Beef, of course, is outlawed for them, and so are onions and garlic, not for religious reasons, but because the strong, lingering taste is supposed to heat the blood and encourage unbridled passion.

With these self-imposed restrictions, Kashmiri Brahmin cooking owes a great deal of its style and inspiration to the Moghlai cuisine. And through the centuries it has modified and refined many Moghlai dishes, and evolved some remarkable specialties of its own—all of them featuring lamb.

Among my favorites of these Kashmiri dishes is a "dry" lamb dish called *qabargah* that a cousin of mine prepares with great skill, using her mother-in-law's classic recipe. She cooks equal amounts of lamb spareribs, milk and water, with salt and spices, in a sealed pan on a slow fire. The *masala* for *qabargah* is not ground to a powder or paste. Instead, caraway seed, dried ginger root, 12 cloves, cinnamon, 12 small and 4 big cardamoms, and a few strands of saffron are tied up in a muslin bag and placed in the liquid with the meat.

In all of Moghlai cooking, and especially in the Kashmiri Brahmin embellishments of the cuisine, the emphasis is always on the greatest possible lavishness. All meat dishes and many vegetables are cooked in *ghee,* which is more expensive and heavier than the vegetable oils of the South. Quantity and the elaborations of the cooking processes are stressed here in direct contrast to the fastidious diversity of texture and taste in Maharashtra, or the simplicity of the far South. The ultimate compliment a Moghlai cook can hope for from a guest is, "There is no reply to such a meal!" The guest should be too full to be more grandiloquent than that.

In many ways the most impressive part of North India is the Vale of Kashmir, that remote, disputed, northernmost part of the country, bordered on the east by Tibet and China, on the north by the Soviet Union and Afghanistan, and on the west by Pakistan, and enclosed on all sides by the towering, snow-capped ranges of the Himalayas. So dramatic is the sight of the incredibly green valley (itself 6,000 feet above sea level, surrounded by frozen peaks) that it has elicited some wildly hyperbolic descriptions—"an emerald set in pearls," for example, or the "earthly paradise." On his deathbed, the Moghul Emperor Jahangir replied to respectful requests from his courtiers for his last wish with the words, "Kashmir—only Kashmir."

Here in the Valley of Kashmir, what is perhaps the most remarkable achievement of North Indian lamb cooking is displayed in the serving of a *mishani,* a meal of the traditional "Seven Dishes"—all lamb preparations designed to accompany happy occasions. One such elaborate event is a Kashmiri wedding, and in present-day Kashmir the rules for the wedding itself and for the accompanying *mishani* remain impressively formalized. The wedding arrangements must move at a becomingly long-drawn-out pace (nobody should appear too eager), and each major advance in the negotiations is celebrated with the *mishani*.

Since the Kashmir Valley is predominantly Muslim, neither the prospective bride, nor any of the women in her family may meet the groom or any of the men in *his* family. (Even among the more orthodox Hindus in the rest of India, the bride and groom are not supposed to set eyes on each other until the actual marriage ceremony.) The preliminary stages of any wedding are handled through a series of intermediaries. The actual proposal must come from the father of the young man through a marriage broker to the girl's father —though it is not unknown for a girl's family to put the word about discreetly in the community, or to the broker, that they have a beautiful and eligible daughter. In any case, the girl's father makes the necessary inquiries, partly through the broker and partly independently, about the young man's family, his education, his financial status and other essential matters. If everything is satisfactory, he indicates that his wife would welcome a visit from the young man's mother. On this occasion, the sister of the groom accompanies their mother on the theory that being of the same generation, she will know her brother's preferences, and be better able to judge the looks and demeanor of the bride.

If everyone approves, at this stage of the proceedings the young man's mother puts a ring on the girl's finger, gives her a token present of money, and sets the date for the official engagement ceremony. It is at the celebration of the formal betrothal that the first of the *mishani* feasts is given at the bride's house—although the groom is not permitted to be present.

The first of the seven *mishani* dishes is an all-purpose *masala* called *warri*, made of onion, cumin, coriander seed, red chilies, *garam masala*, and the juice of a small purple local flower called *mawal*. A paste of these ingredients is formed into small bricks and set in the sun to dry. As a part of the *mishani*, the *warri* may be served by itself or cooked with minced or diced lamb. The dishes that follow include highly seasoned slices of lamb liver, kidneys and shoulder meat, and *kababs* of minced lamb mixed with a *masala* and beaten egg, and then formed into small balls and roasted over a charcoal fire. There is a leg of lamb seasoned with strained aromatic spices, and tender lamb chunks spiced with cardamom, cumin seeds and cinnamon, soaked in milk, then cooked over a low fire and finally fried in walnut oil.

The last *mishani* dish, the one that Kashmiris describe as the masterpiece of their cuisine, the most tedious and difficult to make, and the most delicate in texture and flavor, is *goshtaba*. For this, very tender, fatty cuts of meat are used, especially breast of lamb. The pounding and grinding of the meat with a fairly strong mixture of cardamom, cumin seed, cloves, black pepper and a small, dark-brown dried flower called *badiani*, takes all day. Only when the meat has been reduced to an absolutely smooth paste, with no fibers or tendons to give it an unwanted coarseness of texture, is it mixed with well-beaten curds (made from cow's milk) and formed into large balls, somewhat bigger than tennis balls, and fried in *ghee*.

Between the engagement feast and the actual marriage, anything from a month to a year may elapse, and the wedding day itself has no religious ceremonies. However, the fetching of the bride from her family's house must

The succulent *korma* at left is a special kind of curried lamb distinguished by its sauce, which is flavored and lightly thickened with cashews or another kind of nut.

Overleaf: In an elegant setting of carved rosewood furniture and stained-glass windows, a waiter at the Lake Palace Hotel in Udaipur adds gaily colored lamb *pulau* to the *thalis* on a table set for a lavish North Indian dinner. (An exterior view of the hotel appears on page 27.) Two of the four silver *katoris* on each of the *thalis* contain other lamb dishes that are regular features of de luxe meals in this section: lamb curry and lamb *samosas* (pastries filled with ground lamb). On the serving table at the left is still another North Indian specialty—*masala* roast chicken, garnished with hard-cooked eggs. The other dishes on the serving table contain *puris* (a kind of bread) and a sweet called orange *bonda*.

be performed with all the elegance and formality that the groom can summon. He should arrive on horseback in the evening, accompanied by musicians and torchbearers, with his friends, relatives and guests, all in their grandest clothes, in procession behind him. At the bride's house there is more gift giving and celebration, and a second *mishani*—all seven dishes again —is served to the whole wedding party. Usually the festivities continue until the early hours of the morning when, at last, the bride, still heavily veiled and with a becoming show of reluctance, is lifted into a decorated palanquin and carried, in the returning procession, to her husband's house. The groom always rides immediately behind the palanquin to demonstrate his considerateness, a symbolic gesture to show that he will always place his bride before himself.

The following day, *wathal*, marks the third *mishani*, the biggest celebration and the most lavish feasting of all. This is held in the house of the bridegroom's family, to welcome the bride, to entertain her relatives and to establish her formally in her honored place in her new family. This time, all kinds of additions, embellishments and extra delicacies are expected to accompany the "Seven Dishes."

Only when the final *wathal mishani* has been enjoyed is the celebration of the marriage considered complete. After that, the bride is considered blessed, is offered wishes, in the traditional way, that she give birth to a hundred sons, and everything that the families can do to ensure a propitious future for the young couple has been accomplished.

Raan
SPICED LEG OF LAMB

To serve 6 to 8

2 tablespoons scraped, finely
  chopped fresh ginger root
6 medium-sized garlic cloves, peeled
  and coarsely chopped
The seeds of 2 cardamom pods or
  ⅛ teaspoon cardamom seeds
A 1-inch piece of stick cinnamon,
  coarsely crushed with a rolling
  pin or mallet
8 whole cloves
1 teaspoon cumin seeds
1 teaspoon turmeric
1 teaspoon ground hot red pepper
4 teaspoons salt
¼ cup fresh lemon juice
A 5- to 6-pound leg of lamb,
  trimmed of all fell (parchmentlike
  outer covering) and any excess
  fat
½ cup unsalted, unroasted pistachios
½ cup seedless raisins
¼ cup slivered, blanched almonds
1 cup unflavored yoghurt
¼ cup honey
½ teaspoon saffron threads
3 tablespoons plus 1 cup boiling
  water

Combine the ginger, garlic, cardamom, cinnamon, cloves, cumin, turmeric, hot red pepper, salt and lemon juice in the jar of an electric blender. Blend at high speed for 30 seconds, then turn off the machine and scrape down the sides of the jar with a rubber spatula. Blend again until the mixture becomes a smooth purée.

With a small, sharp knife, make about a dozen slashes 1 inch long and 2 inches deep on each side of the leg of lamb. Rub the spice purée over the entire outer surface of the leg, pressing it as deeply into the slashes as possible. Place the lamb in a heavy casserole large enough to hold it comfortably and set it aside to marinate for 30 minutes at room temperature.

Meanwhile purée the pistachios, raisins, almonds and yoghurt in the blender jar, and spread the mixture evenly over the lamb. Drip the honey on top of the leg, cover the casserole tightly, and marinate the lamb in a cool place for about 24 hours, or in the refrigerator for at least 48 hours.

Preheat the oven to 350°. Drop the saffron threads into a small bowl, add 3 tablespoons of boiling water, and let them soak for 15 minutes. Pour the saffron and its soaking water over the leg of lamb, and pour the remaining cup of water down the sides of the casserole.

Bring to a boil over high heat, cover tightly, and bake the lamb in the middle of the oven for 1½ hours. Then reduce the heat to 250° and bake 30 minutes longer, or until the lamb is tender and shows no resistance when pierced with the point of a small, sharp knife.

Remove the casserole from the oven, uncover it, and let the lamb cool in the sauce for 1 hour before serving.

Nargesi Kofta
GROUND LAMB MEATBALLS FILLED WITH HARD-COOKED EGGS

To serve 6

MEATBALLS
1 pound lean boneless lamb, ground
  twice
1 raw egg plus 6 shelled hard-cooked
  eggs
¼ cup finely chopped fresh coriander
  (cilantro)
¼ cup besan (chick-pea flour)
1 teaspoon salt
½ teaspoon ground cumin
Vegetable oil

First prepare the koftas, or lamb meatballs, in the following fashion: Combine the lamb, raw egg, ¼ cup fresh coriander, besan, 1 teaspoon salt and the cumin in a deep bowl and knead vigorously with both hands until thoroughly mixed. Then beat with a wooden spoon until the mixture is smooth. Divide the mixture into 6 equal portions and shape each one into a flat circle about 3 inches in diameter.

Center a hard-cooked egg on each circle and gently shape the lamb mixture up around it to enclose the egg completely. The finished kofta will be somewhat egg-shaped.

Pour 3 cups of vegetable oil into a 10-inch karhai or 12-inch wok (page 151), or pour 2 to 3 inches of oil into a deep fryer. Heat the oil until it reaches a temperature of 375° on a deep-frying thermometer. Deep-fry the koftas 2 or 3 at a time, turning them about with a slotted spoon, for about 3 minutes, or until they are richly browned on all sides. As they brown, transfer them to paper towels to drain.

In a heavy 4- to 5-quart casserole, heat the ghee over moderate heat until a drop of water flicked into it splutters instantly. Add the onions and, lifting

Scallions, white radishes and carrots accompany the surprisingly sweet yet pungent spiced leg of lamb, or *raan*, shown above.

and turning them constantly, fry for 7 or 8 minutes, until they are soft and golden brown. Watch carefully for any sign of burning and regulate the heat accordingly.

With a slotted spoon, drain the onions of as much *ghee* as possible and transfer them to the jar of an electric blender. Set the casserole aside. Add the ginger, garlic and yoghurt to the onions, and blend at high speed for 30 seconds. Turn off the machine, scrape down the sides of the jar with a rubber spatula, and blend again for about 30 seconds longer, or until the mixture is reduced to a smooth purée.

Reheat the *ghee* remaining in the casserole, and with a rubber spatula scrape in the contents of the blender jar. Stirring constantly, add the *garam masala*, turmeric, red pepper and 1 teaspoon of salt, and cook over moderate heat for 5 minutes. Stir in the tomato purée and the water and add the *koftas*, turning them about gently with a spoon until they are evenly coated with the sauce. Sprinkle the top with the remaining ¼ cup of fresh coriander, cover the casserole tightly, and cook over moderate heat for 5 minutes to heat the *koftas* through.

To serve, arrange the *koftas* attractively on a heated platter and pour the sauce over them.

SAUCE

½ cup *ghee (page 54)*

3 large onions, peeled, cut in half lengthwise, and sliced lengthwise into paper-thin slivers

¼ cup scraped, coarsely chopped fresh ginger root

2 tablespoons coarsely chopped garlic

1 cup unflavored yoghurt

1 tablespoon *garam masala (page 56)*

1 teaspoon turmeric

⅛ teaspoon ground hot red pepper

1 teaspoon salt

1 cup coarsely chopped fresh or canned tomatoes, rubbed through a sieve or puréed in a food mill

½ cup water

¼ cup finely chopped fresh coriander *(cilantro)*

175

½ teaspoon saffron threads

3 tablespoons boiling water

2 teaspoons salt

2 cups imported *basumati* rice or
other uncooked long-grain white
rice, washed and drained (*see "kesar
chaval,"* page 54)

1 to 1½ cups *ghee* (*page 54*)

2 medium-sized onions, peeled, cut
lengthwise in half, then sliced
lengthwise into paper-thin slivers

¼ cup unsalted cashews (*page 196*)

¼ cup unsalted, slivered, blanched
almonds (*page 196*)

¼ cup unsalted pistachios (*page 196*)

¼ cup seedless raisins

1 tablespoon scraped, finely chopped
fresh ginger root

1 teaspoon finely chopped garlic

1 teaspoon cumin seeds

¼ teaspoon ground hot red pepper

2 pounds lean boneless lamb,
preferably from the leg, cut into
1-inch cubes

A 4-inch piece of stick cinnamon

8 whole cloves

6 whole black peppercorns

The seeds of 4 cardamom pods or
¼ teaspoon cardamom seeds

¼ teaspoon ground mace

¼ teaspoon ground nutmeg,
preferably freshly grated

1½ cups chicken stock, fresh or
canned

½ cup unflavored yoghurt combined
with ½ cup light cream

Shahjahani Biryani
SPICED SAFFRON RICE WITH LAMB

Drop the saffron threads into a small bowl or cup, pour in the 3 tablespoons of boiling water, and soak for 10 minutes.

Bring 3 cups of water and 1 teaspoon of the salt to a boil in a 3- to 4-quart saucepan. Stirring constantly, pour in the rice in a slow thin stream and cook briskly, uncovered, for 10 minutes. Drain the rice in a sieve or colander and set it aside.

In a heavy 4- to 6-quart casserole with a tightly fitting lid, heat ¾ cup of the *ghee* over moderate heat until a drop of water flicked into it splutters instantly. Add the sliced onions and, stirring constantly, fry them for 7 or 8 minutes, or until they are soft and golden brown. Watch for any sign of burning and regulate the heat accordingly. With a slotted spoon, transfer the onions to paper towels to drain.

Add the cashews, almonds, pistachios and raisins to the *ghee* remaining in the casserole and, adding up to 2 tablespoons more *ghee* if necessary, fry the nuts and raisins for about 1 minute, or until they are lightly browned. Then transfer the mixture to a bowl.

Add the ginger, garlic, cumin and red pepper to the *ghee* still in the casserole (again add a little more *ghee* if you need it) and, stirring constantly, cook for a minute or so.

Place the meat in the casserole, add the remaining teaspoon of salt, and stir over high heat until the cubes of meat are lightly browned on all sides. Stirring well after each addition, add the cinnamon, cloves, peppercorns, cardamom seeds, mace, nutmeg, ¾ cup of the stock, and the yoghurt-and-cream mixture. Reduce the heat to low, cover the casserole tightly, and cook for 15 minutes. Then remove the casserole from the heat and let it rest covered for 3 to 5 minutes.

With a slotted spoon transfer the cubes of meat and the cinnamon stick to one bowl, the cooking liquid and its seasonings to another. Wash the casserole and dry it thoroughly.

Preheat the oven to 375°. Pour 2 tablespoons of *ghee* into the casserole and tip it from side to side to coat the bottom evenly. Pour in half the reserved rice, smoothing it evenly with a spatula, and sprinkle a tablespoon or so of the saffron and its soaking water over it. Scatter half the meat on top and place the cinnamon stick in the center.

Stir the remaining ¾ cup of stock into the bowl of the reserved cooking liquid and add a cup or so of the mixture to the casserole, pouring it slowly down the sides. Add all of the remaining rice and, over that, the rest of the lamb cubes. Sprinkle the top with the remaining saffron and its water and pour the last of the cooking liquid into the casserole as before.

Cover the casserole with a sheet of foil, crimping the edges to hold it firmly in place, and place the lid on top. Bake in the middle of the oven for 20 minutes, or until the lamb and rice are tender and most of the liquid in the casserole has been absorbed.

To serve, mound the entire contents of the casserole on a large heated platter and sprinkle with the reserved fried onions, cashews, almonds, pistachios and raisins.

In India, this festive dish would be further garnished with small sheets of edible silver leaf.

Shakootee

LAMB WITH COCONUT MASALA

Preheat the oven to 400°. With a small, sharp knife or swivel-bladed vegetable parer, peel the brown skin off about one fourth of the coconut meat. (Set the rest of the coconut aside.) Slice the peeled coconut into paper-thin slivers each about 1½ inches long.

Spread the slivered coconut evenly in a shallow baking dish or cake pan and, turning the slivers occasionally, toast them in the middle of the oven for about 15 minutes, or until they are golden brown. Then remove the dish from the oven and set the coconut slivers aside.

Meanwhile, make two milks from the remaining coconut meat, following the directions on page 134, using 1 cup of the hot water for the first batch and 2 cups of hot water for the second. Keep the two bowls of coconut milk separate.

To make the *masala*, heat a heavy ungreased 8- to 10-inch skillet over moderate heat for a minute or so, until a drop of water flicked into it splutters instantly. Drop in the cinnamon, coriander, cumin, poppy seeds, cardamom, cloves and red chilies, and stir for 3 minutes, until they are lightly toasted. Add the ginger and garlic, and continue stirring for 7 minutes more, until they are browned.

Add the onions and, stirring and turning them constantly, fry for 7 or 8 minutes, or until they are soft and deeply browned. Watch carefully for any signs of burning and regulate the heat accordingly. Pour in the remaining ½ cup of water and stir until all the ingredients are well blended. Remove the *masala* from the heat and set it aside.

In a heavy 6- to 8-quart casserole, heat the vegetable oil over moderate heat until a light haze forms above it. Add the meat and brown it well on all sides, turning the pieces frequently with a spoon and regulating the heat so that they color richly and evenly without burning. Stir in the salt, reduce the heat to the lowest possible point, and simmer for 10 minutes.

While the lamb is simmering, grind the *masala* in the following fashion: Stir the vinegar, turmeric and ¼ cup of the second coconut milk into the onion-and-spice mixture. Pour the mixture, a cup or so at a time, into the jar of an electric blender and blend at high speed for 30 seconds. Turn off the machine, scrape down the sides of the jar with a rubber spatula, and blend again until the mixture is reduced to a smooth purée. As the *masala* is puréed, pour it into a bowl.

When all of the *masala* has been puréed, add any remaining second coconut milk to the empty jar. Blend for a second, stir it into the bowl of purée, and pour the entire mixture over the lamb.

Stirring constantly, bring the casserole to a boil over high heat. Reduce the heat to low, cover tightly, and simmer for 20 minutes. Stir in the first coconut milk, cover again, and simmer for 5 minutes longer, or until the lamb is tender and shows no resistance when pierced with the point of a small, sharp knife.

Remove the casserole from the heat and let it rest covered for about 30 minutes before serving.

To serve, mound the lamb attractively in a deep heated platter or large bowl, pour the sauce over it, and sprinkle the top evenly with the toasted coconut slivers.

To serve 6 to 8

1 fresh coconut, opened and shelled (*page 134*)

3½ cups hot, not boiling, water

A 2-inch piece of stick cinnamon, wrapped in a kitchen towel and coarsely crushed with a rolling pin

2 tablespoons coriander seeds

2 tablespoons cumin seeds

2 tablespoons white poppy seeds, if available

The seeds of 3 whole cardamom pods, or ¼ teaspoon cardamom seeds

6 whole cloves

2 dried hot red chilies, washed, seeded and coarsely crumbled (*caution: see page 39*)

3 tablespoons scraped, finely chopped fresh ginger root

2 tablespoons finely chopped garlic

3 large onions, peeled, cut lengthwise in half, and sliced lengthwise into paper-thin slivers (about 3 cups)

½ cup vegetable oil

3 pounds lean boneless lamb, preferably from the leg or shoulder, trimmed of excess fat, sliced 2 inches thick and cut into 3-by-2-inch pieces

4 teaspoons salt

3 tablespoons distilled white vinegar

1 teaspoon turmeric

Moghlai Kabab
BROILED SKEWERED GROUND LAMB

Sprinkle the saffron threads into a small ungreased skillet and, shaking the pan constantly, toast them over moderate heat for 30 seconds. Drop the threads into a small bowl and, when they are cool enough to handle, crumble them with your fingertips. Pour in the boiling water and soak for 5 minutes or so.

In a deep mixing bowl, combine the ground lamb, onions, fresh coriander, *besan*, almonds, ginger, lemon juice, yoghurt, cumin, ground coriander, 1 teaspoon of the *garam masala* and the salt. Knead vigorously with both hands or beat with a wooden spoon until the mixture is smooth. Beat in the saffron and its soaking water, and let the mixture rest uncovered at room temperature for about 30 minutes.

Light a layer of coals in a charcoal broiler and let them burn until white ash appears on the surface, or remove the broiler pan from the stove and preheat the broiler to its highest point. Divide the lamb mixture into 16 roughly cylindrical equal portions and string them, one at a time, on 3 or 4 long skewers, further shaping the lamb into smooth sausagelike cylinders about 2 inches long. Arrange the skewers on the grill of the charcoal broiler or on the rack of the broiler pan and broil 3 inches from the heat for 5 minutes. Gently turn the *kababs* over and broil for 5 minutes more. The *moghlai kababs* are done when they are browned evenly and no trace of pink shows when the meat is pierced with the point of a small, sharp knife.

To serve, arrange the *salat* on a large platter and carefully slide the *kababs* off the skewers directly on top of it. Sprinkle the lamb with the remaining ½ teaspoon of *garam masala* and serve the *sas* in a separate bowl.

Sas
CREAM-AND-NUT SAUCE

Place the saffron in a small bowl or cup, pour in the boiling water, and set aside to steep for at least 5 minutes.

Combine the pistachios, almonds, cardamom seeds and milk in the jar of an electric blender and blend at high speed for 30 seconds.

Turn off the machine and scrape down the sides of the jar with a rubber spatula. Then blend again until the nuts and cardamom are completely pulverized and the mixture is reduced to a smooth purée.

In a heavy 1- to 2-quart saucepan, heat the *ghee* over moderate heat until a drop of water flicked into it splutters instantly. Add the puréed nut mixture, ½ cup of the cream and the salt. Stirring constantly, with a spoon, bring to a boil. Add the remaining ½ cup of cream and the dissolved saffron, and continue to stir until the sauce thickens enough to coat the spoon heavily. Remove the pan from the heat, cover tightly, and steep at room temperature for about 20 minutes before serving.

To serve, pour the *sas* into a small bowl or sauceboat.

Sas is traditionally served as an accompaniment to *moghlai kabab (above)* and may also accompany *husaini kabab (Recipe Index)*.

To serve 4

½ teaspoon saffron threads
1 tablespoon boiling water
1 pound lean ground lamb
1 cup very finely chopped onions
¼ cup very finely chopped fresh coriander *(cilantro)*
¼ cup *besan* (chick-pea flour)
¼ cup slivered, blanched unsalted almonds, pulverized in a blender or with a nut grinder
2 tablespoons scraped, very finely chopped fresh ginger root
3 tablespoons fresh lemon juice
2 tablespoons unflavored yoghurt
1 teaspoon ground cumin
1 teaspoon ground coriander
1½ teaspoons *garam masala (page 56)*
2 teaspoons salt
Salat (page 143)
Sas (below)

To make about 2 cups

⅛ teaspoon saffron threads
1 tablespoon boiling water
¼ cup unsalted pistachios
¼ cup slivered, blanched almonds
The seeds of 4 cardamom pods or ¼ teaspoon cardamom seeds
1 cup milk
1 tablespoon *ghee (page 54)*
1 cup light cream
1 teaspoon salt

Kabobs broiled over an outdoor fire are a North Indian specialty. The recipe for *moghlai kabab* appears above. Others are shown opposite with marinades and raw ingredients for some. On the grill at top and the tray at center are kabobs of pork; liver; beef, sausage and kidneys; lamb; and cubed mutton.

Korma
LAMB WITH CASHEW-NUT CURRY

To make the *masala*, combine the cashews, chilies, ginger and 1 cup of cold water in the jar of an electric blender. Blend at high speed for 1 minute, or until the mixture is reduced to a smooth purée. Turn the machine off and scrape down the sides of the jar with a rubber spatula. Add the cinnamon, cardamom, cloves, garlic, poppy seeds, coriander seeds and cumin, and blend again until the mixture is completely pulverized. Set the *masala* aside.

Place the saffron in a small bowl, pour in ¼ cup of boiling water, and let it soak for at least 10 minutes.

Meanwhile, in a heavy 10- to 12-inch skillet, heat the *ghee* over moderate heat until a drop of water flicked into it splutters instantly. Add the onions and, stirring constantly, fry for 7 or 8 minutes, until soft and golden brown. Stir in the salt and the *masala*, then add the yoghurt. Stirring occasionally, cook over moderate heat until the *ghee* lightly films the surface.

Add the lamb, turning it about with a spoon to coat the pieces evenly. Squeeze the saffron between your fingers, then stir it and its soaking liquid into the skillet. Reduce the heat to low, cover tightly, and cook for 20 minutes, turning the lamb cubes over from time to time. Scatter 1 tablespoon of the fresh coriander over the lamb and continue cooking, tightly covered, for 10 minutes more, or until the lamb is tender.

To serve, transfer the entire contents of the skillet to a heated platter, and sprinkle the top with lemon juice and the remaining fresh coriander.

Badami Gosht
LAMB WITH YOGHURT, COCONUT MILK AND ALMOND MASALA

Drop the saffron threads into a small bowl or cup, add 3 tablespoons of boiling water, and soak for 10 minutes. Pour the saffron and its soaking liquid into a deep bowl and stir in the yoghurt, caraway seeds and salt. Add the lamb and turn it about with a spoon until all the pieces are evenly coated. Marinate the lamb at room temperature for about 30 minutes.

Meanwhile, combine the almonds and ½ cup of boiling water in a bowl, and soak them for 10 minutes. Pour the almonds and their soaking water into the jar of a blender and blend at high speed until the almonds are reduced to a smooth purée. Set aside. In a heavy 4- to 5-quart casserole, heat the *ghee* over moderate heat until a drop of water flicked into it splutters instantly. Add the cinnamon, cardamom, and cloves, stir for a minute or so, then add the onions, garlic and ginger. Lifting and turning them constantly, fry for 7 or 8 minutes, until the onions are soft and golden brown.

With a slotted spoon, remove the lamb from the marinade, add the meat to the casserole, and stir over moderate heat until it browns evenly. Stir in the marinade and ½ cup of cold water, then add the almond purée and red pepper and cook for 10 minutes, stirring occasionally. Pour in the coconut milk, bring it to a boil, and simmer partially covered for 20 minutes, or until the lamb is tender.

To serve, discard the cinnamon and cloves, mound the lamb attractively on a deep heated platter, and pour the sauce over it.

To serve 4

MASALA

¼ cup untoasted, unsalted cashews

3 dried hot red chilies, stemmed and seeded (*caution: see page 39*)

A 1-inch piece of fresh ginger root, scraped and quartered

A 2-inch piece of stick cinnamon, wrapped in a kitchen towel and crushed with a rolling pin

¼ teaspoon cardamom seeds

3 whole cloves

2 large garlic cloves, peeled

2 tablespoons white poppy seeds

1 tablespoon coriander seeds

1 teaspoon cumin seeds

LAMB

½ teaspoon saffron threads

6 tablespoons *ghee (page 54)*

1 cup finely chopped onions

2 teaspoons salt

½ cup unflavored yoghurt

1½ pounds lean boneless lamb leg or shoulder, cut into 2-inch cubes

2 tablespoons finely chopped fresh coriander (*cilantro*)

1 tablespoon fresh lemon juice

To serve 4 to 6

1 teaspoon saffron threads

2 cups unflavored yoghurt

2 teaspoons caraway seeds

2 tablespoons salt

2 pounds lean boneless lamb leg or shoulder, cut into 3-inch cubes

½ cup unsalted blanched almonds

½ cup *ghee (page 54)*

A 4-inch piece of stick cinnamon

½ teaspoon cardamom seeds

6 whole cloves

2 cups finely chopped onions

2 teaspoons finely chopped garlic

2 teaspoons scraped, finely chopped fresh ginger root

½ teaspoon ground hot red pepper

3 cups coconut milk made from 1 fresh coconut and 3 cups water (*page 134*)

On the colonnade of the Rambagh Palace Hotel at Jaipur, opposite, half a dozen kinds of *barfi* are arrayed on a plate beside a cut papaya and a bowl of whole fruits. For a version of *barfi*, see the Recipe Index.

Since Pakistan is both part of the great Indian subcontinent and yet separate from India—independent politically, overwhelmingly Muslim in religion, distinctive in many food customs—this chapter has been written by a Pakistani, the TIME-LIFE correspondent in Rawalpindi.   by MOHAMMED AFTAB

Pakistan: Muslims Who Live on Meat

The billboard advertisement for cigarettes on a street in Lahore has not seduced the Pakistani seated below the adjacent movie poster from his ancient hookah. Tobacco is an important cash crop in Pakistan, as is sugar cane. The cane is sometimes sold in bundles, like those shown, to be turned by villagers into *gur,* a fudgelike unrefined sugar.

There is an old saying that "you cannot be a good Muslim unless you eat meat and lots of it," and this is nowhere more true than in Pakistan. When my country was formed as a result of the partition of India in 1947, it was conceived as a Muslim state. India had been a house divided between Hindu majority and Muslim minority. But the clamor of the Muslims in the North for a homeland of their own brought about the separation of Pakistan.

Few Westerners may realize it, but Pakistan with over 125 million people is the fifth largest nation. Its two widely separated areas—West Pakistan and East Pakistan—together comprise a land mass greater than that of any European country except Russia. The bulk of this land (85 per cent) lies in West Pakistan, but nearly 60 per cent of the people live in East Pakistan.

The first Muslims to arrive in Pakistan came sweeping down from the Middle East—notably Arabia—early in the Eighth Century. As wave after wave of these invaders came into the area, they brought their own distinctive foods and flavors. Gradually, a synthesis of Middle Eastern and Central Asian cooking developed a distinctive, internationally recognized cuisine.

West Pakistan, where I live, is a land of snow-capped peaks, deserts, and craggy uplands, where the food is basically meat, fowl and fish. The splendid variety ranges from the golden pheasant of the snowy Himalayas to beef, lamb, goat, chicken, fish, duck, prawns, deer and peacock. There are only a few foods that Muslims do not eat. Pork, which is considered unclean, is the most notable example.

Among the most popular Pakistani dishes are *shami kabab* (curried meatballs), chicken *tikka* (grilled chicken), *shish kabab* (skewered lamb, beef or chicken), and beef *biryani* (cubes of beef cooked with rice and various spices).

Pakistani cooking differs in other crucial respects from the Hindu cooking of India. Indian dishes employ a liberal quantity of spices—and the food is hotter. As a general rule, Pakistani dishes are larger, served on platters that are sometimes as much as three feet long and two feet wide.

As recently as a quarter of a century ago Muslim families in Pakistan used to eat sitting cross-legged on the floor, because they believed that this created an affinity among those who were eating together. The floors usually were covered with carpets, and enormous white or flowered sheets were spread where the serving dishes were to be set. In the countryside and small towns, the custom still prevails. But nowadays a great number of Muslims have moved up to regular dining tables.

With a rich cuisine to draw upon and their own natural heavy-eating habits, most Pakistanis are unwilling to settle for a snack for lunch. Most people demand a full meal—with a lamb, chicken or beef dish as the main course, some rice, at least one curry, and supplementary dishes such as curds, whey, *raytas* and salads. Dinners tend to be heavier than lunches. Again, the main courses are lamb, chicken or beef—grilled, roasted or barbecued meats —*shami kabab*, chicken *tikka*, *shish kabab* or *chapli kabab* (minced-meat cakes). These are often accompanied by chicken *biryani* (chicken with rice) or a mutton *pollau*, as well as a curry, mutton *korma (Recipe Index)*, *pasanday* (strips of curried beef) and *nargesi kofta* (meatballs with whole boiled eggs inside). The dinner will also include *raytas*, yoghurt or curds and a salad. It usually winds up with a *kheer*, milk-rice pudding, or a *halva* such as carrot pudding.

Devout Muslims in Pakistan celebrate four main festivals. The ninth month of the Muslim year, Ramadan, when the Koran was revealed to Muhammad, is observed as a time of fasting. Throughout this month Muslims eat only before sunrise and after sundown, but they are forbidden to eat, drink, smoke, sell perfume, or indulge in sinful thoughts from dawn to sunset.

The Ramadan fast culminates in the festival of Id-ul-Fitr—Feast of Alms —the most joyous of all Muslim festivals. Men, women and children break out in new clothes—on which the womenfolk have worked throughout Ramadan. Early on the morning of Id-ul-Fitr, before going to the mosques for prayer, they enjoy a dish of vermicelli in milk, with sugar, dried fruits and nuts. Later they devour a feast that features *korma* curries made with chicken, lamb or beef, *dals*, *pollaus* and a dessert called *shawi*, made of rice noodles fried in butter and then boiled in milk and sugar.

Next in importance among the Muslim festivals is Id-uz-Zaha, "the feast of the sacrifice." This festival falls two months and 10 days after Id-ul-Fitr and commemorates the story in the Koran (and Bible) of the prophet Ibrahim's (Abraham) offer to sacrifice his son Ishak (Isaac) in the name of God. When Ibrahim was about to sacrifice his son, God sent a ram and told the anguished father to sacrifice the animal instead. On the occasion of Id-uz-Zaha adult Muslim men and women slaughter sacrificial animals—lambs, goats, rams, cows or camels—and send them as presents to relatives or friends. Dozens of fine dishes are prepared on the three days of Id-uz-Zaha—*pollaus*, roasts, barbecues, curries, *raytas*. Another occasion for celebration is Shab e Baraat, the day when God distributes riches to men on earth. The celebration features fireworks displays and feasting, and some of the food is

184

kept overnight in the belief that whoever is affluent enough to have food left over at this time will be affluent through the year that follows.

Still another great Muslim festival celebrated in Pakistan is Muharram, commemorating the martyrdom of the saint Hussain who fell in battle against Yazid—the ruler of Arabia—1,400 years ago. On the day of the saint's martyrdom two special dishes are prepared—a sweet rice with saffron called *zarda,* and a milk-rice pudding called *kheer.* These are distributed to relatives and friends and hundreds of poor people are fed during the day.

East Pakistan, which lies 1,000 miles away from the Western part of the country, provides a striking contrast. It is a lush, green, semitropical coastal land. Jute and rice are the principal crops and, while Muslims predominate, there are many Hindus as well. (East Pakistan formerly was a part of the Indian province of Bengal.) An abundance of seafood—fish, shrimp, prawns, crabs—is what marks the principal difference between the diet of East and West Pakistan. East Pakistanis like to cook their seafood in mustard oil, and they like it hot. First they prepare a *masala,* a red one with hot chilies, or a yellow one with turmeric. Then they coat food with the *masala* and cook it in smoking mustard oil. The East Pakistanis also like highly seasoned curries, and for dessert they eat a sweet called *roshgulla,* which is made out of fresh cheese formed into a walnut-sized round ball. They dip the cheese in sugar syrup and flavor it with rose water to provide a spongy but teasingly sweet contrast to their highly seasoned seafood dishes and curries.

Pakistan is a fledgling nation, handicapped by the wide geographic division between the two sections of the country. But religion, which brought the nation into being, is a strong unifying force, and gradually it is forging Pakistan into a single entity with a cuisine of its own.

A passenger bus winds its solitary way through the Khyber Pass, the major road link between Pakistan and Afghanistan. In bygone centuries the armies of Babur the Moghul, Alexander the Great and Tamerlane swept down through the pass into India. Today the route is principally a trade artery, as trucks from Pakistan bearing salt, vegetables, tea, gasoline and machinery lumber into Afghanistan and return laden with fresh and dried fruits, lambskins and carpets.

Herdsmen from a village near Peshawar, West Pakistan, drive sheep and cattle past *busaras* in which straw forage is stored.

Pakistan: An Underdeveloped, Slowly Emerging Land

Pakistan is largely a nation of farmers engaged in a relentless struggle with the land. Water is the great problem. In West Pakistan there is so little of it that the land is parched and brown, and fields must be irrigated before crops will grow. In East Pakistan the problem is reversed: The land is lush and green, and rainfall is so heavy that fields must be drained of excess water. Farming methods in Pakistan are so antiquated that yields are among the lowest on earth. Farmlands are chopped into tiny inefficient parcels; ox-drawn plows and harrows are used to till the fields; modern fertilizers, pesticides and improved seeds are virtually unknown. Absentee ownership has inhibited initiative, and the absence of modern transportation puts most marketplaces beyond the reach of farmers. Yet in spite of all the handicaps, the country produces a broad range of foods. Sugar cane and wheat are the principal crops in West Pakistan, rice and sugar cane in East Pakistan. The country grows fruits and vegetables of almost every description, and produces sheep, goats, cattle, water buffalo, horses and camels. Moreover, Pakistan is a young nation (born in 1947), and the state—through a series of five-year plans—is making a major effort to modernize the country.

In West Pakistan's bucolic town of Tatta, a Muslim holy man *(left)* and a sheepherder pass the time of day in front of a butcher's shop.

188

In the bustling city of Peshawar, tribesmen from Afghanistan and Central Asia, dressed in native garb, mingle with townsmen. Located near the Khyber Pass, which links Pakistan and Afghanistan, Peshawar (the name means "Frontier Town") is a city of 150,000 that serves as an important trading post for both countries. Its principal wares are brightly colored scarves—worn by Pakistanis as turbans—wood carvings, knives and serving trays like those on display in the bazaar shown here. The trays are made of copper, then dipped in a protective silvery coating called *kaley,* which is a mixture of tin and zinc. Above them hangs a sign that reads "dispensary" (in Urdu); it is the shingle of an herb doctor whose clinic is located in the building here.

A spice and nut shop in the Delhi Gate bazaar in Lahore offers a variety of spices most commonly used in Pakistani cooking. On the table *(from right to left)* are a basket of small chilies, a tray of ground turmeric and two trays of ground chilies. (Between the trays of ground chili is a pan of indigo, used for laundering white clothes.) The bags on the floor hold coriander seeds *(right)* and more small chilies, while the baskets and other containers in the background hold dates and nuts.

Vendors of Food on Pakistan's City Streets

Hot chicken-soup for sale in Peshawar.

A rock salt vendor in a Lahore bazaar.

Carrots ready for munching in Lahore.

Peddling unrefined sugar in Peshawar.

Savoring ribs and bread in Landi Kotal.

A poultry salesman in Tatta.

Omar Bakash, 85, and his grandsons sell walnuts, pine nuts, almonds, pistachios, cashews and dried fruits in their Peshawar shop.

Masaledar Raan
CURRIED BONELESS BEEF ROAST

To serve 6 to 8

¼ cup fresh lemon juice
3 tablespoons coarse salt or 2
 tablespoons table salt
½ teaspoon coarsely ground black
 pepper
¼ teaspoon ground hot red pepper
A 5- to 5½-pound boneless sirloin
 roast about 5½ inches in diameter,
 tied securely at 1-inch intervals
2 tablespoons *ghee (page 54)*

Mix the lemon juice, coarse salt, black pepper and red pepper together. Rub the mixture evenly over the surface of the meat and place it in a large bowl. With a long needlelike skewer, make perforations completely through the meat at ¼-inch intervals all over its surface. Then rub it with the 2 tablespoons of *ghee* and set it aside for 15 or 20 minutes.

Meanwhile, prepare the *masala:* Drop the saffron into a small bowl or cup, pour in the boiling water, and soak for 10 minutes. Combine the onions, yoghurt, pomegranate seeds, garlic, ginger, mustard seeds, cloves, cinnamon, fennel, cardamom, coriander and cumin in the jar of an electric blender. Blend at high speed for 1 minute, turn off the machine, and scrape down the sides of the jar with a rubber spatula. Then blend again until the mixture is reduced to a smooth purée. Stir in the saffron and its soaking water.

With your fingers, rub the *masala* over the surface of the roast, and again

In Peshawar's Salateen Restaurant, below, grilled kabobs highlight a menu that also features lamb curries and roast chicken.

perforate it as before. Cover the bowl with plastic wrap, and let the roast marinate at room temperature for 12 hours, or overnight in the refrigerator.

Preheat the oven to 450°. Place the beef fat side up on a rack in a shallow roasting pan and place it in the middle of the oven. After 15 minutes reduce the heat to 350°. Basting the meat occasionally with the ¼ cup of melted *ghee*, roast the beef until it is well done and reaches a temperature of 170° on a meat thermometer. If you are not using a thermometer, you can be fairly sure of the beef's being well-done—which it should be—if you estimate approximately 30 minutes per pound. Start timing the roast after you reduce the heat to 350°.

Transfer the beef to a platter, carve it into ¼ inch slices and serve at once.

Tithar

CURRIED PARTRIDGES

Wash the cavities and bodies of the birds under cold running water and pat them dry with paper towels. Sprinkle each of the birds inside and out with ½ teaspoon of the salt, and truss the birds securely. Arrange them side by side in a large baking dish and sprinkle the lemon juice over them. Chop the livers, hearts and gizzards fine and set the birds and giblets aside.

Drop the saffron into an ungreased skillet and, shaking the pan constantly, toast them over moderate heat for 1 minute. Transfer the saffron to a small bowl, crumble the threads between your fingers and stir in the cream.

In the same skillet, heat 1 tablespoon of the *ghee* over moderate heat until a drop of water flicked into it splutters instantly. Add the chopped onions, the garlic and black pepper, and stir for a minute or so. Then add the chopped giblets and, stirring constantly, fry for 2 or 3 minutes, until they are lightly browned. Remove the skillet from the heat, stir in the remaining ½ teaspoon of salt and the saffron-and-cream mixture. With a rubber spatula, scrape the mixture into a deep bowl.

Wash and dry the skillet and return it to moderate heat. Add the remaining 4 tablespoons of *ghee,* drop in the slivered onions and, stirring them constantly, fry for 7 or 8 minutes, until soft and golden brown. Watch carefully for any signs of burning and regulate the heat accordingly. With a slotted spoon, transfer the onions to paper towels to drain.

Add the cardamom, cloves and cinnamon to the skillet and, stirring constantly, cook over moderate heat for about 2 minutes, until the *ghee* becomes brown and the cinnamon stick splits. Strain the *ghee* into the giblet-and-cream mixture, and discard the whole spices. Add the yoghurt and stir well.

With a rubber spatula or your hands, rub the giblet-and-yoghurt mixture over the birds. Cover the dish tightly with foil or plastic wrap and marinate the partridges at room temperature for at least 12 hours.

Preheat the oven to 400°. Place the partridges on a rack in a large shallow roasting pan. Spoon the marinade over them and sprinkle with red pepper. Pour 1 cup of the water down the sides of the pan. Roast in the middle of the oven for 20 minutes, add the remaining cup of water to the pan, reduce the heat to 350°, and continue roasting for about 30 minutes longer, basting the birds two or three times with the liquid in the pan. When done, the birds should be golden brown. To serve, arrange the partridges on a heated platter, moisten with the cooking liquid, and sprinkle the fried onions on top.

MASALA

1 tablespoon saffron threads
¼ cup boiling water
¼ cup coarsely chopped onions
¼ cup unflavored yoghurt
1 tablespoon dried pomegranate
    seeds *(page 196)*
1 tablespoon coarsely chopped garlic
1 tablespoon scraped, coarsely
    chopped fresh ginger root
1 tablespoon black mustard seeds
8 whole cloves
A 1-inch piece of stick cinnamon,
    wrapped in a kitchen towel and
    crushed with a rolling pin
1 teaspoon fennel seeds
The seeds of 6 cardamom pods or
    ¼ teaspoon cardamom seeds
½ teaspoon coriander seeds
½ teaspoon cumin seeds
¼ cup *ghee,* melted *(page 54)*

To serve 6

6 twelve-ounce oven-ready young
    partridges, or substitute any other
    12-ounce game birds
3½ teaspoons salt
¼ cup fresh lemon juice
The livers, hearts and gizzards of
    the partridges
½ teaspoon saffron threads
¼ cup light cream
5 tablespoons *ghee (page 54)*
2 tablespoons finely chopped onions
1 teaspoon finely chopped garlic
½ teaspoon coarsely ground black
    pepper
1 large onion, peeled, cut lengthwise
    into halves, and sliced lengthwise
    into paper-thin slivers
The seeds of 6 cardamom pods or
    ½ teaspoon cardamom seeds
8 whole cloves
A 3-inch piece of stick cinnamon
⅓ cup unflavored yoghurt
½ teaspoon ground hot red pepper
2 cups water

To serve 6

½ teaspoon saffron threads
2 tablespoons plus 2 cups boiling
    water
2 cups imported *basumati* rice or
    other uncooked long-grain white
    rice
½ cup melted *ghee* (*page 54*)
4 whole cloves
A 1-inch piece of stick cinnamon
2 medium-sized boiling potatoes
    (about ½ pound), peeled and cut
    into ½-inch cubes
2 tablespoons coarsely cut fresh mint
    leaves
2 tablespoons scraped, finely
    chopped fresh ginger root
½ cup unflavored yoghurt
1 teaspoon salt
¼ cup finely chopped fresh coriander
    (*cilantro*)
2 tablespoons finely chopped onions

To serve 6 to 8

MEATBALLS
26 whole blanched almonds
1 teaspoon saffron threads
1 tablespoon boiling water
2 pounds lean boneless beef, ground
    twice
1 egg
⅓ cup plus 2 tablespoons *besan*
    (chick-pea flour)
1 cup finely chopped onions
¼ cup finely chopped fresh coriander
    (*cilantro*)
2 tablespoons scraped, finely
    chopped fresh ginger root
2 tablespoons *garam masala* (*page
    56*)
¼ teaspoon ground hot red pepper
2 teaspoons salt
3 tablespoons cold water
Vegetable oil for deep frying

Hari Chatni Pollau
RICE WITH POTATOES, CORIANDER AND MINT

Place the saffron and 2 tablespoons of the boiling water in a bowl, and soak for 10 minutes. Meanwhile, combine the rice and 3 cups of cold water in a saucepan and bring to a boil over high heat. Stirring often, boil briskly, uncovered, for 5 minutes. Drain the rice in a sieve and set aside.

In a heavy 4-quart casserole, heat 4 tablespoons of the *ghee* over moderate heat until a drop of water flicked into it splutters instantly. Add the cloves and cinnamon and stir for 30 seconds, then add the potatoes and, turning them constantly, fry for 5 to 6 minutes, or until they are golden brown.

Remove the casserole from the heat and sprinkle the potatoes with the mint and 1 tablespoon of the ginger. Spread half the rice on top, smoothing it flat. Combine the yoghurt and salt with the saffron and its soaking liquid, and pour half of it over the rice. Sprinkle the yoghurt-covered rice with the remaining 1 tablespoon of ginger, the coriander and onions, then spread the rest of the rice over the top and pour in the remaining yoghurt mixture.

Carefully and slowly pour the rest of the melted *ghee* and the remaining 2 cups of boiling water down the sides of the casserole. Bring to a boil, cover tightly, and cook over high heat for 15 minutes, or until the rice is tender and has absorbed all the liquid in the casserole.

To unmold and serve the rice, run a long, sharp knife around the inside edges of the casserole. Place a heated serving plate upside down over the casserole and, grasping plate and casserole firmly together, invert them. Rap the plate on a table and the rice should slide out easily. Serve immediately.

Kofta Kari
GROUND BEEF MEATBALLS STUFFED WITH ALMONDS

Place the almonds in a bowl or pan, add enough cold water to cover them by 1 inch, and soak them for at least 4 hours.

Prepare the meatballs in the following fashion: Drop the saffron into a small bowl, pour in 1 tablespoon of boiling water, and soak for 10 minutes. Meanwhile, in a deep bowl, combine the beef, egg, ⅓ cup of chick-pea flour, onions, ¼ cup of fresh coriander, the ginger, *garam masala*, red pepper and 2 teaspoons of salt. Knead the mixture vigorously with your hands, then put it through the finest blade of a meat grinder twice. Pour the saffron and its soaking liquid over the meat and stir together thoroughly.

(If you do not have a meat grinder, ask your butcher to grind the beef two or even three times. Combine the onions, ¼ cup of fresh coriander and ginger and, with a large, sharp knife, chop them into the tiniest possible pieces. Place the beef, the onion, coriander and ginger mixture, the egg, ⅓ cup of chick-pea flour, *garam masala*, red pepper and 2 teaspoons of salt in a deep bowl. Knead vigorously with both hands, then beat with a large spoon until the mixture is smooth. Beat in the saffron and its soaking liquid.)

Shape the *koftas*, or meatballs, in the following fashion: Divide the mixture into 26 portions and pat each one into a slightly flattened round. Drain the almonds and place one in the center of each round. Shape the beef around the nut into a ball, enclosing the almond completely.

Make a thick, smooth batter with the remaining 2 tablespoons of *besan* and the 3 tablespoons of cold water. With your fingers or a pastry brush,

194

spread the batter evenly on all sides of each *kofta*. Arrange the meatballs side by side on a sheet of wax paper.

Pour 2 cups of vegetable oil into a 10-inch *karhai* or 12-inch *wok (page 151)*, or pour 2 to 3 inches of oil into a deep fryer. Heat the oil until it reaches a temperature of 350° on a deep-frying thermometer. In batches of 7 or 8, deep-fry the *koftas* in the oil, turning them about with a slotted spoon for about 3 to 4 minutes, or until they are richly browned on all sides. As they brown, transfer them to paper towels to drain.

In a heavy 10- to 12-inch skillet, heat the *ghee* over moderate heat until a drop of water flicked into it splutters instantly. Add the onions and garlic and, stirring constantly, fry for 7 or 8 minutes, until they are golden brown.

Add the turmeric and ¼ cup cold water, and stir for 2 minutes. Add the tomatoes and cumin, and continue stirring for 5 minutes, then add the yoghurt, salt and remaining ½ cup of cold water. Bring to a boil over high heat and drop the *koftas* into the simmering curry sauce. Sprinkle the top with coriander, cover tightly, and reduce the heat to low. Simmer for 8 to 10 minutes, or until the *koftas* are tender and have absorbed the flavors of the sauce. Serve the *koftas* in a serving dish with the sauce poured over them.

CURRY SAUCE
¼ cup *ghee (page 54)*
1 cup finely chopped onions
1 tablespoon finely chopped garlic
1 teaspoon turmeric
¾ cup cold water
1 cup finely chopped fresh tomatoes
1 teaspoon ground cumin
½ cup yoghurt
1 teaspoon salt
¼ cup finely chopped fresh coriander
  (*cilantro*)

Shahitukra

FRIED BREAD AND NUT DESSERT

To serve 6 to 8

Place the saffron in a small bowl, pour in the boiling water and 3 tablespoons of the cream, and soak for 10 minutes. Meanwhile, with a large serrated knife, remove the crusts from the bread, cutting deep enough to level the top of the loaf if it is mounded. Cut the loaf crosswise into 9 slices, each about ¾ inch thick, and divide each slice crosswise into 2 rectangles.

Drop the almonds and pistachios into a heavy ungreased skillet. Shaking the pan frequently, toast the nuts over low heat for 5 minutes, or until they brown lightly. Transfer the nuts to a plate and set aside. In the same skillet, heat 3 tablespoons of the *ghee* over moderate heat until a drop of water flicked into it splutters instantly. Two or three batches at a time, fry the bread for about 4 minutes, turning the pieces with a spatula and regulating the heat so that they brown evenly on both sides without burning. (Add more *ghee* as necessary.) When brown, transfer the bread to a plate.

Combine the cold water and sugar in a heavy 2-quart saucepan and bring to a boil over moderate heat, stirring until the sugar dissolves. Increase the heat to high and, timing from the moment the mixture comes to a full boil, cook uncovered and undisturbed for 5 minutes, or until the syrup reaches a temperature of 220° on a candy thermometer. Remove the pan from the heat and dip one piece of bread at a time into the syrup for 30 seconds. Arrange half the bread pieces side by side in a single layer in a shallow baking dish about 8 inches square. Reserve the rest of the bread on a plate.

Pour the remaining heavy cream and the milk into the syrup and, stirring constantly, cook over moderate heat for about 3 minutes. Then stir in the saffron and its soaking liquid, and remove the pan from the heat.

Sprinkle half the nuts over the bread in the serving dish and spoon half of the cream and syrup mixture over them. Arrange the reserved pieces of bread side by side on top, sprinkle with nuts and pour in the remaining cream mixture. Refrigerate for 1 hour, or until chilled, before serving.

1 teaspoon saffron threads
1 tablespoon boiling water
1 cup heavy cream
1 loaf unsliced homemade-type white
  bread, about 8 by 4 by 4 inches
½ cup unsalted, slivered, blanched
  almonds
½ cup unsalted pistachios
3 to 6 tablespoons *ghee (page 54)*
2 cups cold water
1 cup sugar
½ cup milk
1 tablespoon rose water

A Guide to Ingredients in Indian Cooking

Most of the ingredients called for in this book's recipes can be found at any grocery store or supermarket. Even the spices are included in the rack of a well-stocked market, although not all of them are widely used by American cooks. When a recipe calls for a whole spice, you may substitute the ground form, using exactly the measurement called for. The flavor of ground spices, however, is less pungent than that of whole spices pulverized at home for immediate use.

In a few cases, the recipes in this book include ingredients available only in Indian or other specialty food stores, such as those in the listing opposite. Some of these ingredients can be approximated by more familiar ones—but substitutes may change the character of a dish. If an ingredient is not available, the best course often is to omit it from the recipe.

ASAFETIDA: Dried gum resin from the roots of various Iranian and East Indian plants. Depending on the variety of plant, it may be reddish brown or pale buff. It has a strong fetid odor and somewhat garlicky flavor; it is definitely an acquired taste and may be omitted from any recipe that calls for it.

BESAN: Flour made by grinding dried chick-peas.

CARDAMOM, POD: Dried fruit of a plant of the ginger family. The pod is about the size of a large pea and may be buff colored if it was bleached; green if dried in an oven; or brown if dried in the sun. Most cardamom pods available in the U.S. are of the bleached variety, but Indian cooks prefer green cardamom. The outer pod itself is not used in cooking but is broken away from the seeds inside and discarded.

CARDAMOM SEED: Small aromatic black seed found in the cardamom pod. (Each pod contains from 15 to 20 seeds.) The pungent, somewhat lemon-like flavor is most pronounced in the seed of the green cardamom. Available in the pod, decorticated (with pod removed), and ground. The seeds of four

whole pods measure approximately ¼ teaspoon.

CHICK-PEAS: *See* Dal, chana.

CINNAMON STICK: Dried reddish-brown bark peeled from a tree of the evergreen family, and rolled into long slender "quills" or "sticks." Available usually in 4-inch lengths, stick cinnamon has a more pronounced and aromatic flavor than ground cinnamon.

COCONUT MILK: Liquid produced by grinding fresh coconut meat and hot water together, then squeezing the pulp or meat completely dry. In India, this process is often repeated with additional water to produce a second coconut milk. The term coconut milk is sometimes applied to the natural liquid inside the fresh nut, but this liquid is not used in Indian cooking.

CORIANDER, FRESH: Aromatic herb of the parsley family. It resembles flat-leaf parsley in appearance, but has a much more pungent flavor. It is sold by the bunch in Latin American stores *(as cilantro)* and Chinese markets (as Chinese parsley). Do not wash the leaves or remove the roots before storing; it will keep for about a week if refrigerated in a plastic bag or damp paper towel. If necessary, refresh before using by soaking it for 5 minutes in cold water.

CORIANDER SEED: White to yellowish-brown round ridged seed of the herb coriander, slightly smaller than a peppercorn. To some it suggests the taste of lemon peel and sage, to others a mixture of caraway and cumin. Available whole or ground.

CUMIN SEED: Yellowish-brown seed of a plant of the parsley family. Shaped like a miniature kernel of corn, it is strongly aromatic and reminiscent of caraway. Available whole or ground.

DAL: The Hindi name for all members of the legume, or pulse, family. In India they are available both as fresh vegetables and as dried beans, peas or lentils. In the United States, some are available in cans.

ARHAR DAL: Small, pale yellow pea-like pulse, somewhat resembling the common split pea. Also called *tur dal* or *toovar dal*. Its English name is pigeon pea; it can be found in many supermarkets and in Latin American stores. Available dried.

CHANA DAL: Round dried pea, ranging in color from pale buff to dark brown, and in diameter from about ¼ to ½ inch. Its English name is chick-pea; its Spanish name is *garbanzo*. Available dried or canned.

MASUR DAL: Small, flat salmon-colored lentil with a brown seed coat. Botanists disagree on whether or not it is the same species as the common European lentil, but the common lentil may certainly be substituted for it. Available dried.

MUNG DAL: Small yellow bean with a moss-green seed coat. Its English name is mung bean and it is available dried in Oriental markets.

LOMBIA DAL: Black-eyed peas.

RAJMA DAL: Red kidney beans. Available dried or canned.

URAD DAL: Small (¼-inch-long) bean with a grayish-black seed coat. The kernel is yellow. It is not the same species as the common American black bean, which should not be substituted for the Indian bean. Available dried, split and hulled.

FENNEL SEED: Yellowish-brown seed of a plant of the parsley family. Shaped like a miniature watermelon, it has an agreeable odor and a licorice flavor. Available whole and, in Oriental stores, ground.

FENUGREEK SEED: Very small reddish-brown seed of a plant of the pea family, it has a pleasant bitter flavor and a strong, sweetish odor reminiscent of burnt sugar. Available whole.

GARAM MASALA: Blend of dried spices combined and ground together in the home for use as a seasoning.

GHEE: Butter oil made by cooking

butter over low heat for a long period of time to clarify it and enrich its flavor. Simple clarified butter is not exactly the same thing but may be substituted for *ghee* if necessary.

GINGER ROOT, FRESH: Gnarled brown root about 3 inches long, with a more pungent flavor than dried ginger. Wrapped in a plastic bag and refrigerated, the fresh root will keep for two or three weeks.

JAGGERY, or GUR: Crude type of raw sugar made from the juice of the sugar cane or, occasionally, from the juice of certain types of palm trees. The juice is purified and boiled to produce sugar crystals lightly coated with molasses. Keep indefinitely in a tightly covered jar. If jaggery is not available, you can make a substitute by combining 1 cup of dark-brown sugar with 1 tablespoon of dark molasses.

MASALA: Spices and other seasonings ground together to provide the base for an Indian sauce. To produce a wet masala, liquid is added during the grinding process.

MUSTARD OIL: Pungent colorless or pale-yellow oil made from black mustard seeds.

MUSTARD SEED, BLACK: Tiny reddish brown to black seed of a variety of the mustard plant, smaller than the common yellow mustard seed and much less pungent in flavor.

NUTS: Most of the nuts used in Indian cooking are familiar varieties like the almond or peanut. The somewhat less well known pistachio and cashew are described below.

In the event that you cannot find the proper unsalted, blanched or toasted form of nut called for in a recipe, you can process nuts in your own kitchen in the following fashion:

To remove salt, rinse the nuts quickly under running water and immediately pat them dry with paper towels. If they still seem moist, place them in an ungreased skillet and, shaking the pan constantly, cook over low heat for minute or two.

To blanch nuts, drop them into pan of rapidly boiling water and et them cook briskly for 2 minutes. Drain at once and peel them with small, sharp knife while they are till hot. To toast nuts, spread them at in a shallow baking pan and, urning the nuts occasionally, bake hem in a preheated 350° oven for to 10 minutes, until they are ightly browned.

CASHEW: Plump kidney-shaped nut native to Brazil and the West Indies, first introduced into India in the 16th Century by early Portuguese explorers. It grows at the base of a pear-shaped fruit called a cashew apple, which is borne in clusters on the low-growing cashew tree.

PISTACHIO: Olive-shaped nut about 1/2 inch long, native to the Orient and the Mediterranean. The inner kernel is green and delicately flavored; the easily split outer shell is naturally tan but frequently dyed red with vegetable coloring or turned white with a heavy coating of salt.

PHOA: Rice that has been pounded into ragged-edged translucent flakes. Deep-fried, *phoa* is eaten as a snack.

POMEGRANATE: Thick-skinned reddish-brown fruit about the size and shape of an orange, the fruit of a tropical Asian and African tree. The outer rind is not edible, but the crimson pulpy seeds inside have an agreeable acid flavor and are eaten fresh or are dried for future use.

POPPY SEED, WHITE: Tiny white seed with a sweet, nutlike taste, from a plant of the poppy family. It is about the size of the familiar blue-black poppy seed, but does not have a similar flavor, so the two kinds of seeds may not be used interchangeably.

RICE, BASUMATI: Long-grain white rice of high quality grown in various parts of India and distinguished by its faintly nutlike flavor and aroma.

RICE FLOUR: Finely ground rice. When made from regular milled or polished grains, the flour is white; when made from brown rice with its outer bran still intact, it has a creamy color.

ROSE WATER: Liquid flavoring distilled from fresh rose petals. Available in pharmacies as well as Oriental specialty stores.

SAFFRON THREADS: Orange-red dried stigmas of a flower of the crocus family. Though chiefly used in cooking to color food a golden yellow, saffron threads also contribute a mildly bitter flavor. Powdered saffron, where available, may be substituted, but in this case use only half the quantity called for in the recipe.

TAMARIND: Edible brown pulp of the seed pod of a tree cultivated throughout the tropical world. The pod is brittle, cinnamon colored and shaped somewhat like a garden pea pod, but 3 to 8 inches long. The pulp is valued for its somewhat acid sweet taste; it is sun-dried or preserved in syrup. The dried variety is the only kind suitable for cooking.

TURMERIC: Pungent spice of the ginger family, used like saffron to color food a golden yellow. Available ground.

Mail-Order Sources

The following stores, grouped by region, accept mail orders for ingredients for Indian cooking. All carry canned and dried ingredients; a few will ship fresh ones. Because policies differ and managements change, check with the store nearest you to determine what it has in stock, the current prices, and how best to buy the items you are interested in. Some stores require a minimum amount on mail orders, ranging from $2.50 to $25.

East
Cambridge Coffee, Tea and Spice House
1765 Massachusetts Ave.
Cambridge, Mass. 02138

Cardullo's Gourmet Shop
6 Brattle St.
Cambridge, Mass. 02138

Sage's Market
60 Church St.
Cambridge, Mass. 02138

S. S. Pierce
133 Brookline Ave.
Boston, Mass. 02215

George Malko
185 Atlantic Ave.
Brooklyn, N.Y. 11201

Sahadi Importing Co., Inc.
187 Atlantic Ave.
Brooklyn, N.Y. 11201

Kalustyan Orient Export Trading Corp.
123 Lexington Ave.
New York, N.Y. 10016

Midwest
Delmar & Co.
501 Monroe Ave.
Detroit, Mich. 48226

Gabriel Importing Co.
2461 Russell St.
Detroit, Mich. 48207

Antone's
2606 Sheridan
Tulsa, Okla. 74129

South
Central Grocery
923 Decatur
New Orleans, La. 70116

Progress Grocery
915 Decatur
New Orleans, La. 70116

West
American Tea, Coffee & Spice Company
1511 Champa St.
Denver, Colo. 80202

Antone's
Box 3352
Houston, Texas 77001

Jamail's
3114 Kirby Drive
Houston, Texas 77006

Samperi's
430 Almeda Mall
430 Northwest Mall
Houston, Texas 77017

Bezjian Grocery
4725 Santa Monica Blvd.
Los Angeles, Calif. 90029

Curl's Fancy Grocery
Stall 430, Farmer's Market
Third and Fairfax
Los Angeles, Calif. 90036

Haig's
441 Clement St.
San Francisco, Calif. 94118

DeLaurenti's Italian Delicatessen
Stall 5, Lower Pike Place Market
Seattle, Wash. 98101

House of Rice
4112 University Way N.E.
Seattle, Wash. 98105

Canada
The Bay—Food Dept.
8th Ave. and 1st S.W.
Calgary 2, Alberta

Woodwards Dept. Store
Specialty Food Floor
Chinook Shopping Center
Calgary 9, Alberta

S. Enkin Incorporated
1201 St. Lawrence
Montreal 129, Quebec

Top Banana, Ltd.
62 William St.
Ottawa 2, Ontario

The T. Eaton Company
Attn.: Specialty Foods Dept.
190 Yonge St.
Toronto 1, Ontario

Glossary

AAB GHOSH: Lamb boiled in milk, a Muslim dish.

ACHAR: Brine pickles.

ALU: Potato.

ANVLAS: Tart, gooseberrylike fruit.

APPAM: Deep-fried pancake, made of rice and lentil flour. Known as *hopper* in South India.

AVIYAL: Vegetable curry.

BALUSHAHI: Crisp, sweet pastry deep-fried in *ghee,* then dipped in sugar syrup.

BARFI: Candylike sweets made from milk that has been cooked slowly over low heat until it is reduced to a fudgelike consistency and then flavored (and sometimes tinted) with the addition of coconut, cocoa, rose water, or any of various kinds of nuts.

BHELPURI: Snack of various savories and chutneys served on a *puri.*

BHUJIYA: Slices of various kinds of vegetables dipped in a batter made with chick-pea flour, and deep-fried. Traditionally eaten as snacks.

BIRYANI: Elaborate dish made from spiced saffron rice cooked with pieces of lamb, chicken or beef, or with shrimp.

BONDAS: Deep-fried snack made from boiled potatoes or chick-pea flour mixed with spices.

CHAPATI: Pancakelike whole-wheat bread fried on a *tava* or other iron griddle.

CHAT: Salty snacks.

CHATNI, CHUTNEY: Highly seasoned side dish made from raw, cooked or pickled fruits or vegetables, and traditionally served as an accompaniment to any curried food.

CHENA: Cottage-cheese-like curd preparation.

CHIURA: Savory dry snack composed of deep-fried chick-pea-flour noodles, nuts and spices.

CHULA: Stove made of baked mud.

DAHI: Yoghurt.

DAM: Method of steaming foods in a tightly covered or sealed pot.

DEGCHI: Indian saucepan, usually made without a handle.

DHERA DUN: Special variety of rice, grown in Dhera Dun in Central India.

DO PYAZA: Literally, cooked with onions; the term is used for a variety of dishes in which onions are featured.

DOSA: Highly seasoned pancakelike bread made from pulverized rice and lentils.

FALSA: Punchlike mixture of several kinds of fruit juice with spices.

GOSHTABA: Lamb and curd meatballs.

HALVA: Puddinglike sweet always made from milk, but flavored with any of several vegetables and fruits such as carrots or pumpkin.

IDLI: Flattened cupcake-shaped bread made from ground lentils and rice and steamed in small saucers.

JALEBI: Pretzellike rings of deep-fried batter, lightly coated with sugar syrup.

JHINGA: Large shrimp or prawns.

KABABS: Small pieces of meat, poultry, seafood, vegetables or fruit strung on a skewer and broiled, often over an open fire.

KARANJIA: Pastries filled with grated coconut and sugar.

KARCHI: Long-handled iron ladle.

KARHAI: Shallow bowllike pan for frying food; it somewhat resembles a Chinese *wok.*

KARI: Tamil word for seasoned sauce, and the source of the English word curry.

KARI LEAVES: Pungent leaves similar in flavoring to bay leaves.

KATORI: Small individual serving bowl.

KHIR: Chilled dessert pudding made of milk and Cream of Rice.

KOFTA: Ground-meat balls.

KOKUM: Acid fruit of reddish color, found in South India.

KORMA: Curry sauce thickened with yoghurt and nuts or poppy seeds.

LADDU: Literally, "sweet."

LASSI: Drink made from yoghurt diluted with water, and seasoned with sugar, spices or herbs.

LOTA: Clay water jug.

MAKTI: Malayalam (Malabar Coast) word for fresh sardine.

MASALA: Spices, herbs and other seasonings ground or pounded together and used as the base for all Indian curry sauces. When yoghurt, coconut milk or other liquids are added, the preparation is called a "wet" *masala.*

MATTAR: Fresh green peas.

MAWA: Milk that is reduced and thickened to the consistency of a soft cream cheese, by being cooked slowly over low heat.

METHI: Fenugreek greens.

MODAK: Cone-shaped dumpling made from rice flour.

MULI: Large, mild horseradish.

MURG: Chicken.

MURUKKU: Crisp and salty pretzellike deep-fried savory.

NAAN: Individual flat bread made of white flour, shaped somewhat like a large teardrop or leaf, and traditionally baked on the inner wall of a *tandoor.*

PAAN: Digestive preparation that Indians chew after meals. It contains betel nuts, spices and lime paste—and sometimes includes tobacco.

PAKORA: Deep-fried savory made from any of various kinds of vegetables, such as eggplant or cauliflower.

PANIPURI: Deep-fried *puri* filled with tamarind.

PANNIR: Cottage-cheese-like preparation of curds.

PAPPADAM: Very light, puffed, crisp bread made from lentil flour.

PARATHA: Pancakelike flat bread made from a batter of unleavened whole-wheat flour and fried on a griddle. *Alu paratha* is a similar bread with spiced potato filling. *Gobi paratha* is filled with spiced cauliflower.

PAYASAM: Semiliquid sweet rice dessert.

PONGAL: Sweet rice dish served during the Pongal festival.

PULAU: Rice cooked with spices, and meat, poultry, seafood, vegetables, dried beans or lentils, or eggs. Called *pollau* in Pakistan.

RAYTA: Saladlike combination of yoghurt and various types of raw or cooked vegetables, flavored with herbs and spices.

ROSHGULLA: Cottage cheese balls cooked in syrup flavored with rose water.

ROTI: Bread. *Tandoori roti* is bread baked in a *tandoor. Rumali roti,* or handkerchief bread, is a kind of *paratha* composed of many layers like a folded handkerchief. Others are *chapatis, puris* and *naan (Recipe Index).*

SAMOSA: Deep-fried pastries filled with mixtures of meats or vegetables.

SAIVE: Savory snack made from vermicelli. Sometimes made with sugar as a sweet snack.

SHAKAR-PARAS: Bits of pastry glazed with syrup.

SHARBAT: Chilled fruit mixture, sometimes liquid enough to be drunk, but sometimes thick enough to be eaten with a spoon. It is the forerunner of the familiar frozen sherbet.

SHIRMAL: North Indian bread.

SONDESH: Creamy candy made from cottage cheese kneaded with sugar and other flavorings.

TANDOOR: Cylindrical clay oven.

TAVA: Heavy iron griddle with a concave surface used for frying.

THALI: Individual serving plate or tray.

TIKKA KABAB, TIKKA MURG: Boned or ground chicken pieces rubbed or mixed with *masala* and then grilled.

UPPAMA: Farina or Cream of Wheat cooked with vegetables.

How to Use Indian Recipes

hanks to the English colonizers and to the American clipper ships of the 19th Century, the curries and chutneys of India are popular throughout the Western world, and to many people the Indian cuisine has a familiar and appetizing ring.

The recipes in this book, of course, go far beyond the rudiments of a simple curry. There are roasted and grilled meats, deep-fried pastries, interesting vegetable concoctions and desserts of all kinds. The basic Indian blendings of spices are neither odd-tasting nor fiercely hot, and the finished dishes lend themselves easily to both Western and traditional menus.

As you will discover, Indian food is made to order for entertaining. The savory fried *chiura* and *bhelpuris* (Recipe Index) are attractive cocktail snacks. The spectacular *shahjahani biryani* of lamb and rice or the *tandoori* chickens presented on a platter of *salat* are elegant *pièces de résistance* for a dinner party. Furthermore, curries improve with age so that you can cook them hours before guests arrive and simply reheat them at dinnertime.

The simplest way to begin to fit Indian food into your menus is to stick with the familiar Western-style organization of courses. As a starter you can try one or two Indian recipes at a time and merely substitute them for equivalent Western ones. Then, more ambitiously, you may compose a whole meal of Indian dishes.

You might start an all-Indian dinner with some kind of *samosa* or *pakora*; or a selection of several if you have time to make them. Then use one of the curried meat, poultry or seafood dishes as your main course, accompanied by a simple rice and a fresh chutney. Try an Indian *salat* or let one of the *raytas* serve as salad. For dessert, experiment with an Indian sweet. Or, more simply, present your guests with fresh fruit—mangoes, papayas or bananas would all be appropriate.

The numbers of servings to expect from the recipes in this book are based on Western practice. Even the service described—on platters or from large bowls—is designed for Western dining.

On some occasions you may wish to serve Indian food in the country's own style. In India, meals are not formally divided into courses. Instead, everything—even the dessert—is brought to the table at the same time.

An Indian hostess serves her guests small portions of many kinds of food rather than large portions of just a few kinds. A menu composed of half a dozen or more different dishes is not unusual. This means preparing many separate foods, but the number of guests a recipe can serve will increase as your menu becomes more elaborate.

Food is ladled out into individual bowls or carved into bite-sized pieces in the Indian kitchen. Each guest's portion is then arranged on a separate tray or *thali*, and brought to the table ready to eat. Indians pick up food with their fingers or small pieces of bread. Your guests may be more at ease using a spoon and fork; place these to the left of the tray in front of the water glass. Finger bowls, though not traditional, would be useful after the trays are cleared away—especially for guests who have chosen to eat with their fingers.

Because of India's great diversity of religious and regional traditions, authentic menus vary enormously. The menus on this page suggest some appropriate combinations of foods.

Vegetarian Menus

South India:
Chaval: plain boiled rice garnished with fresh whole green chilies
Sambar: dal with vegetables
Baingan pakora: deep-fried eggplant
Sabzi bhindi: dry okra, curried
Alu ka rayta: yoghurt with potatoes
Imli chatni: tamarind chutney
Chapatis: whole-wheat bread

North and South India:
Nimbu ka chaval: lime rice
Mung ki dal: yellow dal
Tamatar salat: tomato, onion and beetroot salad
Khumbi bhaji: mushrooms and peas
Dahi vada: lentil cakes in yoghurt
Dhanya chatni: coriander chutney
Firni: Cream of Rice with rose water

North India:
Sabzi ka chaval: rice and vegetable pilaf
Gobhi ki sabzi: curried cauliflower
Baingan ka rayta: yoghurt with eggplant
Dam alu: hot curried potatoes
Rajma: red kidney beans
Phulka: whole-wheat puffed bread
Pudine chatni: mint chutney
Khir: milk and rice and cardamom dessert
Lassi: yoghurt drink

Punjab:
Kesar chaval: saffron rice
Mattar pannir: peas and cheese
Bharta: curried eggplant
Manh ki dal: black lentils
Pakora ka rayta: yoghurt with *pakoras*
Puris: whole-wheat fried bread
Simla mirch: stuffed green peppers
Adrak chatni: ginger chutney
Gajar halva: carrot pudding

Nonvegetarian Menus

Parsi and Coastal:
Machli ki tikka: sole with dill
Jhinga patia: shrimp curry
Bhuna chaval: brown rice
Dhansak: lamb with vegetables
Same ki bhaji: green beans
Tamatar chatni: tomato chutney
Parathas: layered whole-wheat bread
Jalebis: pretzellike sweets

Goan and Coastal:
Jhinga kari: shrimp curry
Machli ki tikka: fish fillets with dill *masala*
Chaval: plain boiled rice
Sorpotel: pickled pork and liver
Cachumbar: salad of tomatoes, onions, lemon and ginger
Corom chatni: mango chutney
Beebeek: layered custard cake

North India Buffet Banquet:
Raan: roast lamb
Korma: lamb curry
Kesar chaval: saffron rice
Murg masalam: spiced chicken
Husaini kabab: skewered lamb
Simla mirch: stuffed green peppers
Naan: oven-baked white bread
Puris: whole-wheat fried bread
Baingan ka tikka: stuffed baby eggplant
Pudine chatni: mint chutney
Pudine rayta: yoghurt with mint
Tali machli: fried sole
Gulab jaman: sweets of milk

North India:
Kheema biryani: minced lamb rice
Murg ilaychi: chicken with cardamom
Machli aur tamatar: halibut with tomatoes

Alu mattar: peas and potato curry
Parathas: layered whole-wheat bread
Kheera ka rayta: yoghurt with cucumber

Bengal:
Nariyal ka chaval: coconut rice
Murgi kari: chicken curry
Sag: broccoli and spinach
Puris: whole-wheat fried bread
Nariyal chatni: coconut chutney
Roshgulla: cheese dessert

North India:
Shahjahani biryani: lamb, rice, nuts, raisins
Nimbu chatni: lemon and date chutney
Kela ka rayta: yoghurt with banana and coconut
Pakki hui machli: baked fish with tomato and chili *masala*
Parathas: layered whole-wheat bread
Khir: milk and rice cardamom dessert

Konkan Coast:
Chaval: boiled rice
Shakootee: lamb curry
Am ki chatni: mango chutney
Jhinga tikka: shrimp cutlets
Chapatis: whole-wheat puffed bread
Alebele: coconut and jaggery pancake

Punjab:
Kaleja kari: curried calf's liver
Chana ki dal: chick-peas
Parathas: whole-wheat layered bread
Kheera ka rayta: yoghurt with cucumber and tomato
Gobhi ki sabzi: curried cauliflower
Pudine chatni: mint chutney
Firni: Cream of Rice with rose water

Recipe Index: English

Recipe Index: Hindi

General Index
Numerals in italics indicate a photograph or drawing of the subject mentioned.

Credits and Acknowledgments

The sources for the illustrations in this book are shown
below. Credits for the pictures from left to right are
separated by commas, from top to bottom by dashes.

All photographs are by Eliot Elisofon except: 4—Top
left Allan Grant—bottom Jehangir Gazdar, Dan Coggin.
13—Map by Mary Sherman. 14—Fotiades. 25—Roloff
Beny. 36—Anthony Linck courtesy Département des
Manuscrits, Bibliothèque Nationale, Paris. 74,75
—Fotiades. 90—N. Ramakrishna. 94,95—M. A.
Chandrakant-Cirrus. 103—Panna Jain-Cirrus. 104
—Drawing from *Hindu Pantheon* by E. Moor from P.
Thomas' *Hindu Religion, Customs and Manners* published
by D. B. Taraporevala Sons and Co., Ltd., Bombay. 106
—Dean K. Brown. 107—Vishnu Panjabi. 112—Brian
Brake from Rapho Guillumette. 146—Raghubir Singh
from Nancy Palmer Photo Agency. 151—Drawings by
Matt Greene. 155—Richard Jeffery. 159—Derek Bayes
courtesy Victoria and Albert Museum. 161,162,163
—Raghubir Singh from Nancy Palmer Photo Agency. 167
—Roloff Beny. 168—John Freeman courtesy of the
Trustees of the British Museum. 180—Fotiades.

For their help in the production of this book the editors
wish to thank the following: *in New York,* Art Asia, Inc.;
Daniel Brooks, Inc.; Dr. Paul Buck, Cornell University;
Grossman-Kohn, Inc.; India Government Tourist Office;
India Nepal, Inc.; Le Tourneau's; Luten-Clarey-Stern,
Inc.; J. Garvin Mecking; Pakistan House; Navnit N.
Patel, Assistant Director, Consulate General of India; Dr.

Theodore Riccardi, Columbia University; James Robinson,
Inc.; Sona the Golden One; S. Wyler, Inc.; Dr. Lekh R.
Batra, United States Department of Agriculture, and Dr.
Suzanne W. T. Batra, Beltsville, Maryland; Dr. S.
Vaidyanathan, University of Pennsylvania, Philadelphia,
Pennsylvania; *in India,* Mrs. Rohini Haksar; Mrs. Dhan
Nanavatty; Miss Thangam E. Philip; Lady Rama Rau;
Mrs. Pommu Waglé.
Sources consulted in the production of this book
include: *The Cambridge History of India,* Vols. I, III, IV,
and V; *The Wonder That Was India,* by A. L. Basham;
The Hindu Tradition, ed. by Ainslie T. Embree; *Shorter
Encyclopaedia of Islam,* ed. by H. A. R. Gibb and J. H.
Kramers; *Muslim Civilization in India,* by S. M. Ikram;
Village Life in Northern India, by Oscar Lewis; *The
Ramayana* of Valmiki, as told by Aubrey Menen; *Myths
of the Hindus and Buddhists,* by the Sister Nivedita and
Ananda K. Coomaraswamy; *India and Pakistan: A General
and Regional Geography,* by O. H. K. Spate and A. T. A.
Learmonth; *India: A Modern History,* by Percival Spear;
The State of Pakistan, by L. F. Rushbrook Williams.

𝕩

PRODUCTION STAFF FOR TIME INCORPORATED

John L. Hallenbeck (Vice President and Director of Production),
Robert E. Foy and Caroline Ferri. Text photocomposed
under the direction of Albert J. Dunn